Advance Praise for
REFINED CONSEQUENTIALISM

"*Refined Consequentialism: The Moral Theory of Richard A. McCormick* makes a significant contribution to the literature focusing on contemporary debates within Roman Catholic moral theology over the proper way to determine whether human actions are morally good or not. The introductory chapter is concerned with the meaning of 'consequentialism' in contemporary ethical discussions, and the second traces the development of 'proportionalism,' which in reality turns out to be a form of 'refined proportionalism,' through such Catholic authors as Peter Knauer, Joseph Fuchs, Louis Janssens, and McCormick. The third chapter is a very patient and comprehensive account of McCormick's own sophisticated version of proportionalism, making it clear that McCormick's proportionalism is indeed a 'refined consequentialism.' The final two chapters provide, in my opinion, an excellent critique of McCormick's proportionalism and his consequentialitic defense of intending so-called pre-moral or non-moral evil for the sake of a 'proportionate' good."

William E. May, Michael J. McGivney Professor of Moral Theology,
John Paul II Institute for Studies on Marriage and Family.
Washington, D.C.

REFINED CONSEQUENTIALISM

PETER LANG
New York • Washington, D.C./Baltimore • Bern
Frankfurt am Main • Berlin • Brussels • Vienna • Oxford

PATRICK ANDREW TULLY

REFINED CONSEQUENTIALISM

The Moral Theory of Richard A. McCormick

PETER LANG
New York • Washington, D.C./Baltimore • Bern
Frankfurt am Main • Berlin • Brussels • Vienna • Oxford

Library of Congress Cataloging-in-Publication Data

Tully, Patrick Andrew.
Refined consequentialism: the moral theory of Richard A. McCormick / Patrick Andrew Tully.
p. cm.
Includes bibliographical references.
1. McCormick, Richard A., 1922– 2. Consequentialism (Ethics) I. Title.
BJ1031.T85   171'.5—dc22   2006019658
ISBN 0-8204-8625-6

Bibliographic information published by **Die Deutsche Bibliothek**.
Die Deutsche Bibliothek lists this publication in the "Deutsche Nationalbibliografie"; detailed bibliographic data is available on the Internet at http://dnb.ddb.de/.

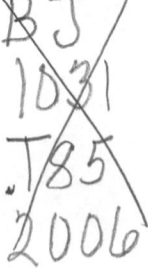

Cover design by Lisa Barfield

The paper in this book meets the guidelines for permanence and durability of the Committee on Production Guidelines for Book Longevity of the Council of Library Resources.

© 2006 Peter Lang Publishing, Inc., New York
29 Broadway, New York, NY 10006
www.peterlang.com

All rights reserved.
Reprint or reproduction, even partially, in all forms such as microfilm, xerography, microfiche, microcard, and offset strictly prohibited.

Printed in Germany

To Mom and Dad, for your love and right choices

To Tracy, for all the sacrifices and for never doubting

To Jim, for your teaching and friendship

To Gerald McCool, S.J., my first and best philosophy teacher, for your example

Table of Contents

Acknowledgment   ix

Introduction   1

Chapter 1: Consequentialism   7
   Two Senses of *Ought*   7
   Two Different Types of Moral Theory   15
   Versions of Consequentialism   25
   Two Approaches to Moral Questions   31
   The Nature of Consequentialism   32

Chapter 2: Proportionalism   41
   The Doctrine of Double Effect   41
   Peter Knauer and Commensurate Reason   45
   Moral Norms   52
   Two Types of Evil   56
   McCormick's Synthesis   60
   Conclusion   64

Chapter 3: McCormick's Proportionalism   75
   The Meaning of *Proportionate Reason*   76
   Purposeful Killing and Proportionate Reasoning   79
   An Abortion Case   80
   Circumstances   82
   The Necessity Principle   84
   The Lynch-Mob Case   87
   Some Non-Consequentialist Standards?   91
   Proportionate Reason and Rights   99
   The Case of Bombing Non-Combatants in Warfare   102
   The Scope of *Proportionate Reason* Reasoning   105
   McCormick's Self-Defense   107
   Conclusion   113

Chapter 4: Purposefully Causing vs. Merely Allowing Ontic Evil   123
   The Traditional Distinction   123
   Norms   129
   The Moral Relevance of the Traditional Distinction   133

McCormick's Philosophical/Theological Anthropology
    and an Exceptionless Prohibition on Moral Evils   138
Conclusion   143

Chapter 5: Acting Against Basic Goods
and Intrinsically Wrong Acts   151
Acting Against a Basic Good   151
Intrinsically Evil Acts   156
Conclusion   165

Bibliography   171

Acknowledgments

My sincere thanks to the Office of Research Services at the University of Scranton for their generous support in bringing this work to publication.

Introduction

In his 1967 article *The Hermeneutic Function of the Principle of Double Effect* moral theologian Peter Knauer argued that "moral evil...consists in the last analysis in the permission or causing of evil which is not justified by a commensurate reason."[1] If Knauer is right, then the Catholic moral tradition's claim that there are certain behaviors which are never morally acceptable to choose must be reinterpreted or abandoned, as must this tradition's exceptionless prohibition against choosing evil as a means to achieving good.[2] Ultimately, what Knauer challenged was his tradition's account of what it is about morally wrong acts that *make* them morally wrong. In very broad and simple terms, he argued that the wrong-making characteristic of any morally wrong act is that the act yields a disproportion between its good end and its evil effect(s). Were the evil effect(s) and the good end of such acts properly proportioned, these acts would be morally licit.[3]

Both criticism of and support for Knauer's thesis and the proportionalist movement it started followed quickly and continues today.[4] The development of proportionalist thought will be detailed in chapter two; for now we may simply note that the theory has hardly gone unnoticed by the community of Catholic moralists. Almost thirty years after the appearance of Knauer's article proportionalism had become, in the estimation of one considered observer, "the most prominent ethical theory among Catholic moral theologians."[5] But it was not just theologians who embraced the theory; Benedict Ashley and Kevin O'Rourke found proportionalism enjoying considerable popularity among Catholic pastoral counselors as well.[6] More recently, Christopher Kaczor judged proportionalism to be "perhaps the most influential moral theory in Catholic circles."[7] He added, though, that it may also be among the most controversial.[8]

A common complaint from the critics of proportionalism has been that it is a form of consequentialism and, as such, commits one to the position that certain acts, like adultery or murder, may be morally justified in certain circumstances.[9] Not surprisingly, proportionalists deny this charge, often asserting that this criticism is unwarranted and grounded in a misunderstanding of their theory. What is unfortunate is that simple-assertion/simple-denial episodes have frequently characterized the proportionalism-as-consequentialism debate. In 1983, just fifteen years after the appearance of Knauer's seminal article, Richard McCormick reported that the state of the debate between proportionalists and their critics was "almost stalemated,"[10] while another observer found things to be at an impasse.[11] At that time McCormick characterized the dispute between proportionalists and their critics as

> growing repetitious, arid, and fruitless, especially so when carefully crafted positions are summarily dismissed with terms such as 'consequentialism' and 'proportionalism'.[12]

In a 1989 update on the state of this debate, McCormick reported that there had occurred "…a quiet theological (even if not magisterial) settling, and a move to other issues in some of these matters."[13] Yet soon after, Kenneth Melchin claimed that "even if McCormick is correct, that a sort of 'settling' has occurred, this settling has involved little movement among the opponents from their positions."[14] Melchin was right; the standoff persisted.

One might have expected Pope John Paul II's 1994 *Veritatis Splendor* to stir things up a bit. In that encyclical the Pope claimed, more and less explicitly, that proportionalist theories in general were consequentialist.[15] Yet this assessment was offered with little supporting philosophical argumentation and did not identify any one of the by-then multiple versions of the theory as its target. Perhaps predictably, proportionalist responses to the encyclical's charge were rather brief and similarly wanting in philosophical content.[16] The problem, as Edward Vacek observed, was that "most proportionalists either were not convinced by the pope's objections or held that the pope rejected ideas they had not proposed."[17]

Ten years after *Veritatis Splendor*, in 2004, Cardinal Joseph Ratzinger, then the Prefect for the Roman Catholic Church's Congregation for the Doctrine of the Faith, demonstrated that this vexing issue had not gone away. Addressing the question of whether it would be acceptable for a Catholic to vote for a political candidate who supported abortion rights, he wrote:

> When a Catholic does not share a candidate's stand in favor of abortion and/or euthanasia, but votes for that candidate for other reasons, it is considered remote material cooperation, which can be permitted in the presence of proportionate reasons.[18]

With these words from the soon-to-be Pope Benedict XVI in mind, the influential Catholic theologian Richard McBrien wondered aloud whether Cardinal Ratzinger should be considered a proportionalist. McBrien's answer? "It would seem so."[19] Unfortunately, though, McBrien offered scant argumentation to support such a significant, and controversial, conclusion. And so, it seems, the stalemate continues.

Just what kinds of choices does the presence of a proportionate reason justify? What role should proportionate reason play in the moral assessment of choices? These questions, at the heart of this bogged-down discussion, remain relevant and significant, and one's answers will go far in determining one's position on a number of today's ongoing debates; debates concerning, for example, voting for pro-choice politicians and whether and when nutrition and hydration may be withheld or removed from a gravely ill patient. The focus of this book, though, is the debate concerning proportionalism and consequentialism, and these most recent flare-ups make clear that the disagreement between proportionalists and their critics is real and unresolved. Indeed, when at this stage in the life of the debate one finds one Catholic ethicist asserting that "proportionalism is a kind of utilitarianism,"[20] while another rejects the notion that the theory implies a "utilitarian calculus,"[21] one is lead rather easily to the conclusion that the stalemate on this critical issue persists.

But it is precisely this stalemate that gives this study its relevance. Is proportionalism a form of consequentialism? As mentioned earlier, proportionalists have usually seemed satisfied that it is not, and their critics have usually seemed convinced that it is and have invested their energies in detailing the flaws and inadequacies of consequentialist ethical theories.[22] Yet a thorough and sustained philosophical case that some one particular version of proportionalism is fundamentally consequentialist has never been offered. For this reason no proportionalist has been provoked into defending any one particular version of the theory against this charge in an equally thorough and sustained philosophical manner. With this in mind, what is offered here is a comprehensive, philosophical case that the proportionalism of the late Richard McCormick (1922–2000) is indeed a form of consequentialism, a charge that James Walter noted McCormick to have "consistently, and rightfully, denied."[23] This denial is supported by a number of those familiar with McCormick's thought, among them Michael Allsopp who offered that "while McCormick's ethics respects the consequences of human action, it should not be classified as a 'consequentialist' ethics,"[24] and Charles Curran, who describes McCormick's version of the theory, remarkably, as "*objecting* to consequentialism and utilitarianism"[25] It seems that someone has gotten McCormick quite wrong.

Focusing on McCormick's version of the theory rather than on proportionalism in general will enable us to avoid what McCormick himself had lamented in this debate: that proportionalists and their critics often "talk past each other, making assumptions and attributing positions that are inaccurate or downright false"[26] When seeking a version of proportionalism to focus upon,

McCormick's is a natural choice. Upon his death, Margaret Farley found him to be "one of the—if not the—premiere Roman Catholic moral theologians of the last half of the 20th century, and that's speaking modestly."[27] Charles Curran characterized him as "a giant and dominating figure in Catholic moral theology in the United States and the world in the last half of the 20th century."[28] And, towards the end of McCormick's career, James Tubbs found him to be the one who

> raises the most powerful and prophetic voice in contemporary American Roman Catholic moral theology, and no Roman Catholic intellectual has contributed more to recent American discussions about religious ethics.[29]

While McCormick's stature as a theologian undoubtedly amplified his voice as a proportionalist, his status within the proportionalist movement itself was well-deserved and hard-earned. Edward Vacek, finding no proportionalist "so pre-eminent in the *P*[roportionalist] school that others understand themselves by reference to his or her position,"[30] nevertheless rightly added that McCormick "is perhaps the one who has spent most time in the trenches."[31] There is no doubt that much of the influence proportionalism has enjoyed, and much of the controversy it has generated, is due to McCormick's work. His efforts in advocating, refining, applying, and defending his version of this theory made him the most notable American proportionalist and the standard-bearer of the movement on this side of the Atlantic. Indeed, one historian of the proportionalist movement dubbed him "the champion of proportionalism in the United States."[32] Now, as we begin this study, the task of chapter one will be to make clear the nature of consequentialist ethical theories, a sensible first step in our case that McCormick's theory belongs in that category.

Notes

1. Peter Knauer, "The Hermeneutic Function of the Principle of Double Effect," *Natural Law Forum* 12, (1967): 140.
2. The *Catechism of the Catholic Church* maintains that "one may not do evil so that good may result from it" (nos. 1756, 1761). This prohibition is scripturally grounded in *Romans* 3:8 (see Pope John Paul II, *The Splendor of Truth*, 99). The issue of licitly doing what is considered an evil in order to achieve a good will be thoroughly discussed in chapter two.
3. What exactly "properly proportioned" means will be seen in chapters two and three. For now allow that it means some sort of acceptable balance between the good and evil effects of an act. The moral decisiveness that proportionalism accords to the proportion between an act's good and evil effects is the reason behind this theory's name. For an account of the genesis of the term *proportionalism* see Bernard Hoose's *Proportionalism: The American Debate and its European Roots* (Washington, D.C.: Georgetown University Press, 1987), p.20 note 1. For a list of proportionalists and their opponents within the Christian moral tradition, see Richard McCormick "Moral Theology 1940-1989: An Overview," *Theological Studies*, 50 1 (March, 1989), 10.
4. I am a critic of this theory, and approach it from the Natural Law perspective of John Finnis, Germain Grisez, and Joseph Boyle. Some recent works dealing with proportionalism are Garth Hallett's *Greater Good: The Case for Proportionalism* (Washington: Georgetown University Press, 1995), Todd Salzman's *Deontology and Teleology: An Investigation of the Normative Debate in Roman Catholic Moral Theology* (Leuven: Leuven University Press, 1995), Christopher Kaczor's *Proportionalism: For and Against* (Milwaukee: Marquette University Press, 2000), Kaczor's *Proportionalism and the Natrural Law Tradition* (Washington: Catholic University of America Press, 2002).
5. Todd Salzman. *Deontology and Teleology: An Investigation of the Normative Debate in Roman Catholic Moral Theology*, 187.
6. Benedict Ashley, Kevin O'Rourke. *Ethics of Health Care*. (Washington, D.C.: Georgetown University Press, 1994), 34.
7. Christopher Kaczor, *Proportionalism: For and Against*, 9. Within the circles of contemporary Catholic ethics, Aline Kalbian sees proportionalism's influence in virtue ethics and feminist ethics ("Where Have All the Proportionalists Gone?" *Journal of Religious Ethics* 30, 1 [2002], 3) while Todd Salzman finds proportionalism ("revisionism") at work in liberation theology ("The Basic Goods Theory and Revisionism: A Methodological Comparison on the Use of Reason and Experience as Sources of Moral Knowledge," *The Heythrop Journal* 42, 4 [2001], 443).
8. Ibid.
9. To appreciate the charge that proportionalism is a form of consequentialism, one might use Bernard Williams' definition of *consequentialism* since it seems to capture what the traditionalist critics of proportionalism find objectionable. Williams defines consequentialism as "the doctrine that the moral value of any action always lies in its consequences, and that it is by reference to their consequences that actions...are to be justified if they can be justified at all" (J.J.C. Smart and Bernard Williams, *Utilitarianism: For and Against*, [Cambridge: Cambridge University Press, 1973], 79).
10. Richard McCormick, "Notes on Moral Theology: 1982," *Theological Studies* 44 (1983), 84.
11. James Walter, "Proportionate Reason and its Three Levels of Inquiry: Structuring the Ongoing Debate," *Louvain Studies* 10 (1984), 30.
12. Richard McCormick, "Notes on Moral Theology: 1982," *Theological Studies* 44 (1983), 84.
13. Richard McCormick, "Moral Theology 1940-1989: An Overview," *Theological Studies* 50 (1989),

19.
14 Kenneth Melchin "Revisionists, Deontologists, and the Structure of Moral Understanding," *Theological Studies* 51 (1990), 389.
15 Pope John Paul II, *Veritatis Splendor*, para. 71-83.
16 See, for example, the proportionalist responses found in *Considering Veritatis Splendor* John Wilkins (ed.) (Cleveland: The Pilgrim Press, 1994).
17 Edward Vacek, review of "Proportionalism: For and Against," *Theological Studies* 63 (2002), 651.
18 Cardinal Joseph Ratzinger, "Worthiness to Receive Holy Communion – General Principles," *L'espresso*, June2004. <http://catholicculture.org/docs/>
19 Richard P. McBrien, "Is Cardinal Ratzinger a Proportionalist?" *The Tidings*, 10/8/04. <http://www.the-tidings.com/2004/1008/essays.htm>
20 Dianne Irving, "Comments: 'Catholic' Bioethicist Thomas Shannon's 'Implications of the Papal Allocution on Feeding Tubes'" <http://www.lifeissues.net/writers/irvi/>
21 Russell Smith, in Jerry Filteau "Theologians Discuss Criteria for Voters When Candidates Back Abortion," *Catholic News Service*, Sept.29, 2004. <http://www.catholicnews.com >
22 See e.g. Germain Grisez, "Against Consequentialism," *American Journal of Jurisprudence* (1978), 21-72; Paul Quay, "Morality by Calculation of Values," *Theology Digest* 25 (1975), 347-364; John Connery, "Morality of Consequences: A Critical Appraisal," *Theological Studies* 34 (1973); Bartholomew Kiely, "The Impracticality of Proportionalism," *Gregorianum* 66 (1985), 655-686.
23 James Walter "The Foundation and Formulation of Norms." *Moral Theology: Challenges for the Future*. Charles E. Curran (ed.) (New York: Paulist, 1990) 149, n.19.
24 Michael Allsopp, "Deontic and Epistemic Authority in Roman Catholic Ethics: The Case of Richard McCormick," *Christian Bioethics* 2, 1 (1996), 100.
25 Charles Curran "Notes on Richard McCormick," *Theological Studies*, 61 (2000), 533. Emphasis mine.
26 Richard McCormick, "Pluralism Within the Church," in *Catholic Perspectives on Medical Morals*. E. Pelligrino, J. Langan, J Harvey [eds.], Netherlands: Kluwer Academic Publishers, 1989: 154).
27 As quoted in the *National Catholic Reporter*, February 25, 2000.
28 Charles Curran, "A Marvelous Exponent of the Living Tradition," *National Catholic Reporter*, 03 March 2000, p.12.
29 Michael Allsopp, "Deontic and Epistemic Authority in Roman Catholic Ethics: The Case of Richard McCormick," *Christian Bioethics* 2, 1 (1996), 98.
30 Edward Vacek, "Proportionalism: One View of the Debate," *Theological Studies* 46 (1985), 287.
31 Ibid., n.1
32 Bernard Hoose, *Proportionalism: The American Debate and its European Roots*, 4.

Chapter 1
Consequentialism

"What *ought* I do?" Posing this question to two moralists who share with Henry Sidgwick the assumptions that "there is something under any given circumstances which it is right or reasonable to do, and that this may be known," may well prompt two answers whose perfect consistency obscures a fundamental ethical disagreement.[1] On the most abstract level, both moralists presumably would believe that one ought to do what is right. The generality of this answer, though, would be unhelpful to one who is wrestling with a real moral dilemma. Both moralists may also agree on a more detailed answer, one addressing the specific situation that prompted the question. Each may conclude that what one ought to do is, say, discontinue extraordinary life-sustaining treatment for their loved one; that choice, they may agree, would be the right thing to do in the given situation. Yet beneath this agreement may lie a fundamental disagreement, a disagreement that would become apparent were one to ask, "*Why* is that the right thing to do?" This second question seeks an explanation of what it is about morally right and wrong acts that make them morally right and wrong.[2] What this question may bring to light is the fundamental difference between a deontological understanding of right and wrong acts, and of one's primary moral duty, and a consequentialist understanding of these things. What follows in this chapter is an explanation of the difference between these two conceptions of just what it is that makes an act morally right or wrong, and precisely what one's primary moral duty demands.

Two Senses of O*ught*

C.D. Broad's well-known *Five Types of Ethical Theory* goes far in helping to lay out the fundamental theoretical differences between consequentialist and deontological moral theories, and so we turn to him. We begin with his analysis of the moral term *ought*. Broad identified three different senses in which the term *ought* is used in moral systems and moral discourse: a *deontological, teleological,* and *logical* sense.[3] Later in this work he argued that these three uses reduce to two, the deontological and the teleological (and it will be seen that the latter of these two plays the defining role in what have come to be called consequentialist moral theories). These different senses of *ought* point to different understandings of what one's primary moral duty is, and of what constitutes the rightness or wrongness of one's choices.

Broad found that *ought* is used in a deontological sense when one asserts that

> there are certain types of action which ought to be done (or avoided) in all or in certain types of situations, *regardless of the goodness or badness of the probable consequences.* [4]

A recent example of this type of assertion may be found in Pope John Paul II's *Veritatis Splendor*. There, one is presented with the traditional belief that the truth of divinely-revealed prohibitions against murder, adultery, stealing, and lying (among other acts) is accessible to human reason. These rather concrete prohibitions constitute part of the natural law and, as such, are appropriately expressed in "ought language" (*One ought not murder, commit adultery*, etc.). The sense of this use of *ought* is indeed deontological because, we are told, the aforementioned prohibitions are

> universally valid. They oblige each and every individual, always and in every circumstance. It is a matter of prohibitions which forbid a given action *semper et pro semper*, without exception, because the choice of this kind of behavior is in no case compatible with the goodness of the will of the acting person, with his vocation to life with God and to communion with his neighbor. It is prohibited—to everyone and in every case—to violate these precepts. [5]

Broad mentioned but did not develop the possibility that there may be a single axiom—say, Kant's categorical imperative—that is primary and from which is derived all other more concrete norms, e.g. *Do not lie, Do not commit suicide, Do not steal*.[6] These derived norms would then prescribe or proscribe concrete acts and would do so using the deontological sense of *ought* (*One ought not lie, commit suicide, steal*, etc.). Fittingly, Broad preferred to call moral theories that use this deontological sense of *ought* deontological theories.[7] Yet whatever name one uses, what is to be noted for our purposes is that each member of this category of moral theories is characterized by

> the view that there are a number of fairly concrete ethical axioms of the general form: 'Any action of such and such a kind, done in such and such a kind of situation, would be right (or wrong) no matter whether its consequences were good, bad, or indifferent'.[8]

As we have seen, Broad described the deontologist's axioms as 'fairly concrete' but, as this is all he said regarding their specificity, one is left a bit in the dark as to what he meant by this phrase and how important norm-specificity is to the distinction between teleological and deontological theories. But one can gather what he meant by 'fairly concrete' by considering his example of a deontological axiom prohibiting lying, where a lie is "a statement made by an agent with the intention of producing a false belief."[9] The specificity of this sort of norm is presumably what distinguishes it in this context from more abstract or formal norms like "Do not act unjustly" and "Act honorably," although, again, Broad did not elaborate on this distinction. Nevertheless, this is no great loss; the degree of specificity of the norm(s) endorsed is not in itself what distinguishes the deontologist from the teleologist. What is characteristic of the deontologist is not the number or degree of specificity of the axioms that he accepts but rather that these axioms are understood to be valid guides to choice regardless of the consequences of the acts they enjoin or prohibit. Indeed, norms as general as "Act justly" and as specific as "Do not engage in intercourse with one who is not your spouse" may each be accepted by both the deontologist and the teleologist. The difference is *why* each would accept them, that is, what it is that grounds their validity, and what role they play in the moral assessment of acts. We will turn to these issues shortly.

However the deontologist believes his axioms come to be known (e.g. through direct divine revelation, through innate ideas, through reason reflecting on natural inclinations, or some other way) they will ground his belief that there are certain acts that are *intrinsically* right or wrong.[10] By ascribing to deontologists the belief that some acts are right or wrong intrinsically, Broad simply meant that these deontologists judge that certain actions, by their nature (a nature reflected in their definition), violate a valid norm. According to these kinds of theories, the moral defect of these acts lie within the act itself, and not in the overall negative consequences that would result were this act to be performed in a particular situation. This is an important point to note because Richard McCormick appears to have supported the notion of intrinsically evil acts and to have rejected the position that the characteristic defect in all morally wrong acts is found in their negative long-term consequences. Together, these elements of McCormick's propostionalism may contribute to the impression that his theory is more deontological than consequentialist. Yet later we will see that such an impression is mistaken. For now let us note that a deontologist's claim that an act is wrong is not necessarily a claim that the act leads to overall bad consequences. J.J.C. Smart helps to make plain the deontologist's separation of an act's rightness or wrongness from its consequences by observing that

> any system of deontological ethics, that is any system which does not appeal to the consequences of our actions, but which appeals to conformity with certain rules of duty, is open to a persuasive type of objection....For though, conceivably, in most cases the dictates of a deontological ethics might coincide with those of human welfare...there must be some possible cases in which the dictates of the system clash with those of human welfare, indeed in which the deontological principles prescribe actions which lead to avoidable human misery.[11]

As the deontologist subordinates the consequences of an act to the question of its nature, and as he accepts a set of norms which prescribe or proscribe certain types of acts according to their natures, he will have the theoretical wherewithal to identify some acts as always wrong, regardless of the consequences of performing them in any particular situation; they are wrong simply because of the type of act that they are.

Broad offered what he considers to be a generally accepted definition of lying to illustrate this deontological notion of intrinsic rightness or wrongness: to lie is to make a statement with the intention of producing a false belief.[12] Were one a deontologist who accepted a norm prohibiting intentionally causing false belief in another, one would be committed to judge every lie as wrong, even those lies that lead to indisputably good effects. For deontologists who accept this definition of lying and a norm against such behavior, to choose to cause false belief in another, regardless of the consequences of this act, is to violate a moral norm and is therefore wrong. That act which by its nature violates a valid norm is by its nature wrong, that is, *intrinsically* wrong, and no amount of good consequences will remove this intrinsic defect from the act.

Now the deontologist is not necessarily committed to the notion that all wrong acts are intrinsically wrong. Were the deontologist so committed, then he would have to judge that if it is wrong to commit act A in situation X, then it must be wrong to commit act A in any situation, since if act A is wrong, it is intrinsically so, thereby making circumstances irrelevant to the judgment. Such a deontologist would be committed to the position that the defect in every wrong act is located in the act itself and not in that act being just contingently inappropriate to a particular situation. But imagine that a deontologist who accepts the somewhat concrete norm *Give aid to people in trouble* finds herself confronted by a hostage taker who holds a gun to his victim's head. The hostage taker tells the deontologist that if she calls out for help, then he will kill his hostage. If, convinced of the sincerity of this threat, the deontologist calls out for help anyway (perhaps out of fear of having to face this situation alone), then her behavior may be judged to have violated the norm to lend aid to those in trouble. But in another case, if circumstances are such that calling out is a legitimate act of helping another in trouble, then the act of calling out for help can be seen to violate a deontological norm in one situation and to conform to the same norm in another situation. For this deontologist, calling out for help, when wrong, is not to be understood as intrinsically wrong since calling out for help does not by its very nature violate a norm (as intentionally causing false belief in another, in our example above, does). The consequences of an act may at times be relevant to this deontologist, but only in the sense that they may aid a judgment as to whether a particular choice in a particular situation is a violation of a relevant norm. For example, in the hostage case above, our deontologist may go through the following assessment: "Because of what I believe the abductor will do if I call out, I believe that my act of calling out will violate the norm to aid those in need. Therefore I ought not to call out." Now, whether it be the case of telling a lie, or the case of wrongly calling out for help, the deontologist's understanding of right conduct does not allow that sufficiently good consequences will somehow eliminate the wrongness of an act which violates a moral norm.

Broad also found that, in contrast to the deontologist, *ought* is used differently by those who believe that "everyone ought to aim at certain ends without any ulterior motive, *e.g.*, at his own greatest happiness, at the greatest happiness of all sentient beings, and so on."[13] The end(s) that these individuals believe everyone ought to aim at are ends that have been judged to be intrinsically good.[14] Now since *ought* is used here to assert that an agent's primary duty is to try to realize intrinsic good(s), Broad classified this as a teleological sense of the term.[15] It is important to note, however, that what here distinguishes the teleological sense of *ought* from its deontological sense is not that the former can and the latter cannot admit a duty to realize good(s) through one's actions. John Finnis's Natural Law theory is an example of a deontological moral theory which includes a recognized duty to realize good(s).[16] At the core of Finnis' moral theory is the notion of practical reasonableness, and he makes a very teleological-sounding assertion when he claims that one of the *requirements* of practical reasonableness is

> the requirement that one *bring about* good in the world (in one's own life and in the lives of others) by actions that are efficient for their reasonable purposes.[17]

Finnis, it seems, would agree that agents ought to try through their actions to realize certain ends, that is, to instantiate in the world certain goods. Yet, distancing himself from those who would employ this teleological sense of *ought* to express every individual's *primary* moral duty, Finnis argues that this requirement of practical reasonableness "is only one requirement among a number,"[18] and that

> every attempt to make it the exclusive or supreme or even the central principle of practical thinking is irrational and hence immoral.[19]

Indeed, he identifies what he believes to be a self-evident principle of reason which properly constrains the duty to realize good(s) in one's actions. This principle forbids an agent from acting directly against any instantiation of any of the basic goods, even in order to promote that same kind of good or some other basic good(s).[20]

Finnis' theory is clearly distinguishable in kind from the sort of moral theory offered by Jeremy Bentham, who claimed that an agent's primary duty is the realization of a particular good. Bentham began developing his teleological theory by identifying happiness as the to-be-pursued end of human action and then proposed a "principle of utility" which, he wrote,

> approves or disapproves of every action whatsoever, according to the tendency which it appears to have to augment or diminish the happiness of the party whose interest is in question: or, what is the same thing in other words, to promote or to oppose that happiness.[21]

He then added:

> Of an action that is conformable to the principle of utility, one may always say either that it is one that ought to be done, or at least that it is not one that ought not to be done. One may say also, that it is right it should be done, at least that it is not wrong it should be done: that it is a right action; at least that it is not a wrong action. When thus interpreted, the words *ought,* and *right* and *wrong,* and others of that stamp, have a meaning: when otherwise, they have none.[22]

More than a century later, G.E. Moore found this same teleological connection between duty and productivity of good(s) when he claimed that it is "demonstrably certain" that the assertion 'I am morally bound to perform this action' is identical with the assertion 'This action will produce the greatest possible amount of good in the Universe.'[23]

Later, Moore made plain just how fundamentally different his teleological sense of duty was from the deontological sense when he claimed that

> Our 'duty,' therefore, can only be defined as that action, which will cause more good to exist in the Universe than any possible alternative.[24]

Keeping in mind the agreed-upon proposition that one *ought* to do what is *right*, the teleological and deontological senses of *ought* point to two fundamentally different beliefs about how acts (possible choices) are to be assessed morally. Rather than identifying right and wrong acts by referring to a set of axioms that are in a significant sense consequence-indifferent, the teleologist morally assesses acts by their consequences, that is, by whether and how well they accomplish (or promise to accomplish) the production of certain good(s).[25] Amartya Sen summarizes well this teleological manner of identifying the right choice. For simplicity sake, allow that our teleologist (whose theory Sen would refer to as *consequentialism*) has before her a number of choices, each of which will have its own unique set of effects. She has, then, a number of different possible "future states" of the world open to her, waiting for realization by her activity. As Sen sees it, for this teleologist (consequentialist)

> there are two quite distinct questions: (i) 'How should I, as an observer, rank the states as outcomes (including descriptions of my actions, if any, that form a part of that state)?' (ii) 'How should I act?'....For consequentialism, the answer to question (ii) is: by taking account just of the answer to question (i) and by acting accordingly.[26]

G.E. Moore expressed quite clearly this teleological approach when he argued that

> to ask what kind of actions we ought to perform, or what kind of conduct is right, is to ask what kind of effects such action and conduct will produce.[27]

Now we should note, with Brian Ellis, that a teleological theory may be either retrospective, maintaining that one may know an act to be right or wrong only after its consequences are seen, or prospective, maintaining that since "the rightness or wrongness of an act depends in some way on the probabilities of its possible consequences," one may know prior to performing a particular act whether that act is right or wrong.[28] Along these same lines J.J.C. Smart's account of utilitarianism distinguishes between the *right* act and the *rational* act. The former is that act which in fact produces the best results, the latter is that act which is "on the evidence available to the agent, *likely* to produce the best results."[29] Yet whether a particular teleological theory is prospective or retrospective, what makes it a teleological theory is its explication of the concept *right* in terms of best results. The implication of this connection is this: one who would do the *right* act is one who would do that act which leads to the best results.[30]

Before moving on to consider the third sense of *ought* identified by Broad, let us return for a moment to the notion of intrinsically evil acts. Recall that the deontologist's understanding of moral rightness and wrongness may provide her with the theoretical wherewithal to maintain that certain acts, by their very nature, violate a valid moral principle. It may now be seen that, unlike the deontologist, the teleologist has no theoretical grounding for the assertion that certain concrete sorts of acts are *intrinsically* wrong in this deontological sense, i.e. that they cannot ever be rightly done because by their very nature they violate a valid moral principle, a principle whose validity does not depend upon its conduciveness to good consequences. For the teleologist, an intrinsically wrong act would have to be one which could never be the right choice for any agent since by its very nature (and regardless of changing circumstances) that act could never be the one among any agent's choices that promises the best consequences. But unless one is able to anticipate all possible future states of affairs, and all possible choices of all possible agents, one will be unable to judge that a certain act (say, genocide) is *intrinsically* wrong in this teleological sense.[31] And since there are no identifiable intrinsically wrong acts for the teleologist, he cannot accept exceptionless prohibitions on any sort of behavior, for any sort of behavior may some day, in some circumstance, be the best (in the teleological sense) among an agent's choices. This consequentialist position on exceptionless prohibitions on specific sorts of acts is well captured by Smart's assertion that:

> If it were known to be true, as a question of fact, that measures which caused misery and death to tens of millions today *would* result in saving from greater misery and from death hundreds of millions in the future, and if this were the only way in which it could be done, then it *would* be right to cause these necessary atrocities.[32]

The consequentialist, then, has no theoretical basis to exclude absolutely, always and everywhere, any sort of behavior based upon the nature of the behavior itself; for any behavior may be rightly done, indeed obligatory, if it is the choice which promises to maximize good(s) in a given situation.[33]

Now recall that in addition to the teleological and deontological senses of *ought*, Broad identified a "logical" sense of this term, one which is employed by those who

> not only do not recognize any types of action as being obligatory apart from all consideration of the goodness of their consequences, but also do not recognize that there are any ends at which an agent ought to aim at.[34]

This *ought* is hypothetical and practical in the sense that it is employed to urge consistency between means and ends: whatever end one chooses to realize, one *ought* to do what one determines will realize this end. Presumably, one ought (in this practical sense) to take into consideration whatever practical constraints one finds one's behavior to be under as the chosen end is sought. As this sense of *ought* urges one toward rational consistency between means and ends, Broad judged it to be a case of the deontological use of the term:

> For we believe that it is within the power of any sane human being to be consistent if he tries. Thus to say that anyone who adopts an end as ultimate for him ought to adopt what he believes to be the means to it is like saying that everyone ought to tell the truth….In fact it seems to me that the logical ought is just a special case of the deontological ought"[35]

Two Different Types of Moral Theory

Having so dealt with the logical *ought*, Broad was left with two fundamentally different senses of this term, with each pointing to a fundamentally different type of ethical theory. These two types of theory offer differing accounts of what every agent's basic moral obligation is, and of what makes for the moral rightness or wrongness of acts. However, a problem appears when one considers what Broad said of the teleologist:

> …he recognizes only what I have called…the teleological and the logical sense of 'ought'. When he says: 'I ought to do X', he always means simply and solely: (a) 'I ought (in the teleological sense) to desire Y'; (b) 'So far as I can see X is the most suitable means open to me for producing Y'; and (c) 'I ought (in the logical sense) to choose the most suitable means open to me for producing what I ought (in the teleological sense) to desire.'[36]

Here, Broad claimed that the teleologist accepts and asserts the logical *ought*, a use of this term that Broad earlier concluded is deontological.[37] Has Broad's division between teleological and deontological ethical theories broken down? Not necessarily. The teleologist's use of the deontological *ought* in statement (c) is conceptually dependent upon, and subsequent to, the teleologist's claim that one's primary duty is to realize certain good(s). While Broad did not explain the meaning of 'suitable' in statement (c), it seems natural to understand it in terms of cost/benefit efficiency in the achievement of the given end(s). If this read of 'most suitable' is correct, then statement (c) asserts that one ought (in the deontological/logical sense) to act in the most optimal ways *because* one's duty (teleological notion of *duty*) is to effect the maximum realization of intrinsic good(s).[38] The teleologist might explain his use of the logical *ought* by observing that it would be rationally inconsistent to maintain that one's duty is to aim for the greatest realization of a given good, and at the same time maintain that one need not aim for this maximization in the most cost-efficient way possible. Still, one might ask the teleologist, "Why *must* I be consistent? Is not this demand for rational consistency between my chosen end and the means chosen to achieve it a deontological demand?" The teleologist might answer that rational consistency is the most effective way to achieve the ends that are to be achieved, and that one who asks the teleologist "What ought I do?" is already committed to identifying and doing what is "best" among their choices, i.e. identifying and doing what maximizes good(s). Indeed, even if there were cases where arbitrary election of means was judged to be the method of choice which would maximize the realization of good(s), the consistent teleologist would then *choose* to behave arbitrarily, demonstrating again that this logical commitment to means/end consistency is grounded in a prior teleological commitment to realize good(s).

The foregoing case that the teleologist's use of the logical *ought* is not sufficient reason to abandon the teleological/deontological division of ethical theories rests in part upon the teleologist's demand for the *maximum* realization of good(s). Bernard Williams found this demand to be characteristic of teleological theories. He noted that

> in any form of direct consequentialism, and certainly in act-utilitarianism, the notion of the right action in given circumstances is a *maximizing* notion: the right action is that which out of the actions available to the agent brings about or represents the *highest degree* of whatever it is the system in question regards as intrinsically valuable...[39]

It may be wondered, though, why one ought to aim at the *maximum* realization of good(s). The teleologist might point out that this demand for maximization is self-evident or a matter of common sense: if X is intrinsically good then, clearly, more X is better and the most X is best and should be pursued.[40] One might reply, however, that this supposedly self-evident rule does not always appear to hold. Consider the good of freedom, for example. It seems reasonable to suppose that a state of affairs in which people enjoy absolute freedom (i.e. a complete absence of constraint) is not at all the *best* state of affairs for these same people. It might be argued that life in a society in which there was an absence of constraint on individuals' actions towards each other would be a life reminiscent of Hobbes's state of nature. Yet the teleologist might well respond that this objection implicitly accepts the disputed point, as a war of all against all is judged to be a less-than-best state of affairs, in part, *because* it is *not* the state of maximum freedom. One may argue that in such a state of nature one's behavior and options are severely restricted in many predictable ways. The law of diminishing returns sees to it that a state of complete freedom is, in reality, not the state of the most practically possible freedom. This being so, the teleologist might comfortably assert that, indeed, the state of affairs that delivers and sustains the most actual freedom is, other factors aside, the best state, with *best* in this context meaning the state that enjoys the most *practically* possible freedom.[41]

The teleologist might continue his defense of this call for the maximization of good(s) by noting that without it his ethical theory would be a rather diminished guide to choice: if the teleological requirement were only that one's acts aim at good(s), without regard to the amount of good(s) realized, then the only guidance that this theory would provide an agent seeking to do his duty would be the admonishment to choose good(s) over non-good(s), an admonishment that seems hardly necessary given that one who asks the moral question "What ought I do?" is, presumably, already convinced of this and is seeking further direction. Now this further direction might include a pointing-out of the good(s) identified by this particular teleological ethical theory. Still, if there were no more direction offered beyond the aforementioned admonishment and an identification of good(s), then one would be left to wonder how this theory would be helpful to one whose choice is *between* goods, or between different amounts of realization of one good? Would the teleologist maintain that there is no relevant difference between alternatives in these sorts of choices? That seems unlikely. Rather, one would expect the teleologist to defend the notion that the concepts *bad, worse, worst, good, better, best* are to be decisively action-guiding and will apply to an agent's choices according to the relative amount of good(s) that each given choice promises to bring about.

We have seen that a teleologist might argue that the logical *ought* serves as a maximizing rule since the efficiency of means/ends consistency in achieving one's ends promises the maximum realization of these ends. Yet, in this context, if statement (c)'s phrase 'most suitable' means something like 'most cost/benefit-efficient,' then the teleologist's call for a *maximization* of good(s) might lead to another difficulty. Consider the situation where one's only two choices are act A which produces 1000 units of good but at the expense of 900 units of evil, yielding a net 100 units of good, and act B which produces 500 units of good but at the expense of 300 units of evil, producing a net 200 units of good. Here, act A produces *more* good than act B, and can be understood in this case to be the maximizing act, while act B may be considered the more efficient act, as it's cost/benefit proportion is more favorable. Which alternative would the teleologist counsel the agent to choose in order to fulfill her duty to maximize good? If one's duty is simply to maximize good, ought one choose the option which promises to bring about the gross maximium amount of good, or that which promises the maximum net good? It seems that the teleologist would be committed to point the agent toward the choice which promises the net maximization of good because of the following: If, when engaged in a teleological assessment of the above alternatives, one believes that all that is to be considered is an act's gross productivity of good, then one is committed to the position that the negative consequences are to be ignored in the assessment process. But, if one were to ignore negative consequences, then what will one do when faced with a choice in which the bad produced outweighed the good? Suppose that act A above generated 1900 units of evil instead of 900. Ignoring these negative consequences would commit the teleologist to the judgment that one's duty is to choose act A over act B, which in this case will undeniably leave the world (which cannot ignore negative consequences) worse off. Such a judgment is inconsistent with a system of ethics the aim of which appears to be to guide agents to the realization of ever more good states of affairs. This being so, it seems reasonable to believe that when the teleologist uses terms like "efficient" and "suitable" to describe the means that one ought to choose in pursuit of an end, these terms refer to net-maximizing concepts.[42]

One might still challenge the distinction between teleological and deontological ethical theories by arguing that the teleologist's assertion that one ought to aim at the maximum realization of certain goods is actually a deontological *ought*, and that this fact reveals that there really is no fundamental difference between a teleological ethical theory and a deontological one, as the former is an instance of the latter. This challenge might maintain that in place of some deontologist's plurality of axioms, the teleologist accepts one (namely, *Maximize good(s)*.) and that, regardless of any differences in content, number, or degree of specificity of their accepted axioms, each ethicist holds to their norm(s) deontologically. This challenge, however, fails once one considers more carefully what it claims. Recall Broad's observation that *ought* is used in a deontological sense to assert that

> there are certain types of action which ought to be done (or avoided) in all or in certain types of situation, regardless of the goodness or badness of the probable consequences.[43]

Consider, too, Broad's summation of Henry Sidgwick's observation that "intuitionist" (i.e., deontological) ethical theories maintain that

> there are a number of fairly concrete ethical axioms of the general form: 'Any action of such and such a kind, done in such and such a kind of situation, would be right (or wrong) no matter whether its consequences were good, bad, or indifferent'.[44]

Finally, recall that when a teleologist states that one ought to aim at certain goods, what is meant is that one ought to aim at the *maximum realization* of these good(s), implying thereby that one's duty is to choose those acts which promise the best (i.e. the most net good) consequences. Now, given the foregoing, it can be seen that to claim that teleologists hold deontologically to their demand to maximize certain good(s) is to claim that teleologists believe one's duty is to aim at the best possible consequences (i.e. at the net-maximum realization of certain goods) regardless of the goodness or badness of the consequences. But what can this claim mean? It is either nonsense or it must be understood to mean that good is to be maximized no matter what one has to do to maximize it. If this latter interpretation is correct, then the objection that the teleological *ought* is a species of the deontological *ought* loses all force; in this case the teleologist will still be committed to the position that the rightness or wrongness of an act is exclusively a matter of the act's net productivity of good(s), a position fundamentally different than that of the deontologist. For the deontologist, certain concrete choices, i.e. certain intentional behaviors like, perhaps, causing false belief in another, are wrong and can be judged so without any knowledge of their net productivity vis-a-vis certain goods because the deontologist does not share the teleologist's belief that the rightness and wrongness of such choices is a function of the net amount of good(s) they produce or promise.

Broad found that

> the fundamental difference between the Intuitionist and the Teleologist is that the former does, and the latter does not, recognize a sense of 'right' which applies to actions and intentions and is not analysable into 'conducive to *good* consequences'.[45]

If one were to connect this observation to the idea that one's duty is to do what is right, then one would see that a deontological theory will assert duties that are not analyzable into "conducive to good consequences." The thought of W.D. Ross provides us with an example of this type of ethical theory. According to Ross,

> in fact there are several branches of duty which apparently cannot be grounded on productivity of the greatest good. There appears to be a duty, for instance, of fulfilling promises, a duty of making compensation for wrongs we have done, a duty of rendering a return for services we have received, and these cannot be explained as forms of the duty of producing the greatest good; we are conscious of duties to behave in these ways even when we have no conviction that the greatest sum of good will be thus produced…[46]

Now some may claim that the duties mentioned by Ross are duties *because* performing the acts they prescribe produces more good than not performing them. Ross, though, anticipated this challenge and turned it around, arguing that performing these duties leads to good consequences *because* they are duties.[47] We need not enter into this debate because our point has already been well illustrated by Ross' position: the deontologist understands the assessment of an act's rightness or wrongness not to be equivalent to an assessment of the goodness or badness of that act's consequences. For the teleologist, the assessment of an act's rightness or wrongness *is* the assessment of the goodness or badness of the act's consequences. In these two theories, one can see a reverse prioritization of norms and consequences. For the teleologist, the duty to maximize good(s) (i.e., the duty to do what promises the best consequences) is primary, with the validity of all norms being subordinate to this duty. The deontologist, however, does not accept the notion that the validity of a norm is dependent upon the consequences of the acts it enjoins or forbids. Rather, in the words of Matthew Kramer, these norms are understood to be valid "irrespective of the consequences that will flow from our heeding of them."[48] The deontologist, then, is committed to a subordination (when there is conflict) of the question of consequences to that of following norms.

The immediate point of all of the foregoing was to respond to the challenge that the teleologist's use of what seems to be an instance of a deontological *ought*, specifically, the teleologist's use of the logical *ought* in statement (c) above, is a retreat from teleological principles and calls into question the depth of the difference between the two types of ethical theory mentioned. The fact, though, is that the teleologist's use of the logical *ought* is required given his prior, foundational commitment to the net-maximization of good(s). This basic commitment is expressed in the teleologist's account of what one's primary duty is, and of how acts are to be morally assessed, and it is this commitment that the deontologist simply does not share.

Broad pointed to yet another possible challenge to the deontological/teleological division of ethical theories, one which suggests that instead of teleological theories being a type of deontological theory, the reverse is true. Of an intuitionist (that is, a deontologist) who accepts a norm prohibiting lying he writes:

> Now it is plain that an action cannot be called a 'lie' without reference to certain of the consequences which the agent expects that it will have. He must expect that his action will produce certain beliefs, and he must hold that these beliefs will be false....The action, then, is judged to be wrong because the agent expects it to have consequences of a certain kind. But, if so, it may be asked, how does Intuitionism differ from a teleological type of ethical theory, such as Utilitarianism?[49]

One way to go about answering Broad's question is to consider the data that each type of theory finds relevant to the moral assessment of acts. Let us use the example of telling a lie and compare the data that a teleologist (say, a universal hedonist)[50] and a deontologist (who accepts a norm against lying) would require in order to morally assess this behavior. For our deontologist, it would be both necessary and sufficient to know the answers to the following questions in order to assess whether the act would be right or wrong: *What kind of act is it? Is this kind of act prescribed or proscribed?*[51] Once the deontologist understands both that the proposed action would be an instance of intentionally causing false belief in another, and that there is a norm prohibiting this, he will be able to make a judgment that this act is wrong and ought not to be done.[52] The consequences that are most relevant to the deontologist's assessment are those that form part of the very nature of the act. To communicate in a way that is intended to cause false belief is to lie and, presumably, to communicate in a way that is intended to cause true belief is to tell the truth. Part of what makes each of these acts to be the act that it is, and not the other act, is what the act produces (or at least aims at producing): true belief in one case, false belief in the other case. These consequences form part of the very nature of the act, and are necessarily connected to what one means by that particular act. These necessary consequences[53] can be distinguished from those contingent consequences that result from an act of this type being performed in certain circumstances. For example, an act of intentionally causing false belief in another in order to save lives, and an act of intentionally causing false belief in another in order to take lives would each be considered a lie.[54] These two acts, despite their dissimilar further consequences, share a classification (lie) because of their common nature, a nature that is understood, in part, by what consequences each act produced or sought to produce, viz. false belief in another. Any further consequences, that is, any consequences that are produced *because* false belief was caused in another in a particular situation, are not relevant to the classification of these acts as lies. This being so, no further consequences will be relevant to the deontologist's question of whether this proposed act complies with or violates a norm prohibiting lying. The deontologist looks at the nature of the act and at the set of norms and, if the former is prohibited by the latter, he understands that he is to forego the former, regardless of what good can be realized by disregarding this duty.[55]

For the teleologist, the manner of morally assessing an instance of intentionally causing false belief in another will be quite different. John Stuart Mill, a teleologist who argued that "the foundation of morals" is the principle that "actions are right in proportion as they tend to promote happiness, wrong as they tend to produce the reverse of happiness,"[56] claimed that an act's consequences vis-a-vis happiness are a "sufficient guide to right."[57] So, the crucial moral question, "What course of action will best accomplish my duty?" will lead the conscientious universal hedonist through a deliberation process fundamentally different than the deontologist's. If, of all the acts open to her at the moment of choice, the universal hedonist determines act X to maximize universal good, then she has what she considers necessary and sufficient data for insight into which act is right—act X. If act X happens to be an intentional causing of false belief in another, our universal hedonist need not be troubled, for the fact that act X consists of telling a lie is relevant to the rightness or wrongness of act X only to the degree that it promotes or undermines the realization of universal happiness, and presumably she has already determined and taken account of this aspect of the act.

While a deontologist can admit that in some cases lying would have overall better consequences than its alternatives, he can also, with consistency, maintain that to lie in those cases would nevertheless be wrong, since "wrong" for him is not equivalent to "overall worse consequences than some possible alternative." Shifting our terminology from deontologist/teleologist to non-utilitarian/utilitarian, and shifting our example from lying to promise-keeping, J.J.C. Smart agreed:

> A non-utilitarian...might agree with us in the evaluation of the relative merits of the total set of consequences of the actions A and B and yet disagree with us about whether we ought to do A or B....He might say: 'The total consequences of A are better than the total consequences of B, but it would be *unjust* to do A, for you *promised* to do B.'[58]

However, for a teleologist to maintain that in a particular case lying promises the best overall consequences and, at the same time, to maintain that it would nevertheless be wrong to lie in that case, is for her to be nonsensical as a teleologist since she would be maintaining that it is not optimific to do what is optimific, given that for her "wrong" is equivalent to "overall worse consequences than some alternative." Even if it were believed that lies usually negatively impact the realization of the consequentialist's to-be-realized good(s), the fact that in *this* particular case lying is judged to be most conducive to maximizing good(s) is decisive. Perhaps the teleologist judges that lying is always a disvalue—and perhaps more so than usual in some one particular case because of some unusual circumstances in this case—nevertheless, she must judge that lying is the right thing to do in this particular case if that is what promises to yield the best consequences. She might note with perfect consistency that, on consequentialist criteria, telling the truth is usually to be preferred to lying, but in this case it would be wrong to do so, as telling the truth is not the act among her choices that she judges will best contribute to the realization of good(s). In this vein, Broad found that unlike deontological theories, "teleological theories would make all statements about the rightness or wrongness of classes of action into empirical propositions about general tendencies."[59] He noted that even if a teleologist were to believe that true belief itself were an intrinsic good and that, consequently, one's duty was to maximize true belief, then

> cases might easily arise in which it would be almost certain that more true belief would be produced by telling a lie than by telling the truth. In such cases a Teleologist of the

kind just described would consider it his duty to tell a lie, while an Intuitionist about lying would still hold that it is wrong to do so.[60]

Bernard Williams used promise keeping to illustrate this deontological separation of the concepts *right* and *maximization of good(s)*. He wrote:

> a non-consequentialist can hold both that it is a better state of affairs in which more people keep their promises, and that the right thing for X to do is something which brings it about that fewer promises are kept.[61]

For the deontologist, we have seen that the demand that our choices aim at the production of the best states of affairs (if such a demand is recognized by the deontologist) will be subordinated to the demand that these choices conform to certain norms that enjoin or forbid certain types of acts regardless of their consequences in some particular context. Paul Hurley explains that such agent-centered restrictions

> are typically generated in cases in which the action that will bring about the best state of affairs is an action that will require the agent to do great harm. They stem from the recognition of requirements to avoid doing harm....An agent-centered restriction results when such requirements to avoid doing harm provide decisive grounds for acting contrary to requirements to prevent even greater harm from happening or promote even greater benefit.[62]

It is because of this ordering of demands that the deontologist can agree with a consequentialist that state of affairs X promises to be better than state of affairs Y (i.e. that X promises or contains more net-good than Y), but can also maintain that one ought not do the act which will bring about X because that act violates a norm.

Given all of the above, it is important to take a moment and draw a distinction between consequentialist ethical theories and a deontological ethical theory which identifies certain human goods teleologically. For example, one may follow the thought of John Finnis, Joseph Boyle, and Gremain Grisez and observe in human beings natural inclinations to certain ends, ends the enjoyment of which constitute the agent's overall good as a human being. One might further judge that all instances of these goods are to be respected unconditionally, i.e., that one may never act against any one of them intentionally. One would thus be equipped to generate a set of somewhat concrete ethical norms to guide choice and to assess acts morally.[63] One's moral theory, then, would be deontological in the sense described above, and would be fundamentally different from one who makes the same observations about human inclinations and the same judgments about human goods, but who also claims that one's primary duty is to maximize the realization of these goods, even if that required intentionally acting against an instance of a good (for example, by killing one person to save five people). As Frederick Carney points out, a deontologist will not necessarily be distinguished from the consequentialist by his method of identifying human good(s), but rather by "the procedures he employs and recommends for deciding whether various acts are morally required, forbidden, or permissable."[64] A deontologist who employs a teleology of the human person to identify the human good is not thereby committed to asserting duties (and assessing acts) in terms of their net-productivity of these goods.[65] For the consequentialist, though, one's primary duty is to realize some specified good(s), and acts will be morally assessed by their net-productivity vis-a-vis this end and in comparison to the agent's other possible choices.

Versions of Consequentialism

At the heart of this deontological/teleological distinction, J.J.C. Smart found a disagreement in principle over whether or not one's primary moral duty is "to produce the best consequences."[66] This disagreement between these two fundamentally different types of ethical theory, is to be distinguished from the disagreement *among* teleologists who, despite their common acceptance of the aforementioned statement of duty, do not always agree about just what good(s) should be considered when evaluating the anticipated consequences of possible choices. A disagreement in this area lends itself to different judgments about which of an agent's choices promises the best (or even good) consequences in a given situation. So, while these teleologists would agree that one's duty is to try to produce the best state of affairs, they may nonetheless differ in their judgments about which among the possible states of affairs set before the agent is best.[67] Smart described these differences among teleologists as "ultimate" and added that

> another type of ultimate disagreement between utilitarians…can arise over whether we should try to maximize the *average* happiness of human beings (or the average goodness of their states of mind) or whether we should try to maximize the *total* happiness or goodness.[68]

We need not try to resolve this disagreement. What is important here is to note that Smart categorized these utilitarians (consequentialists), in spite of some significant differences among them, by their common commitment to a primary ethical principle that good is to be maximized.

It should be noted that consequentialist theories may differ from each other in other respects, too. For example, Smart identified two different ways in which consequentialists apply their foundational belief that "the rightness of actions is to be judged by their consequences."[69] He distinguished an extreme form of utilitarianism from a restricted form of this theory. In the former case, any particular act will be justified or not according to that particular act's consequences, while in the latter case,

> the rightness of an action is *not* to be tested by evaluating its consequences but only by considering whether or not it falls under a certain rule. Whether the rule is to be considered an acceptable moral rule, is, however to be decided by considering the consequences of adopting the rule. Broadly, then, actions are to be tested by rules and rules by consequences.[70]

Although Smart believed that on pain of becoming a form of "superstitious rule-worship"[71] restricted utilitarianism must be abandoned for extreme utilitarianism, he somewhat sympathetically noted two factors that may prompt some utilitarians to adopt the restricted version of their theory: First, one frequently finds oneself in a situation that demands action but which does not allow sufficient time to make all of the appropriate consequentialist deliberations;[72] second, all agents are subject to biases that may in some cases undermine their ability to correctly assess options.[73] In these ways, agents often find it somewhat of a challenge to make consistently correct consequentialist assessments. Given these limitations, one may find that a correct consequentialist choice is best ensured by following rules that have been adopted beforehand because of their demonstrated good(s)-maximizing tendencies. Still, Smart's own extreme utilitarianism was evident in his reply to such restrictive utiltiarian thinking:

> I conclude that in every case if there is a rule R the keeping of which is in general optimific, but such that in a special sort of circumstances the optimific behavior is to break R, then in these circumstances we should break R.[74]

Once again, we need not take a side in this debate in order to note what is helpful for our purposes: whether one is an extreme or a restricted utilitarian, one is a consequentialist since in each case the consequences of performing an act or of following a rule are what morally justify the act or the rule. The agent's primary duty in each of these versions of utilitarianism is the same: aim at the net-maximization of good(s). The differences between the act and rule utilitarian are practical and emerge only as they seek to answer the question of how to realize that common goal.

The distinctions between consequentialist theories mentioned so far are not exhaustive. Robert Adams finds that a consequentialist theory need not maintain that the consequences of either acts or rules are always to be the primary object of a correct moral assessment. Suggesting that he is following the lead of Bentham and Sidgwick, Adams maintains that "the test of utility could be applied in various ways to the evaluation of motives,"[75] and then offers that such a theory would claim

> ...that one pattern of motivation is morally better than another to the extent that the former has more utility than the latter. The morally perfect person, on this view, would have the most useful desires, and have them in exactly the most useful strengths; he or she would have the most useful among the patterns of motivations that are causally possible for human beings. Let us call this doctrine *motive utilitarianism*.[76]

This consequentialist theory would question the usefulness, in certain circumstances, of having an ever-present desire for the maximization of good(s); a desire that would lead the agent to engage in a consequentialist assessment of every choice. There are times, Adams believes, when it may be correct by consequentialist standards to conclude that one's choices ought not to be motivated by the desire for the net maximization of good(s). This consequentialist justification for making some choices non-consequentialistically is plausible because, Adams argues, in certain situations it is the case that good(s) will be maximized only by acting upon desires other than the desire for the maximization of good(s). He uses the example of the love of aesthetic experience bringing one to choose to spend a few hours at Chartres rather than dutifully seeking to do something else during that time, something that would have greater net utility.[77] This particular choice is not to be understood to have been made after, and in accordance with, a consequentialist assessment of all the options open to the agent at the moment of choice. Rather, this choice is to be understood to have been made *absent* such a calculation (or *regardless* of such a calculation), for Adams adds that the agent in this example cares more about seeing the cathedral than about maximizing utility. The point that we are not to miss is that if the motivation that leads this agent to this decision is one that may cause him sometimes to make the wrong consequentialist choice (i.e., choosing in some particular situations the option that does not promise the greatest net good[s]), but which nevertheless promises greater net good overall and in the long run, then it is justified on consequentialist grounds for the agent to be so motivated.

Adams' argument hinges on the claim that there may be some motivations to act that lead to better overall consequences than the pure-hearted consequentialist motivation to maximize good(s). Accepting this claim as true,

> ...the motive utilitarian is led to the conclusion that it is morally better on many occasions to be so motivated that one will not even try to do what one ought, by act-utilitarian standards, to do.[78]

Yet, Adams adds,

> If he performs a mildly unutilitarian action as an inevitable consequence of the most useful motivation that he can have, on the other hand, he is still living as well as possible, by his overall utilitarian standards.[79]

Joel Kupperman says much the same thing about an agent's attitudes. Offering what he describes as "an acceptable consequentialist ethics," Kupperman's theory of "attitude consequentialism" sets itself apart from other teleological theories

> in that the unit judged by the consequentialist standard will be most fundamentally a system of attitudes (and the policies expressing these), rather than the individual moral act or an inviolable moral rule.[80]

Philip Pettit and Geoffrey Brennan seem to agree. They believe that any agent concerned primarily with the maximization of good(s) must be concerned, among other things,

> with his own predispositions. He must ask himself whether he ought to preserve or promote this or that trait or motive or policy, as well as asking whether he ought to perform this or that action. That means that he has to be open to the possibility of deciding to restrict calculation in some areas of action. For to opt for a predisposition will be to accept that some actions – those that manifest the predisposition – will be uncalculatingly generated.[81]

Yet despite motive utilitarianism's and attitude consequentialism's allowance that, at times, choices may be made according to certain desires or attitudes of the agent rather than according to a more traditional consequentialist assessment, these theories are genuinely consequentialist. While they do allow for an agent to cultivate certain motives or attitudes according to which this agent may at times act in a non-maximizing way, their justification for this allowance is found in the net-good consequences that acting according to these motives or attitudes yields. Such theories claim that one may cultivate in oneself motivations or attitudes that may *at times* lead one to act in a non good(s)-maximizing way *if* these motivations or attitudes promise, overall, to maximize good(s). Kupperman refers to this reasoning as a "consequentialist justification for not thinking about consequences." [82] The goal, again, is to act in whatever way one judges will lead to the overall maximization of certain good(s). A helpful summation of the different versions of this basic consequentialist belief is provided by Kupperman, who finds that a consequentialist theory will be committed to one of the following claims:

> Either we should do what has the best consequences (what will maximize X), or we should follow a moral rule or a policy general recognition of or adherence to which would have the best consequences (would maximize X), or we should act on motives or on the basis of attitudes which tend to produce the best consequences (tend to maximize X).[83]

Consistent with Kupperman's observation is Bernard Williams' claim that consequentialism is characterized by the belief that

> the moral value of any action always lies in its consequences, and that it is by reference to their consequences that actions…are to be justified if they can be justified at all.[84]

This being so, we have seen that a consequentialist can justify *any* act, rule, motive, character trait, etc. by reference to its productivity of good(s), and any act, rule, motive, etc. may be found unjustified by applying this same standard.[85]

Now while this notion of maximizing good(s) is alone at the center of the consequentialist assertion of moral duty and is the supreme principle guiding moral assessment, there are several, perhaps countless, data that must be taken into account when applying this principle to concrete choices. If the promised realization of good(s) is that by which the agent's concrete choices are to be assessed, then the consequentialist may not exclude from this deliberation any factor that is judged relevant to a choice's productivity.[86] Indeed, by what principle other than his supreme principle could a consequentialist justify such an exclusion? Bernard Williams noted that an act-utilitarian sort of consequentialist,

> ...must be prepared to consider the utility of anything: his aim is to maximize utility, and anything, of whatever type, whose existence, introduction or whatever has effects on the amount of satisfaction in the world must be a candidate for assessment by the utilitarian standard.[87]

Robert Adams agrees with Williams and points out the necessarily expansive nature of consequentialist assessments:

> If the moral point of view, the point of view from which moral evaluations are made, is dominated by the concern for the maximization of human happiness, then it seems that we must revert to the thesis that the test of utility is to be applied directly to everything...[88]

Indeed, J.J.C. Smart, a defender of utilitarianism, cautioned that when consequentialist deliberation leads to the judgment that a generally accepted moral rule R ought to be broken in a particular case, the consequentialist must be sure to

> consider all the less obvious effects of breaking R, such as reducing people's faith in the moral order, before coming to the conclusion that to break R is right.[89]

To those carrying out consequentialist deliberations about, say, whether or not to cause misery and death to tens of millions of people in order to save hundreds of millions of people from the same fate, Smart had similar words of caution that attest to the thoroughness required of consequentialist assessments:

> We must not forget the immense side effects: the brutalization of the people who ordered the atrocities and carried them out.[90]

And Joel Kupperman adds a bit of specificity to this same point, explicitly connecting it to the consequentialist process of assessment:

> We must remind ourselves that the killings, torturings, etc., that we regard as paradigms of the immoral are in general actions whose consequences include psychological states to which we would assign negative value.[91]

What should be noted from the foregoing is that considerations of character and concerns about the virtue of agents are not sufficient to establish that any particular moral theory is not consequentialist since, as we have seen, such considerations are not at all inconsistent with the consequentialist notions of what one's primary duty is and how one is to assess choices.

Two Approaches to Moral Questions

David Ross identified two general ways in which moral questions are approached, with each of these ways determined by one's sense of the ideal of human life. Taking a moment to consider these different approaches may help make plain the nature of consequentialism. Ross saw that

> in the one case the ideal of human life is envisaged as obedience to laws, in the other as the progressive satisfaction of desire and attainment of ends.[92]

Somewhat consistent with this observation is John Finnis' identification of two fundamentally different conceptions of morality, conceptions that fit well with the deontological/teleological division of ethical theories. Finnis distinguishes these two conceptions of morality according to their differing positions on what is the primary moral task for human beings. In the first instance, one generally orients one's life and morally assesses particular choices according to a basic commitment that

> one's ultimate and immediate responsibility is to bring about good states of affairs in the world and…to prevent the occurrence of bad states of affairs.[93]

As absolute priority is given to bringing about states of affairs in which good(s) is maximized, this understanding of the moral life would quite naturally lead to the development of a teleological (consequentialist) ethical theory. Kupperman's "attitude consequentialism" is a clear example of this type of ethical theory since Kupperman states explicitly that "the goal of morality" is "that events occur that have the best consequences."[94] It is important to note, though, that an ethical theory could maintain that one's supreme duty is to eliminate evil states of affairs, rather than the creation of good states of affairs.[95] This sort of theory would nevertheless be consequentialist; given it's assertion of a primary duty to minimize evil(s), it is a theory which calls for the agent to aim at a certain end(s) and which morally assesses an acts by their success at realizing this end(s).[96] Finnis well captures the decisiveness of consequences in these theories in his summation of the sort of moral deliberation that they seem to require:

> One envisages a determinate goal which can be attained by thoughtful disposition of effective means; scrutinizes alternative courses of action for their efficacy as means and their cost in terms of other goals; and selects and undertakes the action promising to be most effective in attaining the goal with least cost.[97]

The maximization of good(s) or minimization of evil(s) is the agent's primary obligation, and all other obligations will be subordinated to it. With one's priorities and commitments so ordered, it follows that the means selected to realize the end will be morally assessed only by reference to its net productivity of the good(s) or, as the case may be, the net diminishment of evil(s).

The other conception of morality identified by Finnis differs greatly from the one just mentioned in that it is characterized by a different fundamental commitment. Rather than giving the realization of good(s) or the diminishment of evil(s) absolute priority in determining one's duty and assessing acts, one may instead believe one's ultimate and immediate responsibility to be a bit more complex: to honor and to pursue the human good (perhaps the same good or set of goods identified by some consequentialist theories), but never intentionally to destroy, damage, or impede instances of this good.[98] This understanding of one's basic moral task would seem naturally to lead one toward the development of a deontological ethical theory, as the identification of the human good (or perhaps its various aspects), coupled with the prohibition against ever intentionally acting against instances of this good, would generate a set of consequence-immune prohibitions that constrain the agent in ways that consequentialist theories simply cannot.[99] This non-consequentialist conception of morality stands in contrast to the aforementioned teleological theories of Bentham, Mill, and Moore who, according to Smart, all agreed "that the rightness of an action is to be judged solely by consequences, states of affairs brought about by the action."[100]

The Nature of Consequentialism

In this chapter we considered two fundamentally different kinds of moral theory. One kind claims that every agent's primary duty is to act in ways which conform to norms that prescribe or proscribe certain acts; norms whose validity is neither a function of, nor contingent upon, the consequences of following them. This conception of duty lies at the heart of deontological moral theories. A different kind of moral theory maintains that every agent's primary duty is to act in ways which promise to maximize the realization of certain good(s) or the diminishment of certain evil(s). This conception of duty lies at the heart of consequentialist theories.

We have also identified and considered two fundamentally different ways of assessing the rightness and wrongness of choices, each grounded in one of the two different kinds of moral theory. The deontological position holds that to act in a morally correct way is to act in a way which conforms to, or at least does not violate, an ethical norm whose validity is neither a function of, nor dependent upon, the goodness of the consequences of the acts that it enjoins or prohibits. We have distinguished this understanding of morally correct choice from its consequentialist counterpart which maintains that to act in a morally right way is to make a choice which promise the best overall consequences, i.e., the net-maximum realization of good(s) or diminishment of evil(s).

It seems, then, that consequentialist theories, despite differences about what is to be maximized and what is the proper object of moral assessment (acts, rules, attitudes, etc.), are specified by their commitment to either the maximum realization of concrete good(s) or the maximum diminishment of evil(s); that is both the primary duty of the moral agent and the standard by which choices are to be assessed. This commitment will manifest itself not only on the level of a somewhat abstract statement of the theory, but also in the details of the consequentialist's assessments of concrete choices. This point is important to keep in mind as we proceed since it will be seen that Richard McCormick denies that his moral theory is consequentialist, a denial that his case analyses belie. We will attend to that part of our study later. For now it should be noted that these two elements, the understanding of moral duty and the manner of moral assessment, are the defining marks of a consequentialist moral theory, making this kind of theory different in kind from normative ethical theories which either disallow or subordinate a role for consequences both in their notion of moral duty and in their assessment of acts. The chapters that follow will make the case that McCormick's version of proportionalism is consequentialist in the sense described here.

Notes

1. Henry Sidgwick, *The Methods of Ethics* (Chicago: The University of Chicago Press, 1962), *v*.
2. In this context I will use "act" to refer to intentionally chosen behaviors, and I will use "right" and "wrong" to refer to the moral quality of such intentionally chosen behaviors. How the moral quality of an act is to be judged will be discussed in what follows.
3. C.D. Broad, *Five Types of Ethical Theory* (New York:The Humanities Press, 1951), 162.
4. Ibid., emphasis mine.
5. Pope John Paul II, *Veritatis Splendor* (Boston: Pauline Books, 1993) 70.
6. C.D. Broad, *Five Types of Ethical Theory*, 215.
7. Ibid., 206.
8. Ibid., 148. We will use what seems to be the more common term *norms* in place of Broad's term *axioms* when referring to moral rules or principles.
9. Ibid., 209.
10. Ibid., 208.
11. J.J.C. Smart and Bernard Williams, *Utilitarianism: For and Against* (Cambridge: Cambridge University Press, 1973), 5.
12. C.D. Broad, *Five Types of Ethical Theory*, 209.
13. Ibid., 162. Broad did not explain what he meant by the phrase "ulterior motive," but he seems to have used it to convey the idea that a teleologist considers certain ends to be properly final, i.e., that they are ultimate and that all morally right action will somehow or other, either directly or indirectly, aim at or contribute to their realization.
14. Here again Broad did not explain what he meant by something being *intrinsically* good, but let us suppose that he meant something as simple and traditional as what Bernard Williams referred to as "non-consequential value." This type of value or good is judged to be valuable or good in-itself and not because it leads to some other good (J.J.C. Smart and Bernard Williams, *Utilitarianism: For and Against*, 83). What precisely Broad meant here, though, is not crucial to our purposes. What will be seen to be somewhat important is Broad's observation that a teleological theory may identify only one intrinsic good, or several (C.D. Broad, *Five Types of Ethical Theory*, 215). Whichever, one's primary duty is the same: *Aim to realize good(s)*.
15. C.D. Broad, *Five Types of Ethical Theory*, 162, 207. To be precise, he claimed that it is some certain characteristic(s) that is intrinsically good, and that the goodness of any state of affairs is dependent upon the presence in it of intrinsic good(s). Broad noted: "The end aimed at is of course never a characteristic in the abstract; it is always a concrete state of affairs in which a certain characteristic, or characteristics, is manifested" (Ibid., 207, 215).
16. John Finnis, *Natural Law and Natural Rights* (Oxford: The Clarendon Press, 1980), 111-118. See also John Finnis, Joseph Boyle, and Germain Grisez, "Practical Principles, Moral Truth, and Ultimate Ends," *The American Journal of Jurisprudence* 32 (1987), 99-152.
17. Ibid., 111. Emphasis mine. Elsewhere, Finnis refers to basic human goods as basic reasons for action and argues that "practical rationality's fundamental principle is: take as a premise at least one of the basic reasons for action, and follow through to the point at which you somehow bring about the instantiation of that good in action" (John Finnis "Natural Law and Legal Reasoning," in *Natural Law Theory: Contemporary Essays* Robert George (ed.), [Oxford: Clarendon Press, 1992], 137).
18. Ibid., 112.
19. Ibid., 118.
20. Ibid., 111-118. Elsewhere Finnis indicates this fundamental constraint on agents who would seek to realize some basic human goods (i.e. basic reasons for action) by sacraficing others: "One of morality's principles...excludes acting against a basic reason by choosing to destroy or damage any basic human good in any of its instantiations in any human person....These instantiations of human good constitute reasons against any option which involves choosing (intending) to destroy or damage any of them" (John Finnis "Natural Law and Legal Reasoning,"

in *Natural Law Theory: Contemporary Essays*, 147.
21 Jeremy Bentham, "An Introduction to the Principles of Morals and Legislation," in *The Utilitarians* (New York: Doubleday & Company, Inc., 1961), 17.
22 Ibid., 19.
23 G.E. Moore, *Principia Ethica* (Cambridge: Cambridge University Press, 1980), 147.
24 Ibid., 148. Although Moore went on to describe (pages 149-166) epistemological difficulties in *knowing* in any particular case what precisely *is* one's duty, so defined, his teleological connection of duty to consequences remains.
25 The question of whether the right act is the one which, prospectively, *promises* to accomplish the maximization of good(s), or, retrospectively, *actually* accomplishes this maximization will be discussed in a moment, but only in so far as it helps to clarify the distinction between teleology and deontology now being made.
26 Amartya Sen, "Informational Analysis of Moral Principles," in *Rational Action: Studies in Philosophy and Social Science* (Cambridge:Cambridge University Press, 1979), 131.
27 Ibid., 146.
28 Brian Ellis, "Retrospective and Prospective Utilitarianism," *Nous* XV, no.3 (1981), 325.
29 J.J.C. Smart and Bernard Williams, *Utilitarianism: For and Against*, 47.
30 Broad added: "…let us say that what is rational is to try to perform the right action, to try to produce the best results." Ibid., 47.
31 This sort of judgment is not to be confused with judgments of the form '*X* (say, pleasure) *is intrinsically good*,' and, '*Y* (say, pain) *is intrinsically evil*.' These types of judgments may be consistent with consequentialism in that they would merely state that when one is doing a consequentialist deliberation, X is always to carry positive weight in the calculation and Y is always to carry negative weight in the calculation.
32 J.J.C. Smart and Bernard Williams, *Utilitarianism: For and Against*, 63. The citing of this example is not meant to imply that a deontologist will not be theoretically committed to certain choices which may themselves be considered horrible. As Matthew Kramer correctly points out, if we were to choose between these two types of moral theory "we could not rightly base our choice on the ability of either stance to avoid shuddersome results. In various settings, either stance can issue an appalling conclusion" ("How Not to Oppugn Consequentialism," *The Philosophical Quarterly* 46, 183 [1996], 217).
33 We will return to this issue in chapter four.
34 C.D. Broad, *Five Types of Ethical Theory*, 162.
35 Ibid., 163. I believe Broad is correct. It may seem to some that this logical use of *ought* is empty of moral meaning, that is, that choosing means which are consistant with one's end is just a matter of prudence, not morality. Were this so, the logical *ought* would be misplaced in the category of deontological uses of this term. However, one may hold that it is the *duty*— perhaps the only one —of free and rational creatures to be consistent about the means they take to their chosen ends, and that the existence and force of this obligation is manifested in every purposeful behavior. If used in this way, the logical ought does carry a rather deontological sense to it, as Broad noted on p.163. We will return to this issue shortly.
36 Ibid., 210.
37 Recall Broad: "It seems to me that the logical ought is just a special case of the deontological ought." Ibid., 163.
38 While Broad did not incorporate this notion of *maximization* of intrinsic good(s) into his above-cited summary statement of the teleological use of *ought*, he did incorporate it into the two familiar examples of possible ultimate ends that a teleologist might identify: the agents own *greatest* happiness, and, the *greatest* happiness of all sentient beings (emphasis mine; Ibid., 162). The mere absence of his use of this notion in his summation of the teleological use of *ought* is a poor case against it being an important – and characteristic – part of teleological ethical theories. A positive case that it must be included in a teleological ethical theory will be

made shortly.
39 J.J.C. Smart and Bernard Williams, *Utilitarianism: For and Against*, 85. Emphasis mine.
40 Smart, sympathetic to act-utilitarianism (Ibid., 4-5), asserted that *the* act-utilitarian principle is "*maximize* probable benefit "(Ibid.,12), adding that "it is rational to perform the action which is on the available evidence the one which will produce the *best* results" (Ibid., 47. Emphasis mine).
41 One may note in this context Brian Ellis' counsel that "rational utilitarians should start to think more practically about maximizing utility. They should take into account human differences, limitations and frailties in devising strategies for doing so. They should not aim at maximizing utility as much as is *theoretically* possible, *disregarding human limitations*, but to do so as much as possible, *given human limitations*" ("Retrospective and Prospective Utilitarianism," *Nous* XV, no.3 (1981), 335).
42 But consider the following: Choice A promises 10 units of good at the cost of 1 unit of bad, for a 10:1 ratio of good to bad. Choice B offers 100 units of good at the expense of 20 units of bad, for a good to bad ratio of 5:1. Choice A, then, is more cost/benefit efficient but choice B promises to produce more net good. Which, on teleological grounds, is to be chosen? I raise this issue not to attempt to solve it but to point out another of the sort of questions the teleologist must contemplate. In doing so I hope to continue to make clearer the heart of teleological commitments and reasoning.
43 C.D. Broad, *Five Types of Ethical Theory*, 162.
44 Ibid., 148.
45 Ibid., 211.
46 W.D. Ross, *Foundations of Ethics* (Oxford:The Clarendon Press, 1963), 319. See also ibid., 77.
47 Ibid.
48 Matthew Kramer, "How Not to Oppugn Consequentialism," *The Philosophical Quarterly* 46, 183 (1996), 213.
49 C.D. Broad, *Five Types of Ethical Theory*, 209.
50 I will adopt Broads definition of this, pace his critique of it, as the claim that one's duty – i.e. what one *ought* to do – is to maximize Universal Good. (Ibid.,158)
51 The related issues of whether and how circumstances are relevant in determining the sort of act an intentional behavior is will be discussed later in chapter 2. For now, let us accept Broad's suggestion that a deontologist may find the applicability of his norms to be, to a degree, sensitive to circumstances. Broad suggested as much when noting that deontological norms follow a form of prescribing or proscribing certain acts "in such and such a situation" (Ibid., 148).
52 Unlike the rule-utilitarian teleologist, the deontologist does not accept these norms *because* they promise or have shown effectiveness in guiding one to the most good(s)-producing acts, although all or some of them may indeed have this quality. Rather, they are accepted as valid norms for other reasons – e.g. as revealed by God, or as grounded in nature, or as self-evident to reason, or as validly derived from another valid norm, etc.
53 "Necessary" in the sense that without these consequences, the act is not the type of act that it is with them.
54 One might choose to dispute this by claiming that the act that saved lives was not a lie because those in whom false belief was intentionally caused were, for whatever reason, not *due* the truth. This dispute, however, would be generated by differing definitions of *lying* and, as such, it is not helpful to us here to explore this possible difference. Another might choose to dispute our claim that both acts mentioned above are lies by claiming that the act that saved lives was not actually a lie *because* it saved lives. If asked, "Then what sort of act was it?" one might respond that it was an act of saving lives. This approach, though, promises confusion, for what is one to call an act that saves some lives but at the expense of costing other lives? One might respond that if there is a net saving of lives, then it would be an act of life saving.

Yet how would one then distinguish an act of saving lives by lying from one that saves lives by some other means? For now let us assume that our objector will ultimately accept the distinction between an act and at least some of its consequences. When pushed to identify the act S which *accomplished* the saving of lives and which, if not done, would have allowed a different state of affairs to result, our objector would appear to have to allow that act S was "intentionally causing false belief in another." At bottom, then, perhaps the claim that S was not a lie is not a claim that the act was not a causing of false belief in another, but is rather a claim that an act of this nature was morally licit in this situation. What is to be noted here is that this position accepts that act S has an identity that is partly constituted by its causing of false belief but which is also separate and distinguishable from the consequences that result from its being performed in a certain situation.

55 The possibility of genuine conflict of deontologically understood duties is not directly relevant here and will be touched upon in chapters three and four.
56 John Stuart Mill, "Utilitarianism," in *The Utilitarians* (New York: Doubleday & Co., 1961), 407.
57 Ibid., 471. This position stands in stark contrast to the one found in *Veritatis Splendor* claiming that the consideration of consequences "is not sufficient for judging the moral quality of a concrete choice" (John Paul II, *Veritatis Splendor*, 98).
58 J.J.C. Smart and Bernard Williams, *Utilitarianism: For and Against*, 14.
59 C.D. Broad, *Five Types of Ethical Theory*, 212.
60 Ibid., 211. Recall that Broad allowed, correctly I believe, for the possibility that a teleologist may hold that there are several intrinsic goods or intrinsically good characteristics of things that ought to be maximized (Ibid., 215. See also Smart in *Utilitarianism For and Against*, 14, 24, 35). G.E. Moore seems to have been this sort of teleologist, arguing that the quality *good* is simple and indefinable (*Principia Ethica*, 10) and that "very many different things are good and evil in themselves, and that neither class of things possesses any other property which is both common to all its members and peculiar to them" (Ibid., ix-x).
61 Bernard Williams, *Utilitarianism For and Against*, 89. Douglas Portmore observes that "all non-consequentialist theories share this same oddness. They hold that certain acts are immoral even though they bring about what is admittedly the best outcome. For example, deontology prohibits the commission of murder even for the sake of minimizing the commission of murders overall" ("Position-Relative Consequentialism, Agent-Centered Options, and Supererogation," *Ethics* 113 [January, 2003], 304 n.5).
62 Paul Hurley "Agent-Centered Restrictions: Clearing the Air of Paradox," *Ethics* 108 (October, 1997), 120-121.
63 The objection that the deontologist here commits a logical fallacy, deriving statements like '*X ought to be respected unconditionally*' from statements like '*X is a human good*' need not be addressed in this context since it is relevant to the issue of the validity, but not of the type, of such a moral theory. What is important is to note that a deontologist may claim that some norms are identified through and grounded in a teleology of the human person.
64 F. Carney, "On McCormick and Teleological Morality," *The Journal of Religious Ethics* 6 (1978): 84.
65 Indeed, far from it. One may well ask a familiar question: How does '*X is a human good*' entail '*One ought to maximize X without constraint*'? Again, we need not enter into this debate, as our point has been made: the use of a teleology of the human person to identify the human good does not commit one to a teleological ethical theory.
66 J.J.C. Smart and Bernard Williams, *Utilitarianism: For and Against*, 14.
67 C.f. Ibid., 14, 24, 35.
68 J.J.C. Smart and Bernard Williams, *Utilitarianism: For and Against*, 27. Smart, a non-cognitivist (see Ibid., 4) found these differences to be ultimate in the non-cognitivist sense: they are grounded in "our ultimate attitudes or feelings" (Ibid., 7). Also to be noted is that he referred to these teleologists as utilitarians and did not use the term *consequentialism* in this work. Wil-

liams did use and distinguish these two terms, and correctly judged Smart's utilitarianism to be consequentialist in that "any kind of utilitarianism is by definition consequentialist, but 'consequentialism' is the broader term...utilitarianism is *one sort* of consequentialism—the sort...which is specially concerned with happiness" (Ibid., 79). Joel Kupperman would agree, putting the matter simply: "Utilitarian theories are the conjunction of value generalisations of a certain sort with consequentialism" (Joel Kupperman, *The Foundations of Morality* [London: George Allen & Unwin, 1983], 70).
69 J.J.C. Smart, "Extreme and Restricted Utilitarianism," in *Theories of Ethics*, ed. Philippa Foot (Oxford: Oxford University Press, 1967), 171.
70 Ibid., 172. Smart came to refer to extreme and restricted utilitarianism as, respectively, act and rule utilitarianism (*Utilitarianism For and Against*, 9), while Bernard Williams referred to them as, respectively, direct and indirect consequentialism (Ibid., 81).
71 J.J.C. Smart, "Extreme and Restricted Utilitarianism," 176.
72 Ibid., 175.
73 Ibid., 176.
74 Ibid., 181.
75 Robert Merrihew Adams, "Motive Utilitarianism," *The Journal of Philosophy* LXXIII 14 (1976), 468.
76 Ibid., 470.
77 Ibid., 471.
78 Ibid., 477.
79 Ibid. Adams believes that motive utilitarianism may take one of two forms: individualistic or universalistic motive utilitarianism. The former would claim that "a person's motivation on any given occasion is better, the greater the utility of *his* having it on *that* occasion," while the latter would claim that "a motivation is better, the greater the average probable utility of *anyone's* having it on *any* occasion" (Ibid., 480).
80 Joel Kupperman, *The Foundations of Morality* (London: George Allen & Unwin, 1983), 106.
81 Philip Pettit and Geoffrey Brennan, "Restrictive Consequentialism," *Australasian Journal of Philosophy* 64 4 (1986), 441.
82 Joel Kupperman, *The Foundations of Morality*, 106. Pettit and Brennan believe that an occasional non-optimific act is the cost one must pay "for seeking out optimific predispositions as well as optimific actions" (Pettit and Brennan, "Restrictive Consequentialism," 441). Pettit makes this same point as he lays out a consequentialist case for honoring such "interpersonal requirements" as "noninterference, equal consideration, and privacy" ("Consequentialism and Respect for Persons," *Ethics* 100 [October 1989], 116).
83 Joel Kupperman, *The Foundations of Morality*, 70.
84 J.J.C. Smart and Bernard Williams, *Utilitarianism: For and Against*, 79.
85 Even intentionally making some choices (or allowing some choices to be made) for non-consequentialist reasons may be, as we have seen, justified according to consequentialist criteria. Again, see Philip Pettit and Geoffrey Brennan, "Restrictive Consequentialism," *Australasian Journal of Philosophy*; see also J.J.C. Smart and Bernard Williams, *Utilitarianism: For and Against*, 51, 55, 119, 127-135.
86 It may be objected that rule utilitarians do just this, i.e. knowingly exclude data that may be relevant to a consequentialist assessment of certain concrete choices. Two points may be offered in response: One, some utilitarians believe that rule utilitarianism, to remain consequentialist, must collapse into act-utilitarianism and, for this reason, must *not* so exclude data judged relevant to any particular choice's productivity (see Smart, "Extreme and Restricted Utilitarianism" and *Utilitarianism: For and Against*). Two, recall from above that some consequentialists who counsel the exclusion of data relevant to a consequentialist assessment of some choices justify this exclusion on consequentialist grounds (see Robert Merrihew Adams, "Motive Utilitarianism," Philip Pettit and Geoffrey Brennan, "Restrictive Consequentialism,"

Joel Kupperman, *The Foundations of Morality*).
87 J.J.C. Smart and Bernard Williams, *Utilitarianism: For and Against*, 119.
88 Robert Merrihew Adams, "Motive Utilitarianism," *The Journal of Philosophy*. See also ibid., 467-481.
89 J.J.C. Smart, "Extreme and Restricted Utilitarianism," 181.
90 J.J.C. Smart and Bernard Williams, *Utilitarianism: For and Against*, 64.
91 Joel Kupperman, *The Foundations of Morality*, 124.
92 W.D. Ross, *Foundations of Ethics*, 3.
93 John Finnis, *Moral Absolutes: Tradition, Revision, and Truth* (Washington: The Catholic University of America Press, 1991), 14. Elsewhere, Finnis states that this conception of morality finds the creation of good states of affairs to be one's "supreme" or "decisive" moral responsibility (*Moral Absolutes*,15).
94 Joel Kupperman, *The Foundations of Morality*, 125.
95 Finnis believes (*Moral Absolutes*, 14; *Fundamentals of Ethics*, 88), as did Smart (*Utilitarianism For and Against*, 29), that the duty to maximize good(s) and the duty to minimize evil(s) are not necessarily two aspects of one duty. Nevertheless, a theory which asserts either of these two options as the supreme moral obligation will be consequentialist in nature. Smart labeled the sort of theory that asserts the primacy of the duty to minimize evil(s) as "negative utilitarianism." He attributed such a theory to Karl Popper, and finds it to be at least "theoretically possible" (Ibid.).
96 This theory would have to call for the *minimization* of evil (as opposed to its mere avoidance) for the same reasons, *mutatis mutandis*, that those theories which call for aiming at the good must call for the *maximization* of this end (see above).
97 John Finnis, *Moral Absolutes*, 13. Frank Jackson offers a similar outline for consequentialism's approach to choice: "Consequentialism approaches the question of whether an action is right or wrong in terms of a comparison of the possible outcomes of the action with the possible outcomes of each available alternative to that action....and the comparison of the various outcomes is carried out in terms of a consequentialist value function" ("Decision-theoretic Consequentialism and the Hearest and Dearest Objection," *Ethics* 101 [April, 1991] 462).
98 Ibid., 11; see also John Finnis, *Natural Law and Natural Rights*, V.7
99 For this notion of agent-relative constraints see Samuel Scheffler's *Introduction* in *Consequentialism and Its Critics* (Oxford: Oxford University Press, 1988), 4. We will consider these constraints in chapters two, three, and four.
100 J.J.C. Smart and Bernard Williams, *Utilitarianism: For and Against*, 13.

Chapter 2
Proportionalism

Having identified the defining marks of a consequentialist ethical theory, we will now consider the fundamental and characteristic elements of proportionalist thought. Once these elements have been identified and explained, the case will be made that Richard McCormick's brand of proportionalism is consequentialist. So, we turn to the question, "What is proportionalism?"

When answering this question, it is important to note Christopher Kaczor's observation that proportionalists "do not agree on all fundamental matters, not even about how to apply the theory to given cases..."[1] But while Kaczor is surely correct, so too was McCormick when he observed that

> common to all so-called proportionalists is the insistence that causing certain disvalues (ontic, nonmoral, premoral evils) in our conduct does not *ipso facto* make the action morally wrong, as certain traditional formulations supposed. The action becomes morally wrong when, all things considered, there is not proportionate reason.[2]

This common belief regarding what does and does not make an act morally wrong is the characteristic and defining claim of proportionalism. What is needed, and what will follow, is an explication of McCormick's observation as well as a consideration of other fundamental theses characteristic of the proportionalist school of thought. Drawing upon seminal proportionalist works as we proceed, we will examine what this theory claims determines the moral rightness and wrongness of acts, and we will consider the proportionalist rejection of exceptionless prohibitions on certain choices.

The Doctrine of Double Effect

A good way to begin to lay out the nature of proportionalist thought is by considering the doctrine of double effect as it is found in the Judeo-Christian ethical tradition. One does well to start here because, as will be seen, proportionalists place an element of this doctrine at the heart of their theory. This doctrine, as traditionally understood, seems to present consequence-indifferent constraints on agents and their choices, constraints the observance of which are necessary conditions for licit behavior. The details of this somewhat complex doctrine, and what aspect of it proportionalism adopts, will be detailed in a moment. For now, we turn to Joseph Mangan who offered a helpful study of the history of this approach to morally assessing choices.

Mangan found double effect thinking to have been

> understood implicitly many centuries before it was actually formulated. Even as far back as the events of the Old Testament, we find examples of moral actions justified under this doctrine.[3]

He added, though, that it is not until the writings of St. Thomas Aquinas in the thirteenth century that one finds this approach employed as an explicitly formulated tool of moral reasoning, enabling one to judge whether an act which promises to cause a proscribed evil may nevertheless be rightly done.[4] In his *Summa theologiae*, when considering the question of whether it is lawful to kill an agressor in self-defense (killing being generally proscribed in the moral universe of Aquinas[5]), St. Thomas writes:

> Nothing hinders one act from having two effects, only one of which is intended, while the other is beside the intention. Now moral acts take their species according to what is intended, and not according to what is beside the intention, since this is accidental as explained above (43, 3; I-II, 12, 1). Accordingly the act of self-defense may have two effects, one is the saving of one's life, the other is the slaying of the aggressor. Therefore this act, since one's intention is to save one's own life, is not unlawful, seeing that it is natural to everything to keep itself in 'being,' as far as possible. And yet, though proceeding from a good intention, an act may be rendered unlawful, if it be out of proportion to the end. Wherefore if a man, in self-defense, uses more than necessary violence, it will be unlawful: whereas if he repel force with moderation his defense will be lawful, because according to the jurists [Cap. Significasti, De Homicid. volunt. vel casual.], 'it is lawful to repel force by force, provided one does not exceed the limits of a blameless defense.' Nor is it necessary for salvation that a man omit the act of moderate self-defense in order to avoid killing the other man, since one is bound to take more care of one's own life than of another's. But as it is unlawful to take a man's life, except for the public authority acting for the common good, as stated above (3), it is not lawful for a man to intend killing a man in self-defense, except for such as have public authority, who while intending to kill a man in self-defense, refer this to the public good, as in the case of a soldier fighting against the foe, and in the minister of the judge struggling with robbers, although even these sin if they be moved by private animosity.[6]

While Mangan acknowledged but argued forcefully against the position that Thomas did not make use of this doctrine in his assessment of killing in self-defense,[7] that debate is not our concern here. Nor are we concerned with questions about the validity of the doctrine itself.[8] Our focus is on proportionalism's adoption of this doctrine and how that bears upon the question of whether this theory is consequentialist. What is to be noted here is Mangan's observation that

> ...even if, as a matter of cold, objective truth...St. Thomas did not teach the doctrine of the double effect as we understand it today, he still gave the initial impetus to its explanation and application in the authors who follow him even to the present.[9]

So, relying upon Thomas and a variety of moralists who follow him in the Catholic moral tradition, Mangan formulated this doctrine "in its full modern dress" as follows:

> A person may licitly perform an action that he forsees will produce a good and a bad effect provided that four conditions are verified at one and the same time: 1) that the action in itself from its very object be good or at least indifferent; 2) that the good effect and not the evil effect be intended; 3) that the good effect be not produced by means of the evil effect; 4) that there be a proportionately grave reason for permitting the evil effect.[10]

According to this doctrine, one who defends oneself against an agressor by, say, shooting them, though it is known that this method of defense will likely kill the agressor, may still have acted rightly, even in the face of a norm prohibiting intentional killing. If it is allowed that defending oneself is both good (or at least indifferent[11]) and a sufficiently grave reason to resort to possibly fatal violence, then so long as one's intention is self-defense, and so long as one does not intend the death of the agressor, one acts blamelessly. Now because each of the doctrine's four conditions must be met for an act (e.g., self-defense) which promises to cause a prohibited evil (e.g., killing) to be licit, it may be inferred that an act which promises and causes evil will be judged morally wrong if any of the following four elements are present: the object of the act is itself evil; the agent intends the evil effect; the evil effect is produced as a means to the agent's end; the end sought is not serious enough to justify the causing, however unintentional, of the evil.[12]

As mentioned above, the doctrine of double effect allows a deontologist to explain the fact that certain acts which promise to cause an evil proscribed by an exceptionless norm may nevertheless be morally licit. A deontologist who accepts this doctrine may by means of it reason that although an act, X, promises to cause a certain amount of to-be-avoided harm, harm whose intentional production is proscribed, X may yet be morally permissible if it satisfies the conditions that together form the doctrine. In this way, the doctrine allows one to argue that an apparently violated norm has not been violated after all, something that may be an especially helpful guide to choice for those who accept a set of norms which may, in some circumstances, lead to an apparent conflict of duties.[13] Consider, for example, the case of a pregnant woman who discovers that she has a cancerous uterus. If this woman accepts, in the deontological sense,[14] a norm enjoining her to respect and protect her own life and health and a norm enjoining her to protect her unborn child, and if neither of these two norms has priority over the other in any helpful sense, then a conflict of duties seems to arise.[15] The woman certainly cannot meet both obligations; she may look upon the choice to allow the pregnancy to continue as a violation of her duty to care for herself, but at the same time she may look upon the choice to have the diseased organ removed as a violation of her duty to care for her child. The doctrine of double effect, though, may provide some guidance here, pointing out that it is morally acceptable for the woman to fulfill one of these duties even though doing so will apparently violate the other. Whether she chooses to fulfill her duty to her child by continuing the pregnancy and thereby unintentionally exposing herself to death, or whether she chooses to fulfill her duty to her self and, by having her uterus removed, thereby unintentionally causes the death of her child, she will have acted rightly provided the doctrine's conditions are met. Now whether or not there would be a consensus among deontologists that this case is a valid application of the doctrine of double effect is not important. What is important to note in this at least plausible application of the doctrine is the deontological manner of approaching the case and morally assessing the woman's choices.

One may contrast this example of a deontological approach to choice-assessment with a consequentialist approach. A consequentialist would maintain that what one ought to do in such a scenario is that act which promises the net maximization of the relevant good(s). Frank Jackson explains:

> Consequentialism approaches the question of whether an action is right or wrong in terms of a comparison of the possible outcomes of the action with the possible outcomes of each available alternative to that action....and the comparison of the various outcomes is carried out in terms of a consequentialist value function.[16]

According to this approach, the woman's duties to protect herself and her child are obligatory *in this case* to the extent that following them *in this case* promises to maximize good(s), the end by which all choices are measured. The teleologist's supreme duty makes impossible such a conflict between equally valid and unsubordinated duties, thereby rendering the doctrine of double effect, as outlined and applied above, irrelevant.

Far from irrelevant in the Catholic moral tradition, the doctrine became more and more conspicuous over time. After identifying Thomas as the one who first formalized this doctrine for his tradition, Mangan traced its development from Cardinal Cajetan in the sixteenth century, through some of the seventeenth century Salmanticenses, to Joannes Gury's *Compendium Theologiae Moralis* in the nineteenth century. Mangan described how attention to the doctrine gradually increased, with it initially appearing only when needed to assess a limited number of specific cases,[17] but later being acknowledged and discussed as a fundamental doctrine of moral reasoning applicable to the whole range of moral theology.[18] And it remains relevant today. Joseph Boyle recently observed that

> double effect has come to play an important role in non-Catholic applied ethics in several areas, notably thinking about the morality of warfare and about medical ethics – in virtually every area of bioethics from abortion and other 'Catholic' issues to euthanasia, withholding treatment, and concealing information.[19]

An important point which emerges from this analysis, one which will make plain the break with tradition that proportionalism carries forward, is that though the doctrine's role and status in Catholic moral thought developed over time, the conditions that constitute it remained, explicitly or implicitly, intact.[20]

Peter Knauer and Commensurate Reason

Peter Knauer, a moral theologian in the Catholic tradition, offered his 1967 article *The Hermeneutic Function of the Principle of Double Effect* as a critical analysis and correction of what he perceived to be flaws in his tradition's understanding of the doctrine and its function.[21] This reconsideration of the traditional understanding of the doctrine and its place in moral reasoning marks the public beginning of the movement that came to be known as proportionalism and provided a theoretical template for future proportionalists, including Richard McCormick. Indeed, in 1989 McCormick judged Knauer's article to be "the opening shot in a 25-year discussion of the proper understanding of the moral norms within the community of Catholic moral theologians."[22] The significance of Knauer's thought was not lost on those who rejected it, either. What many believed was at stake in this emerging "discussion" was captured by Germain

Grisez, another Catholic moralist and a critic of proportionalism, when he accused Knauer of "carrying through a revolution in principle while pretending only a clarification of ideas."[23] What this putative "revolution in principle" was will be seen in what follows.

Knauer began his article by embracing the doctrine of double effect. He claimed that the doctrine enables one to grasp

> the meaning of the fundamental concepts of traditional morality in their interrelation in the tradition itself,[24]

and he accepted the somewhat simple moral belief that the doctrine articulates and elucidates, namely, that "not every permission or causing of physical evil is a moral evil."[25] He also accepted Mangan's conclusion that the doctrine was first formulated by Aquinas.[26] What caught the attention of friends and foes alike, though, was his call for the following: laying aside the third condition in Mangan's formulation; making the criterion which determines whether the fourth condition has been met (the presence or absence of a proportionate reason) to be the criterion which also determines whether the first two conditions have been met; and expanding the scope of the doctrine's applicability so that it functions as the centerpiece of all moral reasoning. Each of these moves is significant, and each will be considered in turn, beginning now with the last one.

Although, as has been mentioned, the doctrine's scope of relevance within the Christian moral tradition had expanded since its earliest formulation, Knauer called for a still-further widening of this scope; indeed, he called for it to be widened it as far as possible. He claimed that the doctrine (as he interpreted it) is "*the* fundamental principle of *all* morality," and that as it "responds to the question whether in a given case the permission or causing of evil is justified or not," it "reveals itself as a principle which provides the criterion for *every* moral judgment."[27] In making his case for these claims, Kanuer focused upon the fourth condition in Mangan's formulation, the one which asserts that an act which promises to cause evil cannot be licit unless there be "a proportionately grave reason for permitting the evil effect."[28] Knauer made this condition the sufficient condition of all morally licit acts, asserting that moral evil

> consists in the last analysis in the permission or causing of a physical evil which is not justified by a commensurate reason.[29]

He believed that this seemingly heterodox thesis actually follows the thought of Aquinas, and when elaborating his position on what makes a morally wrong act to be morally wrong, he turned for support to Thomas's aforementioned article on killing in self-defense.[30] Knauer understood Thomas to conclude that

> in sinning, man seeks a real good, but his act in its total existential entirety is not proportioned to this good. The evil arising thereby, whether it is desired or not, belongs objectively to the act and is objectively what is intended.[31]

Put simply, Knauer's position was this: if an agent pursues a good in a manner that promises to cause evil which is disproportionate to that good, then one must judge this evil to have been intended by the agent, and this intention of evil makes the act morally wrong. In laying out his position, Knauer altered some of the concepts which the traditional version of the doctrine of double effect employs. Once these alterations were complete, he offered his own modified version of the doctrine and set it to govern all act assessments.

In order to see how Knauer carried out his revision of the traditional doctrine of double effect, let us return to condition two from Mangan's formulation of this doctrine, i.e., the condition that an act's evil effects not be intended by the agent. Knauer accepted this as a necessary condition for a morally licit act but, at the same time, he argued that an agent who was "psychologically concentrated on" causing evil in pursuit of a good may nevertheless not have intended the evil in any morally relevant sense.[32] If one notes that in this context Knauer's *psychologically concentrated on causing evil* means *purposefully causing evil*, one may wonder how it can be argued that an agent may not have intended the evil that this agent purposefully caused.[33] Knauer allowed himself such reasoning by claiming that "the concept of intention in ethics evidently means something different from what it means in psychology."[34] Standing upon this claim, he then asserted that an agent cannot be said to have *morally* intended any evil that this agent purposefully brought about so long as this agent acted for a commensurate reason.[35]

Now Knauer's understanding of the third condition of the traditional doctrine of double effect, i.e. the demand that the evil of a mixed act not be used as the means to a good end, will also be seen to have turned on his notion of commensurate reason.[36] Consider, for example, the tradition's claim that "Direct abortion, that is to say, abortion willed either as an end or a means, is gravely contrary to the moral law."[37] According to the reasoning which supports this claim, any abortion which is purposefully done, either as an end or as a means to a good end (say, as a means of saving of the mother's life) is an act in which the evil of killing is *intended* by the agent (in the tradition's sense of *intend*).

Because this act involves the intention of evil, it is to be judged morally wrong.[38] One may note that this third condition in the traditional formulation of the doctrine of double effect is conceptually linked to the second condition, the prohibition against intending evil. What the third condition adds to this second condition is the claim that one may not licitly intend evil even in order to accomplish a good end. Knauer, though, called for the dissolution of this link between the prohibition against *intending* evil and the prohibition against purposefully *doing* evil as a means to a good end. He wrote:

> Thomas also held that the evil might not be effected directly. According to him, the intention must be accidental (*per accidens*); it must be beyond intention (*praeter intentionem*). The usual explanation of this terminology understands the pair of concepts, 'direct-indirect', in the sense of direct and indirect physical causality; but this explanation is questionable. I say that an evil effect is not 'directly intended' only if there is a 'commensurate ground' for its permission or causation.[39]

Knauer thus committed himself to the position that not all instances of purposefully *causing* evil are equivalent to the traditionally proscribed *intending* evil. Knauer's thesis would allow an agent purposefully to bring about evil as a means to realizing a commensurate good without such purposeful behavior having to be judged morally wrong according to the prohibitions on intending evil and on effecting evil as a means to a good end. For Knauer, the agent's intention in these cases is determined by the presence or absence of a commensurate reason.[40] Such a relationship between the concepts *intention* and *commensurate reason* allowed Knauer to argue that some acts which would have to be judged morally wrong according to the traditional prohibition against intending evil ought instead to be judged morally licit so long as the good pursued is commensurate to the evil purposefully caused.

It should be noted here that while the traditional doctrine of double effect prohibits a means-end relationship between an act's evil and good effects, Knauer rejected the notion that an act's good and evil effects are separable in a manner that can support and answer the question of whether the evil was employed as a means to the good. He proposed that the traditional distinction between an act's good and evil effects be replaced by the more helpful notion of an act's good and evil *aspects*.[41] He would then replace the heretofore morally decisive question of whether an act's evil effects are used as a means to its good end, with the question of whether there is a "correspondence" or a "contradiction" between the good and evil aspects of the act.[42] The consequentialist nature of these alterations will soon become apparent when it is pointed out that

Knauer's notions of a *correspondence* or *contradiction* between the good and evil aspects of an act are, like his notion of *intention*, functions of commensurate reason, a concept to which we shall soon turn.

Having altered the concept of *intention* and having made room for the possibility of licitly causing evil as a means to a good end, Knauer presented his own somewhat shorter version of the doctrine of double effect:

> One may permit the evil effect of his act only if this is not intended in itself but is indirect and justified by a commensurate reason.[43]

This formulation appears to offer three conditions for licitly choosing an act that promises to cause evil: 1) the agent does not intend the evil; 2) the evil is to be produced indirectly; 3) the good pursued must be commensurate with the evil promised. However, these seemingly separate conditions collapse into one. Recall that Knauer believed that any physical evil an agent purposefully causes is unintended in the moral sense if that agent had a commensurate reason for causing it. Add to this his statement that

> there are not two distinct requirements when I speak of the 'indirect causing' of evil and of 'a commensurate reason' for the act.[44]

So what Knauer argued, then, was that any evil purposefully brought about must be judged to have been *indirectly* caused (in the *moral* sense of the term) if the agent brought about this evil for a commensurate good. He claimed that such purposeful evil-doing

> is justified by a commensurate reason; *although the cause is physically direct, it is not direct in a moral sense.*[45]

And so one sees that Knauer proposed a single criterion for determining whether an agent directly or indirectly caused evil, and whether that agent morally intended this evil: the presence or absence of a commensurate reason. If the agent acted for a commensurate good, then the evil forseen and purposefully caused was morally unintended and indirectly produced; the act, therefore, must be judged morally licit.

And so all of the criticisms and conceptual alterations that Knauer offered in his seminal proportionalist article dovetail toward his claim that mixed acts which involve the purposeful causing of evil will be morally licit on one condition: that they aim at a commensurate good.[46] His statement that moral evil "consists in the last analysis in the permission or causing of a physical evil which is not justified by a commensurate reason"[47] may now be more fully understood and its significance more fully appreciated, as may his claim that

> the principle of double effect means that to cause or permit an evil without commensurate reason is a morally bad act.[48]

It seems fair to say, then, that given Knauer's analysis the doctrine of double effect may be more accurately referred to as the principle of commensurate reason. Indeed, As Bernard Hoose puts it, "Knauer effectively reduced the number of conditions in the principle of double effect from four to one: the need for a proportionate or commensurate reason"[49]

We have seen that for Knauer the purposeful causing of evil without a commensurate reason means that the evil chosen was not, in Aquinas's words, *praeter intentionem*. This being so, the act is to be judged as one that aims at (i.e., *intends* in Knauer's moral sense) evil and is, as such, a morally wrong act. One may wonder then how this theory, a progenitor of McCormick's, can be genuinely consequentialist since it incorporates a morally decisive prohibition against ever intending evil. By claiming that an act in which evil is intended is, as such, a morally wrong act, Knauer seems to have offered an agent-relative and consequence-indifferent prohibition. Such a prohibition would seem to be at home in a deontological rather than in a consequentialist ethical theory since the latter type of theory finds only the net maximization of good(s), not the intention of the agent, to be decisive in the moral assessment of acts. Yet the deontological sound of Knauer's prohibition is misleading. Although he did claim that one may not morally intend evil, one must keep in mind that he distinguished the concept of *moral intention* from the concept of *psychological intention*. He relied upon this distinction to argue that an agent may psychologically intend (i.e. purposefully bring about) evil as a means to a good end without being guilty of morally intending this evil, so long as the good the agent aims at is proportionate to the evil purposefully caused. Knauer's assertion, then, of the apparently deontological, agent-relative constraint that one may never licitly intend evil turns out to be, in reality, the assertion that the moral rightness or wrongness of a mixed act is a function of the proportion between that act's good and evil aspects.

In fairness to Knauer, it should be noted that he rejected the notion that to require a mixed act to have a commensurate reason in order to be morally licit is simply to require that "the good must outweigh the evil."[50] Yet, this disavowal aside, Knauer's analysis leads to the conclusion that the moral defect of any mixed, morally wrong act will be that such an act yields a disproportion between the good pursued and the evil effected, an account of morally wrong acts which has at least a strong suggestion of consequentialism.

It was noted earlier that Knauer would like to replace the question of whether an act's evil effects were used as a means to its good end with the question of whether the good and evil aspects of the act correspond with or contradict each other. It was also noted that these two notions, *correspondence* and *contradiction*, are at the heart of Knauer's concept of commensurate reason. We will now look more closely at this account of commensurate reason because, as will be seen, McCormick employs similar notions in his own version of proportionalism and cites them as evidence that this theory is not consequentialist.

Knauer claimed that

> The answer to the question whether the reason for an act is commensurate or not depends on rigorous objective criteria and not on merely subjective or even imaginary good intention.[51]

Furthermore, he maintained that

> It is not my meaning that any act at all is permissible as long as there is a serious reason for it. Such a conclusion would indeed be the most evil form of ethical relativism. But a commensurate reason in my thesis is not the same as a serious reason.[52]

In Knauer's estimation, to ask whether an act possesses a commensurate reason is to ask whether the good and evil aspects (effects) of this act *correspond to* or *contradict* each other. These two notions were explicated by Knauer in terms of the realization of human values, and he presented this element of his theory by considering some specific issues, one of which is contraception. He was working within a moral tradition which maintains a deontological proscription on contraception on the grounds that such acts are contrary to the created nature and finality of the human reproductive act.[53] Yet to the question of whether or not an act of contraception is morally licit, Knauer applied his criterion of commensurate reason. He explained that, in regard to this issue,

> the criterion of commensurate reason means that the value whose achievement is realizable only by contraceptive measures in a premoral sense may not in the last analysis be *contradicted* by these measures *by preventing in the long run the highest possible realization of this very*

value with the smallest possible evil.[54]

In light of this understanding of *correspondence* and *contradiction* in terms of the realization of values, one may now appreciate Knauer's statement that "*only* as it contradicts its own end is the direct permission *or causing* of an evil forbidden."[55] Furthermore, Knauer offered the following as the standard by which acts are to be assessed: "means are to be judged as to whether or not they contradict the highest possible realization of the desired value on the whole."[56] Now if one keeps in mind this criterion of act assessment while also considering his claim that, for agents, "what is fundamental is the affirmative obligation to realize in the best possible way all the values of creation,"[57] then the consequentialist character of his theory becomes more evident. In short, what Knauer did was assert a fundamental duty to realize certain values, and then morally assess acts according to their productivity with respect to these values.

Moral Norms

Four years after Knauer article presented his conceptually retooled doctrine of double effect, Joseph Fuchs added another seminal article to what was becoming the proportionalist movement. Fuchs's *The Absoluteness of Moral Terms* is significant in that it presented an engagement of Knauer's position on commensurate reason as the criterion for morally assessing acts, with the Catholic moral tradition's set of exceptionless material moral norms.[58] In doing so, Fuchs indicated the sort of norms that proportionalist thought would and would not support. Fuchs maintained that only formal norms, not material ones, may be genuinely exceptionless, since a formal norm includes what a material norm leaves out, viz., a judgment of the agent's intention.[59] The problem Fuchs found with material norms was that they pronounce a moral judgment on bare behaviors, as when they prohibit all contraceptive acts, for example. Fuchs, though, claimed that unless one knows the reason why an agent chose a prohibited behavior, one lacks sufficient data for a moral assessment of that choice. Distancing himself from his tradition's set of norms prescribing specific behaviors, Fuchs wrote:

> Undoubtedly there are universal ethical statements in the strict sense. Nevertheless they *always* remain formal in a certain sense, at least in so far as they are not *material* norms of action, i.e. norms which indicate whether actions exactly described materially are ethically permissable or not.[60]

Fuchs considered the traditional norm *Thou shalt not kill*, and found it to be

> too broadly stated; it would be better to say, 'Thou shall not commit *murder*'; that is, 'Thou shall not kill unjustly.'[61]

He would have it noted that the norm *Thou shall not kill unjustly* does not simply specify a behavior (killing) but also contains an element indicating under what conditions this behavior may not (and, by inference, under what formal condition it may) be chosen. And, as will soon be seen, Fuchs's criterion for determining whether such a choice was justified was the presence or absence of a proportionate reason.[62]

Fuchs began to develop the part of his argument with which we are most concerned by returning to the question that the doctrine of double effect is meant to answer: *What if one "intends and effects good, but this necessarily involves effecting evil also?"*[63] Fuchs's answer clearly followed Knauer's, both in the presupposition that one must not intend (in the moral sense) evil, and in the criterion offered for determining whether an agent morally intended an evil purposefully produced. Fuchs's response to the question just posed appears, on first read, to be consistent with at least some of the traditional requirements of the doctrine of double effect. He wrote:

> Here we take up the question: When is human action, or when is man in his action (morally) good? Must not the answer be: When he *intends and effects* a human good (value) – in the premoral sense, for example, life, health, joy, culture, etc. (for only this is recta ratio): but not when he *has in view and effects* a human *non-good*, an evil (non-value) – in the premoral sense, for example, death, wounding, wrong, etc.[64]

Fuchs, like Knauer before him, claimed that to intend evil in an act is to commit a morally wrong act; thus appearing to have embraced a deontological norm prohibiting an agent from intending evil.[65] However, once again like Knauer, Fuchs's notion of *moral* intention was explicated in terms of proportionate reason. While Fuchs accepted the rule that "evil (in a premoral sense) effected by a human agent must not be intended as such...,"[66] his words must be understood in light of his prior claim that

> if the realization of the evil through the intended realization of the good is justified as a proportionately related cause, then in this case only good was intended.[67]

Given Fuchs's explication of moral intention in terms of the proportion between the good and evil aspects of an act, his statement that an action "cannot be judged morally in its materiality (killing, wounding, going to the moon), without reference to the intention of the agent"[68] must be understood to mean that an action cannot be morally assessed without reference to the proportion between its good and evil aspects. According to Fuchs, then, it would be morally licit for an agent purposefully to cause evil if this evil were brought about in order to realize "a proportionately related cause." So long as this requirement for a proportionate reason is met, the agent has not violated the norm not to intend evil.

On first read, Fuchs also appears to be in agreement with the doctrine of double effect's prohibition against using evil as a means to a good end. He wrote "*The end does not justify the means*, that is, the morally bad means. This tenet is, of course, correct."[69] This claim may offer support to those who would argue that Fuchs's position is not consequentialist because he appears here to have embraced a deontological-sounding doctrine according to which an act may be judged but which is not subordinated to the duty to maximize good(s). His position, though, is a bit more complex than this defense suggests. Fuchs argued that once a particular means has been judged to be immoral in its specific context (i.e. as *this* means X to *that* end Y, here and now), one may not licitly use it in that specific context to achieve that particular end. While Fuchs did claim that,

> When and to the extent that it has been established that an action is *morally* bad, it may not be performed as a means toward attaining a good end,[70]

it must be noted that this statement applies only to means that have already been morally assessed according to his proportionate-reason standard.[71] This being so, his claim that a good end does not justify a morally bad means amounts to the claim that one may not purposefully cause any evil that has been judged to be disproportionate to the good that this evil would be employed to realize. And to the more probative question of whether a good end may justify deliberately causing a *physically* evil means, Fuchs replied:

> if there is a question only of evil in the *pre*moral sense, such as death, wounding, dishonor, etc., the intention and the realization of a good can possibly justify the doing of an evil...[72]

Although he did not explicitly state so, what Fuchs meant by the phrase "the doing of an evil," was "the *purposeful* doing of an evil," a notion which seems to be the equivalent of Knauer's notion of being "psychologically concentrated" on causing evil. Consider the example of purposefully killing oneself. The claim that it may be morally licit *purposefully* to kill oneself in order to achieve an appropriate end should be distinguished from the claim that one may only tolerate ones death as the unavoidable side effect of an act which aims at some good. An example of this latter would be throwing oneself on a grenade in a crowded fox hole. This scenario seems to be the sort of moral situation to which the traditional doctrine of double effect would apply, yielding a judgment that one acted licitly, yet not undermining the validity of the tradition's deontological prohibition against purposefully killing oneself. However, Fuchs clearly suggested that purposefully killing oneself may indeed be permissible in certain circumstances. When reflecting upon his tradition's prohibition against killing he asked,

> How could one make a judgment that would take in *all* the human possibilities – even granting that one had succeeded in understanding rightly and judging rightly those possibilities that were forseen?...Is there meanwhile no life situation that might justify suicide, as for example, the only means of preserving a state secret...?[73]

These comments on purposeful killing illustrate Fuch's belief that traditional material norms which have prohibited certain choices without exception ought to be subordinated to the criterion of proportionate reason. He revealed the moral significance he attributed to the proportion between the good and evil aspects of an act when he wrote that

> a behavioral norm, universally valid in the full sense, would presuppose that those who arrive at it could know or forsee adequately *all the possible combinations* of the action concerned with circumstances and intentions, with (premoral) values and non-values. (bona and mala physica). A priori, such knowledge is not attainable.[74]

Put simply, Fuchs maintained that since one cannot know *a priori* whether circumstances may arise in which the only way to realize some particular good is by purposefully causing a proportionate physical evil, norms ought not to prohibit without exception the purposeful causing of any particular physical evil; instead, norms should prohibit the purposeful causing of evil which is disproportionate to the good pursued. We will soon see that Fuchs' subordination of moral norms to an assessment of the good and evil effects of an act was adopted by Richard McCormick, a move that will play a central role in our case that McCormick's theory is a form of consequentialism.

Two Types of Evil

Louis Janssens's 1972 article *Ontic Evil and Moral Evil* continued the refinement of the theory initially laid out by Knauer and applied by Fuchs.[75] In *The Hermeneutic Function of the Principle of Double Effect*, Knauer had commented that

> every human act brings evil effects with it. The choice of a value always means concretely that there is denial of another value which must be given as a price in exchange.[76]

Five years later, Janssens offered his rather thorough analysis of the limitations of humans as agents, an analysis which supported Knauer's comments above and which complemented well Knauer's position that proportionate reason is "a principle which provides the criterion for *every* moral judgment."[77]

Janssens found human agents to be constrained in several inescapable ways. It is, in his estimation, an unfortunate fact that

> when we choose a certain action, we must at the same time, at least for the time being, postpone all other possible acts. This is the meaning of Bergson's words: '*Tout choix est un sacrifice*'; or as the traditional terminology puts it, each commissio (act) is an omissio.[78]

Our inability to do all that we would was identified by Janssens as one of the forms of ontic evil we experience. Human agents know that

> our power to act on things is limited and graded by our corporeal capacities....Our body is a means to action. But it is also a handicap which impedes our action. This hindrance may hurt us as an ontic evil.[79]

Additionally, human beings are able to control the material world

> only imperfectly and partially. Detrimental consequences flow from the use of things in the constant accomplishments of every day, e.g., a walk gives me rest and fresh air but it also wears out my shoes.[80]

Furthermore, although "our human existence is also *being with, by and for each other*," it is nevertheless true that

> community life also means that all of us take something of the products of the corporate enterprise. Whatever is consumed or used by one member of the community is not available to another at the same time.[81]

These observations lead Janssens to conclude that every concrete human act "implicates ontic evil,"[82] that is, "ontic evil is *always* present in our concrete activity."[83] Given this *de facto* inseparability of human activity and ontic evil, Janssens argued that

> it cannot be concluded that it is inevitably morally evil to cause ontic evil or to allow it to remain in this world by our actions. If this were the case, there would not be any way to act morally.[84]

Janssens' analysis of the nature and limitations of human agency does not necessarily separate him from the deontological moral thinking which formulated and employs the traditional doctrine of double effect. Indeed, far from it, since it seems that this analysis would fortify the position of deontologists who accept the traditional doctrine and who argue that it is a necessary tool in the assessment of some choices. Yet one can also see how Janssens analysis and conclusion might fit well with Knauer's argument for the necessity of the criterion of proportionate reason in all act assessments. If it is allowed that all human acts aim at some good but also cause some ontic evil, then it is not unreasonable to believe, with Knauer and others, that the central question for the moral assessment of every human act is, "Was the good pursued proportionate to the evil caused?" In the end, though, what separates Janssens' thought from the deontological commitments expressed in the traditional doctrine of double effect, and what places him in the Knauer-Fuchs camp vis-a-vis the moral assessment of human acts, is his answer to a basic moral question he himself posed: *When and to what extent are we justified in causing or allowing ontic evil?*[85]

Janssens answer to this question is that one is justified in causing or allowing ontic evil if one is seeking to realize a good, and if there is a due proportion between the evil in question and the good being sought. Janssens referred to this basic position as the requirement for due proportion, or *debita proportio*, between means and end. This requirement demands that

> no intrinsic contradiction between the means and the end may be found in the total act when the act is placed in the light of reason. Put into terms of the philosophy of values, this means that the means must be consistent with the value of the end. Or, according to a more abstract formulation, the principle which has been affirmed in the end must not be negated by the means.[86]

And Janssens claimed a universal scope for this requiremnent when he added that

> Knauer pointed out very well that the axiom of the *debita proportio* or of the unwarrantableness of the inner contradiction between means and end is the central norm of *each* human act.[87]

To some, Janssens's position may appear to be deontological in that he offered the notion of some sort of consistency or contradiction between means and end as the standard of due proportion, while offering due proportion as the standard by which all human acts are to be assessed. The consequentialist notion of a net maximization of to-be-pursued ends as the supreme criterion of act assessment is absent, or so it seems, and in its place stands a Kantian-sounding demand for consistency between means and ends. But upon closer inspection, the deontological look of Janssens's position fades and its consequentialist character becomes clearer.

In order to appreciate the consequentialist nature of Janssens's answer to the question, *When and to what extent are we justified in causing or allowing ontic evil?*, one should first consider some other aspects of his moral theory. Janssens believed that "the very object of morality is to promote the truly human growth of the individual and the social communities."[88] Deriving a statement of fundamental moral obligation from this goal, he claimed that

> it is our pressing duty to actualize those possibilities for the well-being of each and every individual. That which can be used to further the development of individuals and society thereby becomes a moral dictate.[89]

Janssens thus identified human growth and well-being as the goal and standard of moral behavior, and explained ontic evil to be the frustration of this goal.[90] But in addition to this account of ontic evil and this statement of moral duty, Janssens made the deontological-sounding claim that "ontic evil should never be the *ultimate* goal of our intention."[91] This assertion, though, must be placed within the context of his Aristotelean-Thomistic explanation that

> any dimension of ontic evil is a lack of perfection, a deficiency which frustrates our inclinations. We label it *evil* when it affects a human subject insofar as it appears to the consciousness as a lack and a want, and to the extent that it is detrimental and harmful to the development of individuals and communities.[92]

And, Janssens believed, "it follows from this definition that we should never per se will ontic evil."[93]

So, bringing the aforementioned elements of Janssens's moral theory together, one finds him having asserted that an agent should never will as the end of his act the frustration of human development (individual and communal), that is, an agent should never *will* against the to-be-pursued end Janssens identified. Now, the consequentialist character of this position becomes apparent when Janssens, after repeating this prohibition on *willing* against human growth, added his account of what *constitutes* such willing:

> ...it is bad to will ontic evil which obstructs this growth. *And this happens from the moment we bring about or tolerate more ontic evil than is necessary to make our actions into effective actions.*[94]

As it turns out, then, Janssens' exceptionless prohibition against willing ontic evil as an end is an exceptionless prohibition against acts which bring about more ontic evil than necessary to achieve his previously identified to-be-pursued end(s). He claimed that

> If our actions contain more ontic evil than they must have to be the proper means, they are not ordered properly to the goals of man and society. *Consequently, they are immoral.*[95]

As Janssens understood it, a morally wrong act is one that produces more ontic evil than necessary in realizing goods, goods whose realization he claimed are the object of morality. It is this recurring account of what makes a morally wrong act to be morally wrong which suggests that this proportionate-reason centered moral theory is consequentialist and different in kind than the theory whose deontological commitments gave birth to the traditional doctrine of double effect.

One is further drawn to the conclusion that what Janssens offered is a consequentialist moral theory when one considers his position on the concrete moral norms of his tradition, norms that place deontological constraints on the behavior of moral agents. At the end of *Ontic Evil and Moral Evil*, he wrote:

> We have undertaken this study to explain the meaning and the significance of the *concrete material norms* of morality. This category of norms prohibits *ontic evil*. They show us that we should not kill, maim someone, utter falsehoods, harm others...fail to act to eliminate ignorance, sickness, hunger, etc. They are reducible to: you shall *neither* bring about (cause by your *actions*) *nor* tolerate (allow to grow by your *omissions*, by failing to act) ontic evil.[96]

Yet, as he believed he had shown, causing ontic evil is an inescapable fact of human activity. With this fact in mind, Janssens urged that these aforementioned norms be regarded only as setting an ideal for human agents. Practically, they function to

> pronounce us guilty of immorality when we bring about or tolerate more ontic evil than is necessary to realize the moral objectives of our human existence.[97]

As if to emphasize this point, Janssens repeated it one page later:

> The concrete norms are *relative*: they only forbid that we cause or tolerate ontic evil which exceeds the boundaries of the measure of means to the actualization of good ends.[98]

Furthermore, his claim that "the fundamental concrete norms which guard the essential values – life, human integrity, truthfulness in societal relations – will always be valid," must be understood in light of the foregoing, that is, they are valid only in the ideal sense he laid out and are in practice subordinate to the supreme criterion of *debita proportio*, a subordination which McCormick accepted.[99]

McCormick's Synthesis

Having considered three seminal works in the proportionalist movement, we turn now to Richard McCormick. We have already indicated in the Introduction McCormick's significance in the field of moral theology. Here it will be seen that McCormick wove together and developed Knauer's position on proportionate reason and intention, Fuchs's position on the force and validity of norms, and Janssens' observations on ontic evil and the limits of human agency. The focus of the chapters to come will be McCormick's developed arguments and case analyses as the characteristic elements of his brand of proportionalism are consider in greater detail. At this point, though, we will briefly lay out the general structure of his proportionalism, indicating some of the places where our consequentialist charge will be made.

We begin by looking at McCormick's 1973 essay *Ambiguity in Moral Choice*.[100] There he reviewed the early development of proportionalism and offered a critical synthesis and development of elements from these earlier positions.[101] In this work McCormick noted Knauer's thesis that "moral evil consists in the permission or causing of a physical evil without commensurate reason," and then offered this account of Knauer's notion of proportionate reason:

> It is not just any reason, meaningful or important as it may be. Rather a reason is com-

mensurate if the value realizable here and now by measures involving physical evil in a premoral sense is not in the long run undermined and contradicted by these measures but supported and maximized.[102]

> wrongfulness must be attributed to a lack of proportion. By that I mean that the value I am pursuing is being pursued in a way calculated in human judgment (not without prediscursive elements) to undermine it.[103]

It should be noted that in McCormick's formulation of Knauer's notion of proportionate reason, one finds the rather practical criteria of *undermining, supporting,* and *maximizing* values. The supremacy that McCormick assigned these criteria in the moral assessment of acts comes through clearly in many of his case analyses, analyses which bear witness to his claim that he accepted "the substance of Knauer's presentation," including (and, for us, especially) "the decisive nature of commensurate reason."[104]

In summarizing and agreeing with Knauer, we have seen McCormick make reference to "physical evil in a premoral sense." It would perhaps be helpful to take a moment to explicate this phrase. McCormick's "physical evil in a premoral sense" is equivalent to Janssens's now familiar "ontic evil," and alludes to an important aspect of proportionalist act-assessment. Knauer, Fuchs, and Janssens at least implicitly took the position that prior to the judgment of whether the ontic evil an agent purposefully caused was caused for a proportionate reason, one may not morally assess the agent's choice; hence McCormick's practice of referring to the evil of this not-yet-assessed act as "physical evil in a *pre*-moral sense." The claim is that if, for example, one knows that X purposefully killed Y then, given that life is a good, one knows that X effected physical evil, that is, evil in a premoral sense. However, not until it is known why X killed Y and whether this end was commensurate to the ontic evil of killing Y can one make the further judgment about whether X's act was *morally* wrong.[105] The moral rightness or wrongness of X's choice to kill Y will be determined by whether the value that X sought to realize by killing Y is "undermined and contradicted" or "supported and maximized" by this instance of killing.

Setting proportionate reason as the supreme criterion in the moral assessment of acts entails the subordination to this criterion of any material norm enjoining or forbidding any specific behavior. For example, a deontologist may accept a norm prohibiting the choice to make an act of intercourse infertile. This norm may be grounded in the belief that since human procreation is a Divinely-created and ordained good, human creatures are under an unconditional duty to respect the nature of this good; hence, one may never purposefully work against this good, as contraception does. Note, for example, the reasoning of Pope Pius XI:

> But no reason, however grave, may be put forward by which anything intrinsically against nature may become conformable to nature and morally good. Since, therefore, the conjugal act is destined primarily by nature for the begetting of children, those who in exercising it deliberately frustrate its natural power and purpose, sin against nature, and commit a deed which is shameful and intrinsically vicious.[106]

Pope Paul VI affirmed and expanded on this exceptionless prohibition against certain specific behaviors:

> the direct interruption of the generative process already begun, and, above all, directly willed and procured abortion, even if for therapeutic reasons, are to be *absolutely* excluded as licit means of regulating birth. Equally to be excluded, as the teaching authority of the Church has frequently declared, is direct sterilization, whether perpetual or temporary, whether of the man or of the woman. Similarly excluded is *every* action which, either in anticipation of the conjugal act, or in its accomplishment, or in the development of its natural consequences, propose, whether as an end or as a means, to render procreation impossible.[107]

These prohibitions against specific behaviors function deontologically in that they articulate an unconditional duty to respect (i.e. never intentionally to act against) the nature of human sexual reproduction. According to this position, to choose to contracept the conjugal act is to choose an act which by its very nature is morally wrong, regardless of the consequences that the act might promise and produce in certain circumstances.[108] Yet this moral reasoning and the exceptionless material norms it grounds are inconsistent with the foundational ethical belief that McCormick found in Knauer and embraced himself, namely, that

> a means can be judged to be evil *only if it is caused without commensurate reason*. One cannot, in other words, isolate certain physical evils and say of them that they are, in all circumstances, moral evils.[109]

We have seen that proportionalist thought is characterized by a subjecting of all prohibitions on specific behaviors to the supreme criterion of *debita proportio*. With respect to contraception, a proportionalist may judge that procreation is indeed a good and that, generally speaking, this good ought to be realized; it is just this judgment that lead McCormick to conclude that "direct sterilization is what we call a *prima facie* evil (or an ontic evil)."[110] Yet, given the primacy assigned to proportionate reason in the assessment of acts, one must allow for the possibility that, in certain circumstances, purposefully causing the ontic evil of contraception will be justified by the promised realization of a commensurate good. McCormick argued in this same way for the permissibility of some acts of sterilization, claiming that purposefully bringing about this ontic evil "is justifiable for a truly proportionate reason."[111] Furthermore, McCormick sympathetically cited a proportionalist justification of purposeful, direct abortion in the case where, without such action, both mother and child would die:

> ...*in such circumstances* the abortion is proportionately grounded, is the lesser evil. When one is faced with two options both of which involve unavoidable (nonmoral) evil, one ought to choose the lesser evil.[112]

One should note, too, that the requirement that one ought to *choose* the lesser physical evil will mean, in this case and others, that one ought purposefully to *do* the lesser physical evil; in this case, abort the child.[113]

McCormick made plain the theoretical difference between his own proportionalist understanding of what makes some acts of contraception, sterilization, and abortion to be morally wrong, and his tradition's assessment of these same acts when he wrote:

> ...When an action is always morally wrong, it is not so because of unnaturalness or defect of right (as recent tradition contends), but because *when taken as a whole*, the nonmoral evil outweighs the nonmoral good, and therefore the action is disproportionate.[114]

Several years later he would add

> this understanding of things is not limited to control of birth. It involves an entire theory. For example, a lie consists in telling what is false without commensurate reason and therefore directly or formally causes the error of another. Theft is the taking of the property of another without commensurate reason. Mutilation is surgery without commensurate reason. Murder is killing without commensurate reason. Contraception is intervention into the fertility of the conjugal act without commensurate reason. In all these instances, when there is a commensurate reason, the moral content of the act is not the physical evil but

the commensurate reason. The physical (or nonmoral) evil is then indirect.[115]

And, one is to conclude, the act is licit. So, as with X killing Y and as with A and B choosing to contracept a conjugal act, an act which purposefully causes physical evil cannot be judged to be *morally* wrong until one judges whether this evil was caused for a commensurate reason.

Conclusion

The focus of the general account of proportionalism laid out in this chapter has been what it is that this theory claims makes morally right and wrong acts to be morally right and wrong. Questions concerning the moral character of agents who perform these acts have not been considered since these two issues, although related, are separate. This distinction is understood by both proportionalists and their critics within their tradition. Bruno Schuller, himself a proportionalist, expressed well this shared belief:

> Someone who is animated by impartial love cannot but choose the course of action he *considers* morally right. But he may make an erroneous judgment and mistake for right what is in fact wrong. In this even his intention is to do what is right. Yet this intention notwithstanding, his action, though morally good, is at the same time morally wrongful.[116]

Having noted this common ground, we return to the task of identifying and explicating the characteristic elements of proportionalist thought as a propaedeutic for considering the details of McCormick's version of this theory. We have already noted McCormick's helpful observation that

> common to all so-called proportionalists is the insistence that causing certain disvalues (ontic, nonmoral, premoral evils) in our conduct does not *ipso facto* make the action morally wrong, as certain traditional formulations supposed. The action becomes morally wrong when, all things considered, there is not proportionate reason.[117]

We have seen that from this principle of proportionalist thought there follows a conditioning of *all* material norms on the presence or absence of proportionate reason, as well as a rejection of any material norm which would, by formulation, unconditionally prohibit an agent from purposefully causing specific physical evils (such as killing and contraception). According to proportionalist thinking, a judgment concerning the moral rightness and wrongness of any act involving the purposeful causing of physical evil cannot be made absent the knowledge of the circumstances of that act, for it is knowledge of the circumstances that will allow one to judge what evil was effected, what good was pursued, and whether the good was proportionate to the evil. In the chapters that follow, the focus will be upon McCormick's adoption and refinement of this basic proportionalist approach as the case is made that his moral theory is consequentialist in the sense laid out in chapter one.

Notes

1 Christopher Kaczor (ed.) *Proportionalism: For and Against* (Milwaukee: Marquette University Press, 2000), 10.
2 Richard McCormick, "Moral Theology1940-1989: An Overview," *Theological Studies* 50 1 (March, 1989), 10. A few years later, McCormick offers the following somewhat modified version of this last sentence: "The action becomes morally wrong when, all things considered, there is not a proportionate reason in the act justifying the disvalue" ("Killing the Patient," *The Tablet* 10/30/93, 1411).
3 Joseph T. Mangan, S.J., "An Historical Analysis of the Principle of Double Effect," *Theological Studies* X (1949), 41. More recently, the *principle* of double effect has been referred to as the *doctrine* of double effect, perhaps because it is composed of more than one principle. Whatever the reason for the change, I will follow my contemporaries and refer to it as a doctrine..
4 The classic example of such an act is killing an agressor [an evil] while defending oneself [a good]. I will refer to such acts henceforth as "mixed acts" in that they promise both good and evil effects. Also, we here limit ourselves to the consideration of acts which "promise to cause" evil instead of those which cause reasonably unforseen evil since generally, or at least in this tradition, one would not be considered morally responsible for the unintended and reasonably unforseen evil effects of their acts. The dilemma that the doctrine of double effect seems designed to resolve arises when one believes that an otherwise good or neutral act will likely cause a proscribed evil.
5 See *ST* II-II 64.7c: "But as it is unlawful to take a man's life, except for the public authority acting for the common good, as stated above (3), it is not lawful for a man to intend killing a man in self-defense..."
6 St. Thomas Aquinas, *Summa theologiae* II-II 64.7c. Translated by the Fathers of the English Dominican Province. Copyright 1947 Benzinger Brothers Inc., Hypertext Version Copyright 1995, 1996 New Advent Inc.; Available: http://www.newadvent.org. For a recent publication of the Latin text with English translation see Christopher Kaczor, *Proportionalism: For and Against* (Milwaukee: Marquette University Press, 2000), 20-24.
7 Joseph T. Mangan, S.J., "An Historical Analysis of the Principle of Double Effect," 43-50. Mangan argues that in Thomas's analysis of licit killing in self-defense one will find Thomas observing, at least implicitly, that each of the four conditions—soon to be listed—that together constitute the doctrine are met. Mangan argues, too, that *ST* II-II 64.7c is not the only place where Thomas employs this doctrine; see ibid., 50-51.
8 Don Marquis surveys four versions of this doctrine and concludes that each is flawed. See his "Four Versions of Double Effect," *The Journal of Medicine and Philosophy* 16 (1991), 515-544. For a defense of the plausibility and relevance of one formulation of the doctrine, see Philippa Foot's "The Problem of Abortion and the Doctrine of the Double Effect," *The Oxford Review* 5 (1967), 5-15. See also Joseph Boyle's "Who Is Entitled to Double Effect?" *The Journal of Medicine and Philosophy* 16 (1991), 475-494.
9 Joseph T. Mangan, S.J., "An Historical Analysis of the Principle of Double Effect," 52. His argument for this conclusion: "Many of the moralists who follow St. Thomas, in their explanation of the principle of the double effect refer to the principle enunciated by St. Thomas in II-II, q. 64, a. 7, and they give no other earlier author as a reference, except to quote one or other example used by these earlier authors. For these reasons, therefore, we claim this article of the *Summa Theologica* as the historical beginning of the principle of the double effect as a formulated principle." Ibid.,52.
10 Ibid., 43. Mangan's formulation of the fourth requirement of the doctrine seems to be rooted in Thomas's claim, in *ST* II-II 64.7c (the above-cited article on self-defense), that "Potest tamen aliquis actus ex bona intentione proveniens illicitus reddi *si non sit proportionatus fini*. Et ideo si aliquis ad defendum propriam vita mutatur *maiori violentiam quam oporteat*, erit illicitum." Emphasis mine. This notion of a proportionately grave reason, though, has generated some

controversy, as there has been a lack of consensus on what precisely constitutes such a reason. On this controversy, see Brian Johnstone's "The Meaning of Proportionate Reason in Contemporary Moral Theology," *The Thomist* 40, 2 (1985), 223-247. Our chief concern will be the proportionalist explication of this notion, an explication that will show this theory to be consequentialist and to which we shall turn in some detail later in this chapter and in great detail in chapter 3.

11 In our example of licit self-defense, physically stopping an agressor is not judged to be in-itself objectionable. Recall the premise from *ST* II-II 64.7c "it is lawful to repel force by force."

12 Not all authors who employ this doctrine adopt Mangan's formulation with its four conditions. For example, Boyle writes: "The double effect doctrine states that such harms may be brought about if two conditions are met: (1) the harms are not intended but brought about as side effects; and (2) there are sufficiently serious moral reasons for doing what brings about such harms" ("Who Is Entitled to Double Effect?" *The Journal of Medicine and Philosophy* 16 [1991], 476). Boyle's first condition encompasses Mangan's first three conditions, and Boyle's second condition is the equivalent of Mangan's fourth. See, too, Boyle's formulation of J.P. Gury's four conditions in "Toward Understanding the Principle of Double Effect," *Ethics* 90 (1980), 527-538.

13 Indeed, Joseph Boyle argues that the doctrine of double effect is superfluous *unless* it is located within a moral theory that maintains exceptionless prohibitions on inflicting specific types of harms. He rests this claim on the fact that only those types of moral theories will generate the apparent conflict of duties that the doctrine is designed to address. See Joseph Boyle, "Who Is Entitled to Double Effect?" *The Journal of Medicine and Philosophy* 16 (1991), 475-494. See also Boyle's "Toward Understanding the Principle of Double Effect," *Ethics* 90 (1980), 527-538.

14 As opposed to, say, the rule-utilitarian sense.

15 Allow too that these two norms are not subordinated to any other norm which may resolve the conflict, or, if they are subordinated to some other norm(s), allow that the norm(s) to which they are subordinated are unhelpful in resolving this conflict.

16 Frank Jackson, "Decision-theoretic Consequentialism and the Nearest and Dearest Objection," *Ethics* 101 (April, 1991), 462.

17 The cases Mangan cited are self-defense, "indirect killing of the innocent, especially in time of war; exposing oneself to mortal danger for a good cause; performing some act which one foresees will result in the passive scandal of others; performing an act from which an otherwise illicit pollution or venerial pleasure will arise, when there will be no danger of consenting; and cooperating materially in another's evil action" ("An Historical Analysis of the Principle of Double Effect," 53-55).

18 Mangan wrote: "The authors who come after the Salmanticenses began discussing the principle more and more in their sections of general moral theology, and then in their sections of particular moral problems they referred back to the more general treatment" (Ibid., 56).

19 Joseph Boyle "Intentions, Christian Morality, and Bioethics: Puzzles of Double Effect," *Christian Bioethics* vol.3, no.2 (1997), 87-88.

20 It should be noted, though, that no one formulation of the doctrine is the standard for the tradition. But it should also be noted that differences in formulation do not necessarily indicate changes in the conditions that constitute the doctrine. For example, Joseph Boyle reduces (but does not eliminate) Mangan's first three conditions to one when he offers his own version of the doctrine: "The double effect doctrine states that such harms may be brought about if two conditions are met: (1) the harms are not intended but brought about as side effects; and (2) there are sufficiently serious moral reasons for doing what brings about such harms" ("Who Is Entitled to Double Effect?," *The Journal of Medicine and Philosophy* 16 [1991], 476). Any choice that would violate any of Mangan's first three conditions would also violate Boyle's first condition, and for the same reason..

21 Peter Knauer, "The Hermeneutic Function of the Principle of Double Effect," *Natural Law Forum* 12 (1967), 132-162. This article was Knauer's revised version of his earlier "La determination du bien et du mal moral par le principe du double effet," *Nouvelle revue theologique* 87 (1965), 356-376. He refers to this earlier work as the "first form" of what he presents in "The Hermeneutic Function..." ("The Hermeneutic Function of the Principle of Double Effect," 132).

22 Richard McCormick, "Moral Theology 1940-1989: An Overview," 10.

23 Germain Grisez, *Abortion: The Myths, the Realities, and the Arguments* (Washington: Corpus Books, 1970), 331. John Finnis sees "morality's very foundations" to be at stake in what would become the debate between proportionalists and their traditionalist opponents (John Finnis, "Beyond the Encyclical," in *Considering Veritatis Splendor*, [Cleveland: The Pilgrim Press, 1994], 74).

24 Peter Knauer, "The Hermeneutic Function of the Principle of Double Effect," 132.

25 Ibid., 133. The distinction between physical evil and moral evil is made here within the context of the Catholic moral tradition and with a Thomistic philosophical anthropology among its presuppositions. It is with these presuppositions in mind that we will accept Louis Janssens' (another proportionalist) account of physical evil (which he refers to as "ontic evil"): "There are evils which disrupt the corporeal life of man, e.g. death (which radically defeats our will to live), pain, sickness....Wear and tear of the body, fatigue, etc., are evils. There is spiritual and mental evil. Every human being suffers from the handicaps and shortcomings of his own psyche – not to mention psychoses and neuroses – which make life difficult for him. And are we not always crippled by our ignorance, which makes us aware of a frustration of our urge to know?...We call ontic evil any lack of a perfection at which we aim, any lack of fulfillment which frustrates our natural urges and makes us suffer" (Louis Janssens, "Ontic Evil and Moral Evil," *Louvain Studies* 4 2, [1972], 134). We will look more closely at Janssens's contribution to proportionalist thought later in this chapter.). Ontic evil, then, may be distinguished from moral evil in that knowledge of how beings may suffer is sufficient to understand the former, while knowledge of the latter requires a grasp of moral norms and a capacity to assess human acts. An example of this distinction may be found in Janssens's argument that every *mendacium* is, by definition, a moral evil and involves a *falsiloquium*, an ontic evil. However, not every *falsiloquium* is a *mendacium*. Janssens writes: "It is true that each *falsiloquium* always runs counter to the faculty of cognition which by its own nature and consequently necessarily and directly is ordered to the truth. This is precisely the definition of ontic evil: each ontic evil runs counter to the aim of one of our *inclinations*....The problem of *moral* evil concerns *the activity*" (Ibid., 145, n.105).

26 Ibid., 133, n.2.

27 Peter Knauer, "The Hermeneutic Function of the Principle of Double Effect," 132-133. Emphasis mine.

28 Joseph Mangan, "An Historical Analysis of the Principle of Double Effect," 43.

29 Peter Knauer, "The Hermeneutic Function of the Principle of Double Effect," 133. In the literature that followed Knauer's article, whether seeking to develop or to critique this theory, the phrases "proportionate reason" and "commensurate reason" are used interchangeably. We will follow that practice here.

30 *Summa theologiae* II-II 64.7c

31 Peter Knauer, "The Hermeneutic Function of the Principle of Double Effect," 134.

32 Ibid.

33 In the moral tradition to which Knauer is reacting, the notion of *intending X* means *purposefully bringing about X*. This sense of *intention* is explained by John Finnis in "Object and Intention in Moral Judgments According to Aquinas." There Finnis explains that "intention is a matter of what one *chooses to do*....In considering oneself (or others) morally responsible for what one intends...one is not attributing any significance to some supposed inner act somehow supple-

menting or reinforcing one's acts of *deliberately doing* (scil. of choosing to do...). There is no such preliminary or in any other way supplementary inner act. Choosing to do something is what intending something is..." (Emphasis mine. John Finnis, "Object and Intention in Moral Judgments According to Aquinas," *The Thomist* 55 [1991], 24-25).

34 Ibid. Because the plausability of this distinction between psychological intention and moral intention, offered without supporting argument, is not our concern here, we will not discuss it.

35 Ibid. He repeated this assertion in various ways: "If there is a commensurate reason for the permitting or causing of the evil, the means is effectively willed only in its good aspect. The effect or, more exactly, the aspect which is physically evil remains morally outside of what is intended" (Ibid., 149). Also, "If an act has a commensurate reason, the latter prevents evil from being willed directly or *de industria* in the moral sense, so that what psychological attention may be concentrated on is in the moral sense beyond intention, *praeter intentionem*" (Ibid., 158).

36 For our purposes, it may be noted that this third condition can be read as claiming that an act which involves the intentional use of evil as a means to a good end cannot be licit. One may here note the tradition's teaching that "one may not do evil so that good may result from it" (*Catechism of the Catholic Church*, nos. 1756, 1761).

37 *Catechism of the Catholic Church*, no.2271.

38 For the tradition's sense of *intend*, see note 34. It has been said above that direct abortion is understood here to be an evil because it is the intentional taking of a human life. It should be noted that the intentional taking of a human life is judged an evil because "God alone is the Lord of life from its beginning until its end: no one can under any circumstances claim for himself the right directly to destroy an innocent human being." (*Catechism of the Catholic Church*, 544; quoting the encyclical *Donum vitae*) Richard McCormick explained this specific teaching as follows: "a long tradition has maintained that if an abortional intervention must be said to be directly intended, it is never permissible. For it involves the direct taking of human life. If, however, the death of the fetus is the foresen but unavoidable byproduct of surgery aimed at removal of a pathological organ (for example, a cancerous uterus), the abortion was said to be only indirectly intended, and justifiable if a truly proportionate reason were present" (*Doing Evil to Achieve Good* R. McCormick and P. Ramsey (eds.), [Chicago: Loyola University Press, 1978] 5).

39 Peter Knauer, "The Hermeneutic Function of the Principle of Double Effect," 137.

40 More will be said on this in a moment.

41 Peter Knauer, "The Hermeneutic Function of the Principle of Double Effect," 134. He s, too, that he is in agreement with Aquinas on this point. (Ibid.)

42 Ibid., 135-136. The question of whether a mixed act's evil effects were used as a means to its good end is morally decisive in that it asks whether a necessary but not sufficient condition of licit choice has been met. Its moral decisiveness consists in, and is limited to, the fact that an answer of 'yes' to the question is sufficient to judge the act morally wrong, but a 'no' to this same question is not sufficient to judge the act right given the necessity of the other three conditions.

43 Peter Knauer, "The Hermeneutic Function of the Principle of Double Effect," 136.

44 Ibid., 137.

45 Ibid., 149. Emphasis mine.

46 And this is not an oversimplification of Knauer's position. McCormick wrote, "Knauer's basic thesis could be worded as follows: the causing or permitting of evils in our conduct is morally right or wrong depending on the presence or absence of a commensurate reason" ("Moral Theology 1940-1989: An Overview," 9).

47 Peter Knauer, "The Hermeneutic Function of the Principle of Double Effect," 133. What exactly constitutes a commensurate reason will be discussed in detail later.

48 Ibid., 141.

49 Bernard Hoose, *Proportionalism: The American Debate and its European Roots*, 81.

50 Ibid., 142.
51 Ibid., 154.
52 Ibid., 155.
53 Consider, for example, the following: "Since, therefore, the conjugal act is destined primarily by nature for the begetting of children, those who in exercising it deliberately frustrate its natural power and purpose, sin against nature, and commit a deed which is shameful and intrinsically vicious" (Pope Pius XI, *Casti Connubi*, IV, 1930. Copyright 1947 Benzinger Brothers Inc., Hypertext Version Copyright 1995, 1996 New Advent Inc.; Available: http://www.newadvent.org.). We are not concerned here with the merits or failings of this position and its supporting argument. What we are focused upon is Knauer's analysis of an act of contraception.
54 Peter Knauer, "The Hermeneutic Function of the Principle of Double Effect," 161. Emphasis mine.
55 Ibid., 156. Emphasis mine.
56 Ibid., 161.
57 Ibid., 156.
58 Joseph Fuchs, "The Absoluteness of Moral Terms," *Gregorianum* 52 (1971). In this context, *material* norms are distinguished from *formal* norms. Material norms prescribe or proscribe the choice of specific behaviors, as in *Speak the truth*, or, *Do not contracept a human reproductive act*. Formal norms prescribe or proscribe more abstractly and by reference to values or virtues, as in *Act charitably*, or, *Do not act unjustly*. Richard McCormick cited the prohibition on artificial insemination and the duty to respect one's neighbors as, respectively, examples of a material and formal norm proposed by his tradition (Richard McCormick "The Natural Law: Recent Literature," *Readings in Moral Theology No.7: Natural Law and Theology*, C. Curran and R. McCormick eds., [New York: Paulist Press, 1991] 176).
59 We will see, however, that Fuchs's notion of moral intention is, like Knauer's, understood in terms of proportionate reason.
60 Joseph Fuchs, "The Absoluteness of Moral Terms," 452.
61 Ibid., 449.
62 Although Fuchs does not use the exact phrase "proportionate reason," he does use the phrases "proportionally related cause" and "appropriate reasons." See *The Absoluteness of Moral Terms*, 444-445.
63 Joseph Fuchs, "The Absoluteness of Moral Terms," 444.
64 Ibid., 444.
65 Ibid., 445.
66 Ibid., 444.
67 Ibid.
68 Ibid.
69 Ibid., 446
70 Ibid. Emphasis mine.
71 Indeed, it seems that Fuchs's statement here is a truism, once one grasps his meaning of the term *morally bad*. It will be seen in a moment that, for Fuchs, a morally bad means is one that does not justify a given end in a given context. So, Fuchs's claim that a morally bad means cannot justify a good end is equivalent to the claim that a means which does not justify a given end in a given context does not justify that given end in that given context.
72 Joseph Fuchs, "The Absoluteness of Moral Terms," 446.
73 Ibid., 450.
74 Ibid., 449.
75 Louis Janssens, "Ontic Evil and Moral Evil," *Louvain Studies* 4 2 (1972), 115-156.
76 Peter Knauer, "The Hermeneutic Function of the Principle of Double Effect," 145.
77 Ibid., 133. Emphasis mine.

78 Louis Janssens, "Ontic Evil and Moral Evil," 134.
79 Ibid., 135.
80 Ibid., 136.
81 Ibid., 137.
82 Ibid., 134.
83 Ibid., 138.
84 Ibid., 139.
85 Ibid.
86 Ibid., 142. The notion of the means *negating* the value pursued as end is repeated at 149.
87 Ibid., 143.
88 Louis Janssens, "Ontic Evil and Moral Evil," 150. We need not examine more thoroughly and critique what he means by this, for it is stated clearly enough for our purposes.
89 Ibid.
90 Recall his words "We call ontic evil any lack of a perfection at which we aim, any lack of fulfillment which frustrates our natural urges and makes us suffer" ("Ontic Evil and Moral Evil," 134). Consider too his claim that all forms of ontic evil "by their definition hamper the development of human beings and communities" (Ibid., 154).
91 Ibid., 149.
92 Ibid., 140.
93 Ibid.
94 Ibid., 150. Emphasis mine.
95 Ibid; emphasis mine. Janssens' believed he found support for his position in Aquinas, claiming that Thomas's requirement that there be a *debita proportio* between the evil and good effects of a mixed act is a requirement that "the value realized in the direct effect *must at least counterbalance* the bad, indirect effect" (Ibid.,139. Emphasis mine). For further support Janssens immediately added, "Mangan claims that this principle is a Thomistic one," and cites Mangan's *An Historical Analysis of the Principle of Double Effect* (Ibid). It should be noted that the work of Janssens being cited here was written in Flemish and translated into English by another person (Ibid., 115). We may assume, then, that the presence of the word *counterbalance* in the preceding citation from Janssens is the translator's rendering of a Flemish word or phrase used by Janssens. But we will also assume that Janssens understood and accepted his translator's rendering, for Janssens has published a number of works in English (Ibid.) What exactly is meant by *counterbalance* is not yet clear, but we will attempt to elucidate this concept in a moment. Let us note here, though, that Janssens does not tell his readers which Latin word or phrase from which of Thomas's texts supports the use here of the English *counterbalance*. Let us also note that nowhere in his article does Mangan use this term and, therefore, nowhere does he attribute it to Thomas.
96 Ibid., 153.
97 Ibid., 154.
98 Ibid., 155.
99 Ibid.
100 Richard McCormick, "Ambiguity in Moral Choice," in *Doing Evil to Achieve Good*, R. McCormick and P. Ramsey (eds.), (Chicago: Loyola University Press, 1978). This essay was first presented in 1973 at Marquette University; see "Ambiguity in Moral Choice," (Milwaukee: Marquette University Press, 1973).
101 He does later reconsider and "fine tune" some of the details of his synthesis offered in *Ambiguity in Moral Choice*, and these will be noted as they become relevant.
102 Richard McCormick, *Doing Evil to Achieve Good*, 10.
103 Richard McCormick, "A Commentary on the Commentaries," in *Doing Evil to Achieve Good*, 265.

104 Richard McCormick, *Doing Evil to Achieve Good*, 11. Again, McCormick's theoretical statements and his analyses of cases will be considered in detail in the chapters that follow. Here we are simply laying out a general account of his proportionalist thought.

105 One may wonder whether *X's killing Y* and *Y's death* are really two distinct evils, with the former containing all of the evil that the latter holds, as well as whatever further evil X's *killing Y* may entail. In the following chapters we will see that McCormick is sensitive to this distinction, for now we will let it pass.

106 Pope Pius XI, *Casti Connubi*, IV, 1930; Hypertext Version Copyright 1995, 1996 New Advent Inc.; <http://www.newadvent.org>.

107 Pope Paul VI, *Humanae Vitae*, 14, 1968. Emphasis mine. Hypertext Version Copyright 1995, 1996 New Advent Inc.; <http://www.newadvent.org>.

108 The previous citation from *Humanae Vitae* continues: "To justify conjugal acts made intentionally infecund, one cannot invoke as valid reasons the lesser evil....In truth, if it is sometimes licit to tolerate a lesser evil in order to avoid a greater evil to promote a greater good, it is not licit, even for the gravest reasons, to do evil so that good may follow therefrom; that is to make into the object of a positive act of the will something which is intrinsically disordered, and hence unworthy of the human person, even when the intention is to safeguard or promote individual, family or social well-being. Consequently it is an error to think that a conjugal act which is deliberately made infecund and so is intrinsically dishonest could be made honest and right by the ensemble of a fecund conjugal life" (Ibid.). We will look more closely at these issues in subsequent chapters.

109 Richard McCormick, *Doing Evil to Achieve Good*, R. McCormick and P. Ramsey (eds.), (Chicago: Loyola University Press, 1978), 10. Emphasis mine. To appreciate the unresolved status of this disagreement, consider these recent words of Pope John Paul II: "...the opinion must be rejected as erroneous which maintains that it is impossible to qualify as morally evil according to its species the deliberate choice of certain kinds of behavior or specific acts, without taking into account the intention for which the choice was made or the foreseeable consequences of the act for all persons concerned" (Pope John Paul II, *Veritatis Splendor*, [Boston: Pauline Books & Media], 103).

110 Richard McCormick, *How Brave a New World?* (London: SCM Press, 1981), 278.

111 Ibid., 275.

112 Richard McCormick, "Reflections on the Literature," in *Readings in Moral Theology No.1: Moral Norms and Catholic Tradition*, Charles Curran and Richard McCormick (eds.), (New York: Paulist Press, 1979), 331. The decisive role that the balancing of good and evils plays in this reasoning contrasts markedly with the deontological theory of, say, John Finnis. Finnis argues that a principle of morality excludes "choosing to destroy or damage any basic human good in any of its instantiations in any human person" (John Finnis, "Natural law and Legal Reasoning," in *Natural Law Theory: Contemporary Essays*, Robert George (ed.), [Oxford: Clarendon Press, 1992], 147). The difference here between Finnis and proportionalists like McCormick does not necessarily arise when determining which of the two possibilities represents the lesser physical evil. Presumably Finnis would agree that the death of both mother and child would be, in some sense, worse than the death of either of them alone. The fundamental difference in moral theory arises when one considers what principle each would propose to govern one's choice in such circumstances. McCormick cited the rule that one ought to choose/do the lesser physical evil. Finnis, would presumably cite the above mentioned principle and exclude the direct abortion (see Finnis, *Natural Law and Legal Reasoning*, 145-148).

113 We will return to this issue in the chapters that follow.

114 Richard McCormick, "Reflections on the Literature," *Readings in Moral Theology, No.1*, C. Curran and R. McCormick (eds.), (New York: Paulist Press, 1979), 322. We will return to his understanding of acts that are "always morally wrong" in chapter five.

115 Richard McCormick, *How Brave a New World?*, 417. See, too, Knauer: "Murder, for example, consists by definition in causing the death of a man without a commensurate reason" ("The Hermeneutic Function of the Principle of Double Effect," 138). Hence Finnis' observation that the proportionalist movement "concerns not contraception so much as the whole of sexual morality, not sexual morality as much as morality's very foundations..." (John Finnis, "Beyond the Encyclical," in *Considering Veritatis Splendor* [Cleveland: The pilgrim Press, 1994], 74).

116 Bruno Schuller, "The Double Effect in Catholic Thought: a Reevaluation," in *Doing Evil to Achieve Good*, R. McCormick and P. Ramsey (eds.), (Chicago: Loyola University Press, 1978), 183. For an account of some confusion caused by forgetting the distinction between the moral goodness of an agent and the moral rightness of an act, see chapter 3 of Bernard Hoose's *Proportionalism: The American Debate and its European Roots* (Washington, D.C.: Georgetown University Press, 1987).

117 Richard McCormick, "Moral Theology 1940-1989: An Overview," 10.

Chapter 3
McCormick's Proportionalism

In chapter one, we identified the nature of consequentialist ethical theories by considering their criterion for the rightness and wrongness of acts, by observing the method of act assessment that this criterion suggests, and by noting what these two elements imply about every agent's primary moral duty. In chapter two, we looked briefly at the history and the characteristic theses of the relatively recent movement within the Christian moral tradition that has come to be known as *proportionalism*, finishing with a brief consideration of the thought of proportionalism's most notable and vocal proponent in the English speaking world, Richard A. McCormick. We will now look more closely at the details of McCormick's brand of proportionalism, focusing upon the notion that stands at the center of his moral theory, that of *proportionate reason*. We will proceed by considering some of McCormick's more theoretical explications of *proportionate reason* and its role in act assessment before turning to some of his case analyses, analyses which will give us occasion to identify and consider a few *proportionate reason*-grounded principles that he employs in act assessment.

We begin by considering again McCormick's summation of the basic proportionalist position. As both an historian and advocate of the theory, one may be confident that his words are free of oversimplification and caricature. According to McCormick, proportionalists in general believe that

> causing certain disvalues in our conduct does not by that very fact make the action morally wrong, as certain traditional formulations supposed. These evils or disvalues are said to be premoral when considered abstractly, that is, in isolation from their morally relevant circumstances. But they are evils….The action in which they occur becomes morally wrong when, all things considered, there is not a proportionate reason in the act justifying the disvalue.[1]

When one notes what we shall soon see, namely, that the "proportionate reason" referred to in this quote is some good at which the agent aims, then it becomes clear that McCormick believed that the criterion for the moral rightness and wrongness of an act is the proportion between the good and the evil that the act promises to generate.[2] If the proportion between these two elements of the act were to favor the ontic good, then that good would be judged proportionate to the evil and, as such, would excuse the causing of the evil, however purposeful such causing may be. But if the good-to-evil proportion were reversed, then the act would be judged disproportionate, i.e., the ontic good would not be sufficient to justify the causing of the ontic evil. Now since McCormick believed that *proportionate reason* has such a profound role to play in the moral assessment of acts, it makes sense to consider in greater detail his account of this crucial concept.

The Meaning of *Proportionate Reason*

Throughout his writings, McCormick provided his readers with a few phrases that he used as synonyms for *proportionate reason*. In some places he referred to this act-justifying element as the "greater good,"[3] in other places it is called the "lesser evil,"[4] in still other places one reads that to say that an act has a proportionate reason is to say that "in the action as a whole, the good outweighs the evil,"[5] or, that performing this act promises to cause "less harm" than not performing it.[6] Consider, too that when McCormick claimed that an evil-causing act had a proportionate reason, he meant that the act was "justified."[7] Add to these statements his claim that the rightness or wrongness of any evil-causing act is to be judged "teleologically," that is, by the presence or absence of proportionate reason[8] and it becomes clear that, for McCormick, any evil-causing act is justified so long as, in its circumstances, it promises less evil or greater good than the agent's other possible choices.[9]

In addition to the familiar but perhaps somewhat vague concepts *greater good* and *lesser evil*, McCormick used the paired notions of *undermining* and *serving* a good to explicate further his concept of proportionate reason. For McCormick, any doing-evil-to-realize-good which promises to undermine the realization of the pursued (or more important[10]) good must, due to that undermining effect, be judged to be disproportionate, i.e. unjustified, morally wrong, etc.[11] He wrote that proportionate reason "means that the value being sought will not be undermined by the contemplated action,"[12] and he provided a rather generalized example:

> Where there is a question of taking life, such taking is proportionate only if it is, all things considered, the better service of *life itself* in the tragic circumstances.[13]

Now to claim that an evil-causing act is proportionate because, all things considered, it "serves" the value it seeks, and that an evil-causing act is disproportionate because, all things considered, it "undermines" the value it seeks is simple enough, but such claims say nothing about what it means for a value to be undermined or served by an act. What exactly McCormick meant by an act undermining or serving a particular value will become clear, and will support the case that his theory is consequentialist, when we examine his case analyses below. For now it should be noted that his explication of proportion and proportionate reason in terms of *undermining* and *serving* a good is, despite the perhaps confusing change in terminology, consistent with his explication of proportionate reason in terms of *greater good* and *lesser evil*. We will see that his use of these notions clearly indicates his belief that to say that an act is, in the circumstances, in the best service of a value is to say that this act is proportionate, which is to say that it promises the least evil or greatest good among an agent's choices.[14]

Before turning to some case analyses in which McCormick applied and elucidated his notion of proportionate reason, analyses that will show his moral theory to be consequentialist, it will be helpful to consider for a moment an element of McCormick's thought which Sanford Levy refers to as McCormick's "theory of associated goods."[15] More a principle within his moral theory than a theory in itself, McCormick believed that "the goods that define our flourishing are interrelated..."[16] This claim, at home in a value-theory or in a philosophical anthropology, found a role in McCormick's moral theory because such an interrelationship among human goods would mean that an act which aims at one particular good may also affect, positively or negatively, the realization of other goods. What is more, the affect on these related goods may then redound negatively on the good originally sought. It seems clear that, if true, such interrelationships must be taken into account if one is to assess correctly and thoroughly the good and evil that any act promises, and the proportion thereof. Indeed, McCormick's claim that

> one who *unjustifiably* takes a human life also undermines other human goods, and these human goods once weakened or undermined, will affect the very good of life itself,[17]

is a rather clear example of what he had in mind when he observed, more generally, that

> ...there being an interrelationship of all the values, a consideration of these values would or could illumine the matter of proportionality within the act with regard to the value at stake.[18]

We will soon see this association between human goods being invoked, and playing a decisive role in judgments of proportion, in some of McCormick's case analyses.

Now although McCormick asserted that the interrelated goods that define human flourishing are incommensurable,[19] he also claimed that their interrelationship "provides the context—a kind of single scale—in which decisions are possible and reasonable…"[20] The sort of decision that McCormick believed is made possible and reasonable by this interrelationship between incommensurable goods is, again, a decision about proportion, that is, a decision about where among an agent's choices lies the greatest good or least evil. McCormick himself suggested as much when he cautioned that

> the interrelatedness of human goods, their associatedness, means that in a sense there is a single scale, but the means of assessing the greater and lesser evil are more difficult, uncertain and obscure because the assessment must be done at times through associated goods.[21]

But even though he added, elsewhere, that "it is the characteristic of teleological considerations that they are open to reassessment,"[22] still the aim of every assessment and reassessment is the same: to identify among an agent's possible actions that one which promises the greatest good/least evil.

Having seen McCormick offer an account of proportionate reason in terms of greater good and lesser evil, one may well gain a better understanding of the nature of his moral theory by substituting these phrases into his claim that an evil-causing act "becomes morally wrong when, all things considered, there is not a proportionate reason in the act justifying the disvalue."[23] This substitution yields the proposition that an evil-causing act becomes morally wrong when, all things considered, there is not a greater good in the act justifying the disvalue (or, a bit more awkwardly, that the disvalue caused is not a lesser evil than the disvalue that not performing the act promised).[24] Such substitution emphasizes McCormick's commitment to the position that a morally wrong act is morally wrong because it does not promise a greater pre-moral good or lesser pre-moral evil than some alternative. When a moral theory proposes such a proposition as the supreme criterion of act assessment, as has been done here, and when it is asserted that an agent ought to choose according to such a criterion,[25] then the consequentialist character of this theory becomes apparent.

Purposeful Killing and Proportionate Reasoning

McCormick made clear his foundational position on purposefully causing evil in order to achieve good when he wrote, "we may directly will and directly cause a nonmoral evil if there is a proportionate reason for doing so."[26] Summarizing and agreeing with the position of Bruno Schuller, another proportionalist, McCormick separated himself from the Doctrine of Double Effect's deontological, agent-constraining demands that any causing of evil be *praeter intentionem* and indirect:

> Once it is granted that the killing of an innocent person is the destruction of a fundamental but nonmoral value, there is no need for the distinction direct-indirect. Rather the assessment is made 'teleologically,' i.e. from consequences. Schuller is correct, I believe.[27]

The practical import of what McCormick embraced here becomes clearer when we join his claim that the killing of an innocent person is a premoral evil with two other claims he makes: that "it is legitimate to intend premoral evil *in ordine ad finem proportionatum*,"[28] and that "it is legitimate to intend a disvalue *in se sed non propter se*."[29] The conclusion that this set of propositions validates is that it is legitimate for an agent to intend the death of an innocent person for a proportionate reason, which means, more precisely, that it is morally licit for an agent intentionally to cause the death of an innocent person when such a killing promises lesser evil or greater good than the agent's other choices. Even if McCormick had added to this reasoning the explanation that because the value of any human life is so great,[30] there is in fact no proportionate reason which could ever justify the purposeful killing of an innocent person, his reasoning would nevertheless remain consequentialist because such a practical prohibition on this act would be justified by an assessment of the good and evil that the act and its possible alternatives promise.

In fact, though, McCormick did not claim that there is no proportionate reason which could ever justify the purposeful killing of an innocent person. In his review of an article by Albert Outler,[31] McCormick accepted the position that

> human life, as a basic good and the foundation for the enjoyment of other goods and rights, *should be* taken only when doing so is the lesser of two evils, all things considered.[32]

He added that

to qualify as the lesser of two evils there is required, among other things, that there be at stake a human life or its moral equivalent. *'Moral equivalent' refers to a good or a value* that is, in Christian assessment, comparable to life itself.[33]

We have already seen that McCormick judged *life* to be a nonmoral value,[34] so his moral reasoning once again takes the form of an assessment of the ontic good(s) and evil(s) promised in each choice, with the agent's obligation being to choose that option which promises the greater good or lesser evil. One may note that McCormick's reasoning here does not seem sensitive to the distinction between one's purposefully *killing* an innocent person and one's *allowing* an innocent person to die.[35] In contrast to his tradition's deontologically grounded exceptionless prohibition against intentionally killing an innocent human being,[36] McCormick urged that

> when one says that 'direct killing of the innocent' is forbidden, he need not and should not imply that such killing is morally wrong 'independently of whatever reasons the agent might have had.' He may and ought to imply that the conceivable *reasons for killing* in such circumstances are, under careful analysis, *not proportionate to the harm done*.[37]

It is important to note that McCormick here did not maintain simply that one may *allow* or *risk* the death of an innocent person for a proportionate reason. Rather, by eliding the distinction between an agent *doing X* and an agent *allowing X*, he implied that this distinction is not relevant to the determination of the rightness and wrongness of such acts; the deontological, agent-relative constraints of his tradition are abandoned and the focus in the act assessment is entirely upon the ontic good and harm the act promises.[38]

An Abortion Case

Let us turn now to an even more concrete example of McCormick's application of his supreme criterion, *proportionate reason*. Consider the predicament of a pregnant woman whose medical condition is such that both she and her unborn child are certain to die, but that aborting the child will likely save the mother's life. McCormick rejected an analysis that would invoke the traditional Doctrine of Double Effect and argue that abortion in this case may be justified on the grounds that such an intervention would be an act which aimed exclusively at saving the mother's life while only unintentionally and indirectly causing the death of the child (say, by removing a cancerous uterus). In such an analysis, it might be argued that all four conditions of the traditional DDE were met and that, therefore, the exceptionless prohibition on intentionally killing an innocent was not violated.[39] McCormick, agreeing that abortion in this case is licit (and we will soon see that he actually judges it obligatory), nevertheless found such traditional reasoning to miss the mark:

> This is not, in my judgment, the *justification* at all....What is the true justification of allowing abortion here?...What is the justification – or proportionate reason? Is it not that we are faced here with two alternatives (either abort, or do not abort)? Both alternatives are destructive but one is more destructive than the other. We could allow both mother and child (who will perish under any circumstances) to die; or we could at least salvage one life. Is it not because, *all things considered*, abortion is the lesser evil in this tragic instance? Is it not precisely for this reason, then, that abortion in this instance is proportionate?[40]

It is crucial to note that in his analysis McCormick reasoned from the premise that one death is a lesser evil than two to the conclusion that it is obligatory purposefully to cause the one death.[41] This analysis is an example of the application of a rule he repeatedly employed but never explicitly stated, namely, that agents are morally obligated to choose the least ontic evil/greatest ontic good among the options before them.[42] Perhaps the closest he came to stating this rule plainly was when he wrote that where killing is concerned, the "key question" is,

> when and on what grounds must a killing action, for example, be said to be *necessary* (namely, if omitted, more harm to life will be inevitable)?[43]

Consider, too, his claim that

> if one is steering a runaway tram and there are two directions in which it can be turned (both involving killing people), one *ought* to steer the tram in the direction where the smaller number will be killed, other things being equal. I believe there is a similar commensurability in some rare abortion decisions where the alternatives are to save one or lose two...[44]

Given the putative similarity of the tram and abortion cases, one is left to infer that in the abortion case being considered, one similarly *ought* to abort. Indeed, one may well wonder what proposition would make valid these recurring inferences from an assessment of the good and evil promised in an agent's alternatives to the identification of the morally right and obligatory choice for that agent, other than this implied premise that one ought to *do* that act among one's choices that promises the lesser ontic evil or the greater ontic good. In our abortion case, McCormick's focus was upon assessing the ontic good and evil of the two states of affairs that would be realized by the two alternatives, abort or not abort, and, given his prior commitment that one ought to *do* the lesser ontic evil (take one life) when the alternative would be to *allow* a greater ontic evil (lose two lives), the results of this assessment will be morally decisive: "harm to the mother…can *and should* be avoided."[45] He suggested an even stronger condemnation of the choice not to abort in these circumstances when, after providing as another analogue to this case the case of a non-swimmer entering the water in an impossible attempt to save a drowning man, he wrote that it would be "immoral" for the non-swimmer to attempt such a rescue, presumably because the loss of two lives is a greater evil than the alternative (the loss of one life) and is chosen anyway; one may again infer, given the fundamental parallel he claims exists between these two cases, that a refusal to abort in the given circumstances is morally wrong.[46] It is clear, then, that what McCormick believed to be morally decisive is the amount (or type, as we shall see) of ontic good and evil promised by each of the agent's possible choices. Indeed he claimed as much when he wrote, concerning the abortion case under consideration, that "*taking* one life rather than *losing* two is the lesser evil. This is the *sole root warrant* for the intervention."[47]

Circumstances

In his analysis of the abortion case we have been considering, McCormick noted that the ontic evil of the child's death is certain, regardless of the choice the mother makes. It seems that for McCormick this fact simplifies the decision-making process, allowing the ontic good of saving the mother to tip the scales in favor of the choice to abort. The important and, for many, overriding, deontological consideration of just *how* this preferred[48] state of affairs would be brought about, that is, what its realization would require an agent purposefully to *do* (viz, to kill the fetus intentionally, and perhaps directly), was left out of McCormick's assessment of the alternatives.[49] Writing on behalf of his fellow proportionalists (whom he refers to as "revisionists"), McCormick focused directly upon this fundamental difference between his moral reasoning and that of the Catholic tradition:

> What is at issue is the reason for the conclusion. The defenders of the traditional distinction would argue that the conclusion is correct in so far as, and only in so far as, the death of the fetus can be said to be indirect. The revisionists, so to speak, would argue that the real reason for the conclusion is that *in such circumstances* the abortion is proportionately grounded, is the lesser evil.[50]

Elsewhere, to this analysis he added, "in other circumstances it would not be the lesser evil, and would not be proportionate."[51]

Since McCormick found the "circumstances" of the abortion case under consideration to provide morally decisive data, it is perhaps a good idea to examine this notion. He claimed that an act's morally relevant circumstances are "factors that go into determining proportion,"[52] but he failed to offer a more detailed account than this. Nevertheless, he did suggest elsewhere what he believed constituted an act's morally relevant circumstances. He observed that

> in recent theological and magisterial literature....certain kinds of actions (directly killing an innocent person, direct sterilization) have been proscribed as always wrong regardless of circumstances or consequences.[53]

He then suggested what he meant by "circumstances" when he explained the proportionalist dissatisfaction with this traditional position, noting that revisionists (like himself) argue

> that one cannot isolate the object of an act and say of it that it is *always* wrong in *any* conceivable circumstances. One can, of course, begin to add a variety of circumstances to the description of an object so that such an action is always wrong. For instance: abortion of a fetus in order to avoid a medical (delivery) bill.[54]

Here, then, the morally decisive "circumstance" turns out to be nothing more complex than the good that the agent pursues and the evil that is caused in pursuit of this good. According to McCormick's analysis, the premoral evil of purposeful, direct abortion is disproportionate when measured against the premoral good of avoiding a delivery bill; an abortion in such circumstances is therefore morally wrong. If, however, the circumstances were such that the good that an abortion would realize (or help to realize) was proportionate to the evil of that abortion, then that particular abortion would have to be judged differently, as in the abortion case considered earlier.

Our argument that McCormick's reference to a particular act's circumstances was simply a reference to the goods and evils that are at play in that particular act finds further support in his claim that the statement, *It is morally wrong to kill a human being merely to give pleasure to a third party*, "exhaustively states the circumstances."[55] Consistent with this is his explanation that a chosen behavior may be judged morally right or wrong

> only when sufficient circumstances have been added to complete the picture. Thus, one breaks a promise (e.g. to attend a wedding) in order to give a dying accident victim life-saving first aid. *That* is patient of a moral assessment and we would all agree that the act is morally right.[56]

Such passages also indicate that McCormick's method for identifying the morally right choice in any particular situation consisted of weighing against each other the goods and evils at play in that situation. Underlying this method was his assumption that the option which promised the greatest good/least evil was to be chosen, and this process of assessment and choice was to play out absent any overriding, consequence-indifferent constraints on the agent.[57] To save a life *instead of* keeping a promise when one cannot do both is justified because the greater good is realized, and to have an abortion *in order to* save money, or to kill a human being *in order to* give pleasure will each, in like manner, be judged by reference to this greater good/lesser evil standard. Whether one chooses one good instead of another, as in the first case, or sacrifices one good for another, as in the second and third cases, the greater good/lesser evil assessment is the sole decisive element in determining the moral quality of the choice.

The Necessity Principle

Elsewhere, though, McCormick indicated that he understood the morally relevant circumstances of an act to include the causal relationship that the good(s) and evil(s) at play in that act have with each other. He claimed that the amount and type of ontic good(s) and evil(s) yielded by any evil-for-the-sake-of-good choice will be determined in part by the presence or absence of an "essential and necessary causal relationship" between the evil means and the good end. McCormick seems to have adopted this position from Bruno Schuller. He wrote:

> ...Schuller has defined wrongful behavior as that which does more harm *than necessary*. Yet he has given us no systematic explanation of the factors that make some harms necessary and others unnecessary.[58]

It is significant that McCormick here did not take issue with the principle offered by Schuller, but only asked for a criterion which would make this principle useful in practice. Hoping to fill this lacuna, McCormick offered his own criterion for determining whether some particular instance of purposeful evil-doing was "necessary":

> harm done stands in a necessary relationship to evil to be avoided or good achieved *when it is the only way possible, essentially and deterministically, for the evil to be avoided or good achieved*—as in the case of saving at least the mother versus allowing both mother and child to die when these are my only alternatives.[59]

Here then, besides confirming his agreement with Schuller that wrongful behavior is behavior that does unnecessary harm, McCormick offered his "necessity principle"[60] as the explanation for what makes the purposeful causing of a particular harm in a particular situation necessary. To understand just how McCormick used this principle in the moral assessment of acts let us return to the abortion case just cited.

Recall that in his analysis of this case McCormick at times backed off from an assessment which considered *only* the fact that one option (abortion) would save one life at the cost of another, while its alternative (doing nothing) would cost two lives while saving none. He explained that this case is not "*simply* a save-one vs. lose-two dilemma. It is not *simply* quantitative." [61] Yet far from dismissing these numbers as irrelevant in determining the morally right choice in this case, McCormick claimed that the assessment of the alternatives must not focus *exclusively* on the number of lives saved and lost. When assessing the choice to abort, he urged, one must also take into account the causal relationship between the evil means and the good end. With this in mind, he included the following in his justification of the choice to abort:

> the deadly deed is intrinsically and inescapably connected with the saving of the mother's life, whether that deadly deed be a craniotomy or the removal of the fetus to get at a life threatening aneurysm. That is to say, there is in the very nature of the case no way of saving the mother. There is an essential link between the means and the end.[62]

While McCormick never cited the necessity principle as an element in his moral theory that saves it from consequentialism, Lisa Cahill identifies this principle as one "refinement" that enables his theory to "avoid utilitarianism."[63] Perhaps mindful of McCormick's words that the abortion case at hand is not "simply a save-one vs. lose-two dilemma," Cahill argues that his necessity principle prevents the 'wedge' effect, i.e., a multiplication of exceptions to the general rule not to sacrifice life, thereby "precluding the killing of innocents for utilitarian reasons...."[64]

It is fair to say that as a defense against the charge that McCormick's proportionalism is simply crass utilitarianism, Cahill's argument may be effective. Yet as a defense against our charge it certainly fails, leaving one wondering just how McCormick's allowance for fewer exceptions to a life-protecting norm than some other form of consequentialism (say, crass utilitarianism) makes his moral theory non-consequentialist in nature; to prove that it is not one kind of consequentialism is not to prove that it is no kind of consequentialism. In addition to this, recall that McCormick offered a consequentialist justification for the necessity principle itself: he maintained that when ontic evil is purposefully caused in the pursuit of a good, this evil-doing, if not causally necessary to realize the good, may have an undermining effect on this good.[65] That undermining effect must be accounted for if one is to judge proportion correctly. He wrote:

> What is the difference between a means with a necessary causal connection to the urgent good to be preserved (maternal life) and one without such a necessary causal relationship?...When there is no essential and necessary causal relationship, then other basic values are brought into play or affected, and in a way that can be undermining of the good of life itself, or whatever urgent good is being preserved through ontic evil.[66]

McCormick's necessity principle, then, adds a certain amount of complexity and nuance to his moral reasoning, distinguishing it from rudimentary utilitarianism. Nevertheless, this reasoning, however complex it may be, remains fundamentally consequentialist in that what is sought as the morally correct choice among an agent's options is that one choice which promises the greatest net good or least net evil. The necessity principle is consistent with this type of choice assessment, standing as McCormick's acknowledgment of a reality that may impact the amount and type of evil(s) promised by any particular act. Adding force to our case is McCormick's suggestion that any act of purposeful evil-doing is to be considered "necessary" if refraining from it promises "more harm," or, if choosing it promises "less harm," to the relevant good(s).[67] This more-harm/less-harm criterion makes the consequentialist nature of McCormick's proportionalism even more apparent.[68] Implicit in his explanation and application of this necessity principle was his belief that it would aid in the identification of the option which promised the greater good/lesser evil. Now while other consequentialists, perhaps traditional utilitarians, might disagree with this principle (as Cahill suggests), such disagreement seems insufficient to aquit McCormick of the charge that his moral theory is consequentialist. Indeed, it is not even certain that the adoption of McCormick's necessity principle would be sufficient to make an otherwise utilitarian moral theory non-utilitarian. Sanford Levy, referring to the necessity principle as "NP," explains:

> It is possible for a proponent of a clearly quantitative moral principle, e.g., an act-utilitarian, to adopt NP on the grounds that the existence or nonexistence of the necessary connection affects the quantities of value produced. This is, in fact, the sort of move I read McCormick as making…"[69]

The Lynch-Mob Case

In McCormick's explanation and application of the necessity principle there are suggestions that he believed the goods at stake in any particular act may be related in such a way that harming one may unavoidably harm another. Such relationships, if they exist, would have to be taken into account when determining the amount and type of evil a particular choice might yield. We have already seen McCormick claim that if no necessary causal connection exists between an evil means and its good end, "then other basic values are brought into play or affected."[70] One may understand better the moral relevance McCormick found in both the necessity principle and the relationship between goods by considering his thoughts on what is known as the lynch-mob case. His analysis of this case makes it apparent that he considered these two elements to be morally relevant insofar as they aid in correctly assessing the overall ontic good and evil that an act will yield.

The lynch-mob case refers to the predicament of a sheriff in a small town where a rape has been committed. A large group of townspeople, on the verge of rioting, have assembled to demand that the perpetrator be found. It is believed that their rioting, were it to occur, would certainly cost the lives of several innocent people. It is also believed that quickly producing, convicting, and executing a suspect would satisfy the mob, thereby saving the innocent lives that would be taken in a riot. The question posed is, Should the sheriff frame an innocent person in order to avert the riot? Consistent with his position on the abortion case above, McCormick rejected the simple sacrifice-one-to-save-many argument, and did so despite allowing that

> the immediate indictment and conviction of the suspect would save many lives and prevent many harmful consequences.[71]

Furthermore, he believed that this rejection saved him from the charge of consequentialism. We shall return to this defense soon. For now it will do simply to note that some genuinely consequentialist thought may be a bit more sophisticated than the rather simple consequentialist reasoning he rejected. The claim here has been that his is a rather nuanced form of consequentialism, a charge that his analysis of the lynch-mob will be seen to support.

McCormick counseled against the framing of the innocent man because he sensed that

> taking the life of this innocent man in these circumstances would represent a capitulation to and encouragement of a type of injustice *which in the long run would render many more lives vulnerable*.[72]

Elsewhere, he gave a more properly philosophical explanation for his conclusion:

> The manner of protecting the good (human life – by framing one innocent person) will undermine it in the long run by serious injury to an associated good (human liberty), for by killing an innocent person to prevent others from unjustly killing five innocent persons, one equivalently denies the freedom of these others.[73]

How, one may ask, is the freedom of the brewing lynch-mob undermined?

> One supposes by his action that the cessation of others from wrongdoing is necessarily dependent on my doing harm or nonmoral evil. Such a supposition denies and therefore undermines human freedom.[74]

Here, McCormick invoked the association of goods and argued that in these circumstances the undermining of human freedom would lead to an undermining of life. This easily-overlooked consequence, a product of the relationship between the goods *freedom* and *life*, makes the evil of framing the innocent man disproportionate, i.e., not the lesser evil among the alternatives. He explained,

...because such freedom is an associated good upon which the very good of life itself depends, undermining it in the manner of my defense of life is undermining life itself—is disproportionate.[75]

Supporting McCormick's defense against our charge, Paulinus Odozor finds that this theory of associated goods

helps McCormick to give persuasive answers to critics who charge that proportionate reasoning cannot apply to cases of justice without employing a utilitarian calculus.[76]

And it is indeed true that McCormick's assessment of the alternatives in the lynch-mob case cannot fairly be described as a simple "one vs. many" consequentialism; his judgment of proportion, i.e. his assessment of the good and evil that the alternatives promise, was surely more complex than that. Furthermore, he added yet another element to his assessment of the ontic evil promised by the framing of the innocent person when he claimed that the choice here

is not simply a matter of the life of one v. the life of many others; the entire institution of criminal law is at stake. And that is how proportion must be read.[77]

According to McCormick, then, in addition to the evils of killing the framed man and of denying the mob's freedom, one must consider the evil of undermining the good of criminal law when trying to determine in these circumstances which of the sheriff's alternatives promises the greater good or lesser evil. Yet despite the complexity of this assessment of ontic goods and evils, McCormick's consequentialism is apparent in his assertion of the moral decisiveness of this assessment:

When one states that in conflict situations where either alternative involves nonmoral evil the lesser evil should be chosen, he supposes that a proper assessment of what is truly the lesser evil has been made. He supposes that one has attended to the association of goods....Once this has been done and the lesser evil established, it is true to say that it is patently absurd to choose the greater evil.[78]

It is plain, then, that although McCormick cautioned that a correct assessment of the ontic goods and evils promised by any option may at times be none too simple, his fundamental principle of duty and act assessment remained simple and consequentialist: one is to choose (*do* or *allow*) that among one's options which promises the greatest ontic good or least ontic evil.

In his analysis of the lynch-mob case, we have seen McCormick claim that killing an innocent victim is a form of extortion. In his assessment of this choice he asked, "What is wrong with a little extortion if it prevents even greater nonmoral evils?"[79] His answer indicates both his consequentialism and its complexity:

> ...Extortion by definition accepts the necessity of doing nonmoral evil to get others to cease their wrongdoing. The acceptance of such a necessity is an implied denial of human freedom. But since human freedom is a basic value associated with other basic values (in this case, life) undermining it *also thereby undermines life*. In sum, extortion, as life undermining...is disproportionate."[80]

It must be noted, too, that McCormick's claim that extortion is wrong in this case because it is "life undermining" and "disproportionate" was simply a claim that

> the very value at stake, for example, life, will suffer more if the killing is done. That is, the action is disproportionate.[81]

The necessity principle and the notion of an association of goods were used by McCormick to argue that in the lynch-mob case the evil of sacrificing an innocent person will not yield greater good than its alternative. As a matter of fact, McCormick's words suggest that he believed the choice to frame the innocent person will in the end yield greater evil than allowing the riot, thereby making that act the morally incorrect choice. What is to be noted in all of the foregoing is that, all of the theoretical complexities aside, the purposeful killing of an innocent person was judged morally wrong in this case (and not in the abortion case) because, and only because, this act was judged to promise greater ontic evil than its alternative. Claims that such purposeful killing is forbidden regardless of circumstances and for non-consequentialist reasons are absent from McCormick's analysis. The moral defect in the act of purposeful killing in the lynch-mob case was not attributed to the evil of an innocent person's death, nor was it attributed to the agent purposefully causing this evil. Rather, the moral defect of this particular act of sacrificing an innocent life in order to save other innocent lives was attributed to the amount and kind of evil that such an act, in the specified circumstances, promised to yield. And it is just this sort of reasoning, *mutatis mutandis*, that lead McCormick to judge abortion to be the morally correct choice in the case considered above. As Sanford Levy explains

McCormick believes that it is wrong to do evil to achieve good if there is no proportionate reason for the evil, and that there is no proportionate reason when the evil means undermine (or are not in the best service of) the kind of value being sought, where, in the cases McCormick is concerned with, the undermining takes place via the undermining of associated goods. This undermining effect occurs when the evil means are not necessary for the attainment of the good.[82]

Some Non-Consequentialist Standards?

At one point, though, McCormick seemed to waver a bit from his consequentialist analysis of the lynch-mob case. Recall that in *Ambiguity in Moral Choice* he found the moral defect in the choice to sacrifice the innocent person to be that this choice

> in these circumstances would represent a capitulation to and encouragement of a type of injustice which *in the long run* would render *many more* lives vulnerable.[83]

Such a forward-looking analysis was called for given his belief that the "meaning" (presumably the moral meaning) of an act is constituted in part by "its repurcussions and implications, and therefore what will happen to the good in question over the long haul."[84] Yet a few years later, in *A Commentary on the Commentaries*, despite continuing to maintain that the evil promised by the choice to frame was, in the circumstances, disproportionate to the good pursued, he added that the long-range evil consequences of this framing do not "constitute the disproportion; they help to reveal it."[85] He explained,

> the term consequences, as I would read it, refers to the present support or undermining of the value being sought, a support or undermining that occurs through association with other goods.[86]

This clarification was placed within the context of the claim, offered earlier in this same piece, that the basic question in the moral assessment of any act is,

> [I]s the good end being sought by means involving nonmoral evil promoted and not undermined in this action or is it undermined?[87]

Later, in chapter four, we will look more closely at this supposed abandoning of the position that the moral defect of a morally wrong act is located in the act's long-term consequences. For now, though, we will focus upon this notion of "the present support or undermining of the value being sought" because it sounds as though McCormick may here have proposed a non-consequentialist standard of act assessment, one not tied to long-term consequences.

What must be done to settle the question of whether this is indeed a non-consequentialist standard is to determine what McCormick meant by a value being undermined or supported/promoted by a particular act. If he was proposing that morally wrong acts are morally wrong because they undermine on a conceptual level (perhaps "contradicts" would be a better term, as those who act unjustly in the name of justice conceptually contradict themselves) the value they seek,[88] then our case that McCormick gave absolute priority to a consequentialist criterion of act assessment becomes substantially weakened. If, however, he was proposing that morally wrong acts are morally wrong because they undermine the good they seek in a non-conceptual, practical sense (for example, as those who exercise excessively may undermine, in a tangible, substantive sense, the health that they seek by exercising), then our case that he was proposing a consequentialist moral theory will be strengthened. Put simply, if *undermine* and *support* turn out to refer to tangible effects on substantive goods, then they must be seen to have been offered by McCormick simply as another way of stating his now familiar supreme criterion of act assessment, namely, greater ontic good/lesser ontic evil. It was suggested earlier, and will now be argued, that McCormick's notions of an act supporting and undermining a value have this latter, real-world sense.

McCormick's *undermining/supporting* standard ought to be understood in a concrete, consequentialist sense rather than in a conceptual (perhaps Kantian) sense for two reasons: one, what he meant by his repeatedly invoked notion *lesser evil*, and how he related this notion to the *undermining/supporting* standard makes natural a consequentialist interpretation; two, his abortion and lynch-mob case analyses support a consequentialist interpretation. First, consider his repeated use of the phrase "lesser evil." The evil so qualified is, as we have seen, ontic evil in Janssens' sense, i.e., it is a real-world, palpable, measurable (in some sense) evil that human beings suffer in one way or another. One may get a clearer sense of what McCormick meant by ontic evil by considering how he compared this concept to the Catholic moral tradition's concept of *malum physicum*::

> Contemporary theologians rightly think the word *physicum* is almost invariably misleading, as suggesting and being restricted to bodily harms and harms due to commission. The concept is far broader. It includes not only harm to reputation, etc., but even the imperfections and incompleteness due to our limitations. Thus Janssens writes: 'We call ontic

evil any lack of perfection at which we aim, any lack of fulfillment which frustrates our natural urges and makes us suffer.'[89]

Evidence that McCormick's notion of ontic evil referred to substantive, real-world states of affairs may be found in his comment that, where unmarried teenagers are concerned,

> we can agree that intercourse without pregnancy following is a lesser evil than intercourse with pregnancy ensuing.[90]

Consider, too, his claim that "certainly the death of one innocent man is a lesser evil than the death of five innocent men,"[91] as well as his claim that, in the abortion case we have been discussing, "it is *better* on all counts in such circumstances to save one life where my only alternative is to lose two"[92] Furthermore, McCormick at times referred to ontic evil as "harm," as when he wrote that "because of the association of basic goods, an assault on one (liberty) will bring harm to another (life),"[93] and when he wrote that a judgment of proportion is "a judgment as to whether we are causing less harm by performing the action or omitting it."[94] Such language, taken together, makes it difficult to maintain that McCormick's notions of *undermining* and *serving* a value were offered as non-consequentialist standards of conceptual consistency. Indeed, were that the case, then McCormick would have been committed to the rather far-fetched position that our actions may bring varying degrees of harm to concepts, and that these abstract or ideal objects may suffer such harm. Such a position, with all of its inherent difficulties aside, seems not to be what McCormick was advocating given what we have seen.[95]

To emphasize our point here, recall McCormick's counsel in the abortion case we have been considering:

> ...that alternative should be chosen which is *in the circumstances* the best service of life. The 'in the circumstances' allows us to isolate those characteristics of the situation (feature-dependent aspects) which alone make the action the best service of the basic value of life, make it proportionate, make it the lesser evil.[96]

Here, McCormick explicitly equated *best service of* a good with *lesser evil*, i.e. lesser *ontic* evil. Indeed, in this context, where one is obligated purposefully to take one innocent life because the alternative is to lose two, there is no other plausible account of the meaning of *undermining* and *best service of* other than the concrete, substantive sense of greater ontic good/lesser ontic evil.[97] One may well wonder according to what criterion other than this tangible, consequentialist standard can the purposeful taking of an innocent human life, in the name of innocent human life, be correctly judged to be the act which best serves life.

Finally, consider that in counterposition to his set of synonyms describing morally right acts (*best service of a value, lesser evil, proportionate*) McCormick placed this set of equivalent terms to designate morally wrong acts: *undermine a value, not lesser evil,* and *disproportionate*.[98] Given that he equated the notions *best service of* and *lesser evil*, and given the fact that, to him, *lesser evil* meant lesser *ontic* evil, one can see that McCormick's explication of morally right and wrong acts in terms of *serving* and *undermining* a value (and his explication of disproportion in terms of undermining a value) is not to be understood as an endorsement of some sort of non-consequentialist standard of act assessment. Rather, his explication of right and wrong acts in these terms is to be understood as entirely consistent with his call to assess all of one's choices in any particular situation according to what each choice promises vis-à-vis the realization of, or harm to, the relevant ontic good(s).

One last point will conclude our argument that McCormick's notions of *undermining* and *serving* a good are consequentialist and entirely consistent with his greater good/lesser evil notion of proportionate reason. Sanford Levy explains that

> when McCormick speaks of an act's undermining or not being in the best service of the value being sought, he does not mean that the act fails to attain the instance of value the agent is seeking....His act is wrong because it undermines the kind of value an instance of which is being sought.[99]

Similarly, Brian Johnstone understands McCormick's notion of undermining to mean "undermining the value in a generalized sense," as opposed to "a particular negation of the value (e.g. by direct killing of an innocent)."[100] These explanations of McCormick's position, offered by two of his critics, invite the question, What can "undermining the kind of value an instance of which is being sought," and "undermining the value in a generalized sense" mean for McCormick? We can begin to answer this question by recalling what McCormick said about the choice to frame the innocent man in the lynch-mob case:

> Because of the association of basic goods, undermining one undermines others, and thus the very value at stake, for example, life, will suffer more if the killing is done. That is, the action is disproportionate.[101]

Here it may reasonably be asked just how one goes about serving or undermining *life* if not by serving or undermining individual lives. There is no evidence that McCormick was referring to some sort of Platonic form *Life* which is distinct from the many individual lives that participate in it, and which can be served and undermined by human agents. If, then, we reject the possibility that McCormick was some kind of Platonist in this regard, we seem to be left with the conclusion that his position that *life* may be served or undermined by an act of purposeful killing meant that *life* may be served or undermined in a tangible, substantive sense; that is, that the quality/quantity of particular lives may be affected by such an act. This seems to be the only way that McCormick could reasonably defend what he suggested in our abortion case, namely, that an act which purposefully takes a particular life nevertheless serves life. Indeed, what is being served if not some other particular life or lives? It seems, then, quite reasonable to express McCormick's position here as, *It may be licit, even obligatory, purposefully to take the life of some human being(s) in order to save or promote the life (or lives) of some other human being(s)*. This formulation of his position is supported by his assertion that "human life" is a "basic good" which "should be taken only when doing so is the lesser of two evils, all things considered."[102] How, it may be asked, is this justification of some acts of purposeful killing not consequentialist, especially when McCormick explicitly claimed that the evil of killing an individual is justified by being the "lesser evil" among the agent's alternatives? It is indeed for good reason that Levy defends interpreting McCormick's "Undermining Principle" as "a maximizing principle."[103]

But it is not just this *undermining* and *serving* terminology that may lead some, on first read, to believe that McCormick's moral theory is not consequentialist. His analysis of the lynch-mob case provides two other incidences of rather vague language which may sound to some like he is offering a non-consequentialist standard of act assessment. Concerning the choice to frame the innocent man, he wrote that "what appears to be a lifesaving action...is really at odds with the very value of life—is disproportionate."[104] He also explained that such an act

> is not *material apta* to the goal (preservation of life) because it denies in the means the very value sought in the end.[105]

These passages imply that an act which is "at odds with" or "denies" the value it seeks is, for that reason, morally wrong (disproportionate). Now if McCormick's criterion for what makes an act to be at odds with, or to deny, its end were non-consequentialist, then the case that his overall moral theory is consequentialist would meet a significant challenge. It will be seen, though, that this somewhat vague standard, like his *undermining/serving* standard, is simply another formulation of his fundamentally consequentialist standard of act assessment.

Let us begin with his notion of an act being *at odds with* the value it seeks. One can determine what McCormick meant (and did not mean) by this phrase by comparing his assessment of the choice to take an innocent life in the lynch-mob case with his assessment of that same choice in the abortion case previously discussed.[106] Recall that he found it morally acceptable purposefully to kill in the abortion case, while condemning that same choice in the lynch-mob case. Recall, too, that in the lynch-mob case he found the choice to sacrifice an innocent life to be at odds with the value *life*. Given these elements of these two case analyses, one may well wonder why he did not find the choice to abort also to be at odds with the value *life*. If the standard employed in these analyses were a non-consequentialist one which required conceptual consistency between means and end, or which disallowed any purposeful taking of innocent human life no matter what good it promised, then would not both choices be found to fail in that they each propose the taking of innocent life in order to save innocent life?[107] Indeed, given this similarity, sould not both choices be judged similarly? McCormick thought not. He found the morally decisive difference between these two cases to be that in the abortion case there is an "essential" connection between means and end, a connection which McCormick believed would prevent other goods from coming into play and possibly undermining the good being pursued. In the lynch-mob case, however, he found no such connection and, as we have seen, he believed that

> when there is no essential and necessary causal relationship, then other basic values are brought into play or affected, and in a way that can be undermining of...whatever urgent good is being preserved through ontic evil.[108]

Now if we note that McCormick used the phrases *undermining* and *at odds with* to explicate his understanding of *disproportion*, and if we recall that his concepts of *undermining* and *disproportion* are to be understood in terms of greater ontic good/lesser ontic evil, then it becomes clear that when he claimed that the choice to frame the innocent man is, unlike the choice to abort, "at odds with" the value sought by means of that choice, what he meant was that, overall, this choice did not promise the greatest ontic good/least ontic evil vis-a-vis the value(s) in question. McCormick's *at odds with* terminology, then, meant simply that a particular choice was disproportionate, i.e., that in his estimation it did not promise greater ontic good or less ontic evil than its alternative.

What, then, of McCormick's suggestion (from his analysis of the lynch-mob case) that an act is morally wrong if it "denies" the end it seeks? Might he have embraced a non-consequentialist standard of act-assessment here? It seems not, given what little he said on this matter and given his prior committments. For McCormick, to deny a value cannot have meant simply that one sacrifices an instance of the value sought, because he advocated such sacrifice when it promises a proportionate good. Recall that in the abortion case he urged the sacrificing of the child in order to save the mother, a good that he judged proportionate to the evil of the child's death; in that case he did not condemn such sacrificing as a "denial" of the good *life*. Elsewhere, he implied that "to deny" a value meant "to harm" that value, as when he stated in the lynch-mob case that judicial murder brings "harm to life through harm to an associated good (liberty)…"[109] Still, harming a value, like denying a value, cannot have meant simply harming an instance or instances of the value in question because, again, he advocated such sacrifice in certain cases.

What, then, did McCormick mean when he claimed that certain choices *deny* the value they seek? He never directly answered this question, a fact which is not surprising since it had not ever been put to him. And perhaps it is for this reason that substantial and compelling evidence of precisely what he meant by this term is wanting. Still, it seems most consistent with his more clearly-stated and frequently-used moral principles to conclude that he employed this term to convey a negative judgment about the efficacy of a particular act vis-a-vis the realization of the goods in play. He wrote, for example, that the framing of the innocent person in the lynch-mob case "is not *materia apta* to the goal (preservation of life) because it denies in the means the very value sought in the end."[110] Having already eliminated the possibility that his condemnation of this choice was grounded in the fact that he judged it to violate an exceptionless norm against purposefully killing innocents, his claim seems to have been that the choice to frame is wrong because it does not accomplish the goal for the sake of which it is chosen, namely, the maximization of the relevant good (life) or the minimization of the relevant evil (death of innocent people). The implication, too, is that if the choice to frame did promise a proportionate good, then it would be morally acceptable. It seems, then, that when McCormick claimed that an act was morally wrong because it denied the good it sought, he was simply conveying a prudential judgment about the efficacy of that act with regard to the maximization of the relevant ontic good(s); it was not an introduction of a new standard of moral rightness and wrongness designed to replace his standard of proportionate reason.

It is worth lingering a bit longer on just how this consequentialist interpretation of McCormick's criteria of *undermining* and *serving* a value is confirmed by his analyses of the abortion and lynch-mob cases. In his analysis of the abortion case, an analysis he repeated throughout his writings, McCormick remained unpersuaded by two possible deontological objections: one, that his counsel to abort contains an implicit, conceptual incoherence—namely, that one will purposefully take innocent life in the name of saving innocent life—and, two, that his counsel calls for the violation of an exceptionless, prohibition against intentional killing.[111] Yet it is not surprising that both of these objections, perhaps forceful and decisive to many, were unpersuasive to McCormick given his position on his tradition's norm against killing and given the priority he assigned to the maximization of ontic good and/or the minimization of ontic evil in one's choices. Consider this comment he offered concerning his tradition's commandment *Thou shalt not kill*:

> The rule is, in a sense, as acceptable as it is capable of being *restricted to accommodate* our sense of right and wrong, and *our firm commitment to save more lives than we lose* in situations of conflict.[112]

Here McCormick subordinated the norm against purposeful killing to a demand to save more lives than one would lose in conflict situations; that is, he subordinated the norm against purposeful killing to a greater ontic good/lesser ontic evil standard.[113] As his analysis of the abortion case illustrates, in McCormick's estimation one may purposefully kill an innocent human being so long as one is assured that doing so promises greater good or lesser evil than the alternative. That he embraced such a consequentialist principle is also evident in his assessment and rejection of the choice to frame the innocent man in the lynch-mob case. Recall that his belief in an association of goods and in a necessity principle lead him to conclude that the framing of the innocent man was not proportionate, that is, would not promise a lesser evil or greater good than its alternative. Recall, too, that that disproportion constituted the wrongness of the choice to frame. Finally, recall that concerning the interrelationship between the good *life* and the good *liberty* in the lynch-mob case he wrote:

> Because of the association of basic goods, undermining one undermines others, and thus the very value at stake, for example, life, will suffer more if the killing is done. That is, the action is disproportionate.[114]

Given McCormick's account of what is morally wrong with the choice to frame in the lynch-mob case, one is left to conclude the following: if the situation were such that the framing of the innocent man would not jeopardize the institution of criminal law, and if the claims that the mob's freedom would be undermined and that this undermining would redound negatively on the good of life were found to be implausible (or at least implausible in this case), then the sheriff ought to frame the innocent man. His analysis makes it quite reasonable to conclude that McCormick would endorse the choice to sacrifice if those elements which he cited as preventing this choice from yielding the greater good were to be removed. What is to be noted here, above all, is that McCormick's complex analyses were, at bottom, his attempts to identify the right choice among an agent's options, with 'right choice' meaning the choice which promised the least ontic evil or the greatest ontic good.

Proportionate Reason and Rights

There is still more to be gleaned about the nature of McCormick's moral theory from his analysis of the lynch-mob case. It is significant that by explicating the moral defect in the choice to frame an innocent man in terms of greater good/lesser evil, McCormick eschewed the sort of moral theory that would support an *a-priori* judgment that such an act is morally wrong because it violates the victim's right(s). The implication is that McCormick found no standard or principle to be superior to, and to constrain, the demand on agents to do that among their options which promises to maximize ontic good or to minimize ontic evil. Indeed, were one to object that the choice to frame an innocent person violates that person's right(s), and that such a violation is sufficient to judge this choice to be unjust (morally wrong) regardless of the balance of ontic good(s) and evil(s) it promises, there is good reason to believe that McCormick would have argued that the greatest good/least evil standard functions as the conceptual ground and justification for any invocation of rights.[115] He claimed that

> behind and before the ascription of what is just and unjust is a prudential judgment—in a world of conflict and tragedy—of where the lesser evil lies.[116]

A few years later he joined this reasoning to rights-talk, asserting that

> *before* one ascribes rights, one must *first* discuss what is right and wrong. If we agree that it is wrong to kill a human being in certain circumstances, *then* such killing may be said to violate the victim's rights....Whenever one concludes that life may legitimately be taken, he must simultaneously assert that such taking is not a violation of a right.[117]

These words, when coupled with his greatest good/least evil standard determining when life may purposefully be taken, demonstrate that McCormick subordinated rights, even the right to life, to this proportionate reason standard. Using capital punishment as an illustration, he explained this subordination:

> If some urgent good or avoidance of evil justifies taking the life of a criminal (and I seriously doubt that it does) then one does not say that the benefits outweigh that right, as if it were legitimate to violate rights at times....It can never be morally right (an objective act of beneficence) to do an injustice.[118]

In short, McCormick's position was that human life may be taken purposefully when there is a proportionate reason for doing so, i.e., when doing so promises a greater ontic good/lesser ontic evil than not doing so. In his own words,

> whatever taking of human life is justified (we can disagree about the range of instances), is justified precisely by the good end—and that only.[119]

And, as McCormick understands it, this position cannot come in conflict with a legitimate right to life because, as we have seen, he stipulated that when there is a proportionate reason for taking a human life, the taking is not a violation of this right, and is therefore not an injustice. Put simply, he argued that if a proportionate reason to kill is present, a right to life is not.

Having laid out McCormick's understanding of the relationship between *proportionate reason* and *rights*, we turn now to respond to another element in Lisa Cahill's argument that McCormick is not a utilitarian.[120] Cahill claims that

> the utilitarian notion of justice entails no requirement that all have an equal right to essential material, social, and moral goods included in the *telos*; nor, far less, does it presuppose that the *telos* is only constituted fully by the participation of all who are oriented to it by nature.[121]

Given this understanding of utilitarianism, she finds it to be committed to the position that the sacrifice of individuals is licit when such sacrificing accomplishes or contributes to a maximizing of happiness. Yet, Cahill understands McCormick to have held that no individual is to be treated as a

> *bonum utile*, a means or object to be subordinated to the purposes of others. Every individual is a *bonum honestum*, an 'end in itself' in Kant's sense. This precludes at the very outset minimizing the dignity of some to maximize the welfare of others.[122]

Because of his position on the status of the individual, Cahill finds McCormick's theory to be non-utilitarian.

What can be said of Cahill's argument, specifically her suggestion that McCormick would not allow one human being to be sacrificed for the sake of some other human being *because* such sacrificing would treat the sacrificed human being as a *bonum utile*? It is true that McCormick believed that no human being has any greater intrinsic value than any other. Yet it must be noted that this belief was grounded in his understanding of the *ordo bonorum*. It is simply a fact, as he understood things, that human beings are equal in value.[123] This value judgment, though, is not sufficient to separate McCormick's proportionalism from consequentialism given what we have seen him argue, namely, that the presence or absence of a proportionate reason is what alone determines the moral quality of acts of purposeful killing. When McCormick judged certain instances of purposeful killing to be wrong (recall the lynch-mob case, the case of abortion in order to avoid a delivery bill, and, we will soon see, the case of bombing civilians in order to shorten a war) he did not do so by invoking a norm prohibiting such acts *a-priori*, regardless of the consequences, because they treat a *bonum honestum* as a *bonum utile*. In fact, he wrote:

> As to the principle of 'never treating an individual merely as a means,' I would suggest that this is a highly indeterminate notion, and when pushed begs the very question we are concerned with. Under analysis, it really means *abused*....[124]

McCormick then made a move reminiscent of his setting proportionate reason as the criterion for proper *moral* intention. He asserted that

> [W]hen killing represents the lesser evil, it does not involve one in treating an individual as a mere means....As for myself, I would only suggest that a person must be said to be used as a means only when he can be said to be reasonably unwilling (even by construction) that the action visiting harm on him be done.[125]

Notice, too, that McCormick's accounts of what precisely was wrong with each of the aforementioned examples of sacrificing individuals for the sake of some other good detailed how the evil entailed by the act in question was actually *disproportionate* to the good it would realize. In his analyses there was no reliance on the *bonum honestum/bonum utile* distinction, indeed there was no reference to this distinction at all. Furthermore, despite his belief in the equality of individuals, we have seen McCormick allow (even demand) the purposeful sacrificing of one human being for the sake of another when the sacrificing promises the lesser evil among the agent's choices, as in our abortion case where he argued that because the purposeful killing of the child in order to save the mother is judged to be a lesser evil than the alternative, "we ought to abort."[126]

Given all that we have seen, one may accept Cahill's claim that McCormick's theory is different than utilitarianism because the latter "permits equality to be set aside for considerations of utility."[127] But this observation misses the mark if it is aimed at distancing McCormick's theory from consequentialism in general. McCormick's analyses of cases involving the purposeful killing of some human beings for the sake of some other good (or for the sake of the good of some other human beings) indicate that he was reluctant to set aside equality precisely for consequentialist reasons, namely, because doing so would undermine the goods that are to be realized in one's choices. These analyses also show that despite this reluctance he would nevertheless allow such sacrifice if it were for the sake of a proportionate reason (greater good). In the end, then, McCormick's understanding of what grounds and what dissolves rights, along with his thoughts on treating individuals as means, are entirely consistent with his understanding of proportionate reason, and, as such, are entirely consistent with his consequentialism.

The Case of Bombing Non-Combatants in Warfare

McCormick's moral assessment of the choice to bomb non-combatants in warfare confirms that his moral theory, while somewhat complex, is consequentialist in nature. Writing specifically about the atomic bombing of Japan at the end of World War II, McCormick noted a familiar consequentialist argument in support of this choice:

> Those who would defend such counter-people (versus counter-combatant) attacks argue that they will save more lives. This was Truman's argument....If I am right (that proportionate reason reigns even where the taking of human life is concerned), then there must be a way of showing that Truman's understanding of proportion was wrong—if we hold it to be such, as I do. I believe there is.[128]

Relying upon the necessity principle and invoking the association of goods, he went on to argue that such bombing would actually undermine *life*, presumably even if it were true that more lives would be lost by allowing the conventional war to continue. He explained,

> Making innocent (noncombatant) persons the object of our targeting is a form of extortion in international affairs that contains an implicit denial of human freedom. Human freedom is undermined when extortionary actions are accepted and elevated and universalized. Because such freedom is an associated good upon which the very good of life heavily depends, undermining it in the manner of my defense of life is undermining life itself—is disproportionate.[129]

This case analysis provides another example of McCormick's somewhat complex but altogether consequentialist manner of act assessment. Here, McCormick did not argue that such bombing would violate the right to life of each innocent victim and, because of this fact, ought not to be chosen whatever good it may promise. Instead, he sought to demonstrate that such an act, despite its apparent promise to save more lives than its alternative, would in reality not yield such good consequences when all was said and done. He wrote:

> When our actions deny by implication the freedom and responsibility of the agressor, they deny that same freedom and responsibility in ourselves. And by doing that they remove the conditions for rationality in the conduct of war....Is anyone willing to assert confidently that there is no connection between Nagasaki-Hiroshima and the senseless slaughters that occurred in South Vietnam? Once the manner of our protection of a basic good reduces or removes by implication the basis for rational limitation of violence (liberty), then irrational (disproportionate) things are going to happen.[130]

McCormick's reasoning here is consistent with utilitarian J.J.C. Smart's counsel to those who would carry out a consequentialist analysis of the choice to cause misery and death to tens of millions of people in order to save hundreds of millions of people from the same fate. Smart cautioned that when assessing the consequences of this choice,

> we must not forget the immense side effects: the brutalization of the people who ordered the atrocities and carried them out.[131]

Or, as Joel Kupperman puts it,

> the killings, torturings, etc., that we regard as paradigms of the immoral are in general actions whose consequences include psychological states to which we would assign negative value.[132]

Notably, McCormick did not challenge the consequentialist nature of the reasoning he ascribed to Harry Truman. Instead, he embraced such reasoning but provided a more complex assessment of the overall ontic good and evil promised by the choice to bomb. He considered not only the number of lives saved and lost in each option, but also the negative effect that the choice to bomb would have on the choices of future agents. In doing so, McCormick followed a simple consequentialist principle noted by Paul Ramsey:

> ...[A]ll possible consequences is the test in any consequentialism. That always included consequences flowing from intimate involvement in doing the nonmoral evil means, as well as any other attitudes or corruptions of moral agents.[133]

After considering McCormick's analysis, one is left to conclude that he would approve of this bombing if somehow it were assured that this putative act of extortion would not be "accepted and elevated and universalized." Such a conclusion is reasonable because, given the assurance in question, those elements of the choice to bomb which McCormick believed would lead to disproportionate ontic evil would be absent. Indeed, with his analysis of this case in mind, one should recall his more general statement that

> when one says that 'direct killing of the innocent' is forbidden, he need not and should not imply that such killing is morally wrong 'independently of whatever reasons the agent might have had.' He may and ought to imply that the conceivable reasons for killing in such circumstances are, under careful analysis, not proportionate to the harm done...[134]

In the end, then, McCormick's analyses of the aforementioned abortion, lynch-mob, and civilian bombing cases demonstrate that his implied prohibition against "undermining" a value, X, was not offered as an exceptionless prohibition against ever purposefully harming an instance of X. Rather, this prohibition is to be understood as forbidding purposefully harming an instance of X *unless doing so promotes* X. These case analyses make plain that McCormick believed that acting against any instance(s) of any good (say, *this* human being's life, or, *these* lives) was to be justified or condemned according to the promise, or lack thereof, of a greater overall realization or lesser overall diminution of this same, or an associated, good. We have seen this belief at work in various places: in his counsel to abort the child in the case discussed above, in his identification of just what is wrong with the choice to frame an innocent person in the lynch-mob case, and in his condemnation of the choice to bomb noncombatants to shorten a war. In each case, the greater realization of (or lesser material harm to) a to-be-pursued value, X, was the criterion by which a choice purposefully to harm an instance, or instances, of X was morally assessed. Such moral reasoning is clearly consequentialist in the sense laid out in chapter one.

The Scope of *Proportionate Reason* Reasoning

It is important to note that what McCormick said about proportionate reason and its decisive role in the moral assessment of human acts was to be applied to *every* human act. This point needs to be made because at times McCormick appears to have limited his consequentialist statement of duty and standard of act assessment to what he referred to as "cases of conflict," i.e. cases in which evildoing is unavoidable. He suggested this limitation when he asserted that

> When one is faced with two options both of which involve unavoidable (nonmoral) evil, one ought to choose the lesser evil.[135]

But given the unavoidable limits on human agency which he accepted, it is clear that the principle just mentioned must apply to every choice in every situation. The universal scope of the rule to choose the greater good/lesser evil (a rule which, it should be recalled, was to apply not only to those instances in which the lesser evil would simply be *allowed* to occur, but also to those instances where the lesser evil would have to be purposefully *caused* by the agent) becomes evident when one notes McCormick's claim that "whenever one chooses to do a good he leaves another undone."[136] These recurring instances of ontic good left "undone" are themselves instances of ontic evil. McCormick was careful to point this out, explaining that the concept of ontic evil

> includes not only harm to reputation, etc., but even the imperfections and incompleteness due to our limitations. Thus Janssens writes: 'We call ontic evil any lack of perfection at

which we aim, any lack of fulfillment which frustrates our natural urges and makes us suffer.'[137]

We have already seen that Louis Janssens's account of ontic evil, an account embraced by McCormick, attributed part of this "lack of perfection" and "lack of fulfillment" to the fact that

> when we choose a certain action, we must at the same time, at least for the time being, postpone all other possible acts. This is the meaning of Bergson's words: *'Tout choix est un sacrifice.'*[138]

This practice of considering unrealized ontic good to be a type of ontic evil is consonant with Peter Knauer's claim, noted in chapter two, that

> *every* human act brings evil effects with it. The choice of a value always means concretely that there is *denial of another value* which must be given as a price in exchange.[139]

McCormick's agreement with his proportionalist predecessors on this point is further evidenced by his claim that

> right reason tells us that we may choose to pursue this good of our neighbor only if it is at least as beneficial to him as the value we leave undone.[140]

It is consistent with all that we have seen of McCormick to believe that he found this dictate of right reason to be reasonable because he believed that ontic good left undone is, as an unrealized opportunity, itself ontic evil. As one of McCormick's former students, Christopher Kaczor, explains

> The agent's inability to realize all the values that one could potentially realize is ontic evil. Joseph Fuchs, Louis Janssens, Richard McCormick, and Bruno Schuller, among many others, have agreed with this analysis. Since every act is necessarily an omission of goods that could have been realized, the nonrealization of these goods is a premoral evil.[141]

Now if it is indeed true that every choice is a choice which leaves another good undone, and if this aspect of every choice is to be judged an ontic evil, then it is true that every choice is, in McCormick's terms, a situation of conflict. Drawing all of this together he wrote

> Every human choice, being a finite choice, will fail to realize all possible values. It can realize only certain limited values, and in doing so must at times do so to the neglect of other

values or at the expense of associated disvalues. In this light, every choice represents the resolution of a conflict.[142]

Given his position here, McCormick's statement of obligation in conflict situations, and the criterion of right action which it implies (i.e. that the right act is that act among an agent's possible choices which promises the least evil/greatest good) must apply to every human choice in every situation. Indeed, by what principle, one might wonder, could McCormick restrict this obligation to choose the lesser evil, given all he has said? Would not such a principle violate "right reason" by allowing for morally acceptable instances of not choosing the least ontic evil or greatest ontic good? It seems that his theory left no room for such a principle.[143]

McCormick's Self-Defense

Wanting to distinguish his version of proportionalism from consequentialism, McCormick went right to the heart of his theory and explained, "The phrase 'proportionate reason' is not convertible with the notion of 'better results' or 'net good.'"[144] He faulted Paul Ramsey for interpreting *proportionate reason*

> as if it meant 'greatest net good,' and 'net measurable good' as if it meant weighing all the values against each other and then trying to produce the greatest net good. Thus he suggests that proportionate reason means 'quantity of benefits.' This is a form of consequentialism, as I understand it, and that is certainly not what I mean by proportionate reason.[145]

Prompted by such misunderstanding, McCormick returned to the now-familiar standard of *undermining/serving* a good to clarify his position: purposefully causing ontic evil is justified if it is done for a *proportionate reason*, that is, if

> the value being sought will not be undermined by the contemplated action....Thus, where there is a question of taking life, such taking is proportionate only if it is, all things considered, the better service of *life itself* in the tragic circumstances.[146]

We have already considered a few examples of how McCormick employed this *undermining/serving* standard to assess and explicate the moral character of acts. But he also relied upon this criterion in his moral analysis of contraception, an analysis he was sure proved his theory to be non-consequentialist.

McCormick believed that sexual intercourse directly involves two basic and related human goods: the communicative good and the procreative good.[147] While acknowledging that an act of contraception is, by nature, "a nonmoral disvalue"[148] he nevertheless argued that the moral character of any particular act of contraception is determined by whether that particular act is in the best service of the procreative good, or undermines it. This judgment is made more complex, he continued, given the relationship between the two goods directly involved:

> a consideration of what happens to the communicative good when contraception is used or not can illumine whether the use or nonuse of contraception is the best service of the procreative good. For the communicative good is an associated good whose treatment either supports or undermines the procreative good.[149]

Having thus identified a relationship between goods that must be taken into account when morally assessing a choice to contracept, McCormick went on to note just how his assessment of such a choice would *not* proceed in order to illustrate that his proportionalism was not consequentialist:

> It is not as if we were carving off a little bit of procreative good, a little bit of communicative good, and a little bit of other goods, toting them all up and using the net or sum to tell us which action 'produces the best consequences,' or 'the greatest good for the greatest number.' It is not as if we were holding up two basic and incommensurable values, seeing them conflicted, then choosing one as greater or subordinating one to the other on the grounds that this produces the best overall results.[150]

Lisa Cahill, believing with McCormick that some of his critics incorrectly characterized his notion of proportionate reason as "a narrow and utilitarian advantage," adds to this line of defense.[151] She begins by asserting that

> the bottom line in a utilitarian theory of morality is the sum total of welfare, conceived in a relatively immediate, empirical, and quantifiable sense.[152]

She goes on to cite McCormick's sensitivity to the association of basic goods and his *undermining/serving* criterion as features of his act assessments which are foreign to utilitarian act-assessments:

> since the values in the association are all equal and interdependent, to choose against one is to violate all of the others. Thus, to conclude that an act which aims at one value is dis-

proportionate in itself, it is necessary simply to show that the act damages another value in the group.[153]

As Cahill understands it, McCormick's version of proportionalism makes it "unnecessary to calculate the relative worth of discrete goods" in order to morally assess an act, a fact which she believes "dissociates" this theory from utilitarianism.[154]

What can be said of this defense? Several things. It is true that McCormick's disavowal of the notion *greatest net good* appears to have been an attempt to make clear that he did not mean to advocate a simple utilitarianism, one which identified a single good, X, to which all other goods reduce and whose net-maximization is the ultimate *telos*. In this vein, Cahill notes G.E.M. Anscombe's description of utilitarianism, a description that Cahill suggests does not fit McCormick's proportionalism:

> the goal of human acts is the pursuit of 'the greatest good for the greatest number' or the greatest sum total of social welfare, understood temporally and empirically or at least quantifiably.[155]

And it appears to be just these aspects of utilitarianism that McCormick tried to distance himself from when he wrote,

> proportionate reason as I understand it can be explained in several different ways, no one of which need reduce to 'greatest net good.'[156]

Yet when considering McCormick's words here, one must keep in mind this crucial fact: he believed that when utilitarians measured "total net good," they restricted their scope to "mere welfare values."[157] Given this understanding of utilitarianism, McCormick's claim that *proportionate reason* does not reduce to the utilitarian's *greatest net good* should be understood as meaning simply that judgments of *proportionate reason* are not to be so restrictive as to consider only the determinate set of goods (welfare values) to which he believed utilitarians clung. This claim, so understood, fails as a defense against our charge because while it does distinguish McCormick's value theory, with its multiple and associated *maximands* (the basic goods), from the value theory of one form of utilitarianism (one identifying only welfare values as commensurable *maximands*), it does not separate McCormick's proportionalism from consequentialism in general. It is a mistake to conclude that his moral theory is not consequentialist simply because he did not maintain that *proportionate reason* was to be understood by reference to one particular set of goods, namely, "welfare values." While it may be true that McCormick's proportionalism is not the sort of utilitarianism he described and rejected, it is also true that, in the words of Bernard Williams, utilitarianism is only *"one sort* of consequentialism."[158]

The root of the problem with McCormick's defense here is suggested by Joel Kupperman's observation that "utilitarian theories are the conjunction of value generalizations of a certain sort with consequentialism."[159] Thus, the fact that one particular moral theory (say, McCormick's proportionalism) differs from another (say, utilitarianism) with respect to the *maximand(s)* each identifies does not entail that they cannot both be consequentialist. Indeed, there exists a variety of consequentialist ethical theories distinguishable from each other by their respective notions of the good. Neera Kapur alludes to this fact when she observes that a "monistic and utilitarian" theory of the good is "standardly rejected" by contemporary consequentialists in favor of "a richer theory of the good," one which is "designed to accommodate various things, including friendship, as intrinsic goods."[160] Kapur cites one particular consequentialist theory which proposes that the good *happiness* "is neither an inclusive nor a dominant value, but one among other intrinsic values."[161] Given these facts about consequentialist theories, McCormick's disavowal of utilitarianism is an ineffective rebuttal to our charge that his brand of proportionalism is consequentialist. The supreme principle shared by McCormick and other consequentialist ethical theories, the principle which justifies their being considered of a kind despite their differences in value theory, is: *do that among one's choices which promises the least net-evil/greatest net-good.* So, while we may grant that McCormick was not a utilitarian, we do not thus grant that he was not a consequentialist. As Sanford Levy explains, "another way of putting the point is that he is not a consequentialist in quite the same way that the act-utilitarian is."[162]

Yet another problem with the defense offered by McCormick is that it employed a rather rudimentary form of a consequentialist act assessment. In doing so, it again misses the mark. It has not been contended here that McCormick's act assessments are as simple as the caricatured example he held up as the fruit of some generic consequentialism. What has been argued here is that his moral theory is a complex and nuanced version of consequentialism, one that is surely not so crude as to yield the sort of simplistic assessment of contraception he disavowed. It is true that in some cases (the abortion dilemma, for example) he found the assessment to be rather simple:

> ...[T]he evils involved in the only available alternatives are commensurable, the lesser evil clear, and *that* is why it is morally right to save the one life that one can.[163]

In other cases, though, e.g. the bombing of non-combatants and the sacrificing of an innocent person to a lynch-mob, he found that the circumstances of the act and the association of goods made the assessment of where the greater good/lesser evil lay to be more complex. In such cases, he cautioned, "commensuration is obviously not a simple, uncomplicated thing."[164] However, guiding all of his case analyses was his goal of identifying the greatest good/least evil among the agent's options, with the underlying conviction that there lay the morally right and obligatory choice. Simply to point out that his assessment of the good and evil promised by some particular option would be different than the assessment carried on in some rudimentary version of utilitarianism is, again, to distance his theory from that type of consequentialism, but not from consequentialism itself.

Finally, there is one more element in McCormick's moral analysis of contraception that bears some scrutiny. In the passage on contraception cited above, he seemed to suggest that his proportionalism should not be considered consequentialist because it did not advocate the subordination of any basic good to any other basic good, presumably even if such a subordination promised to produce the best overall results. Perhaps picking up on this suggestion, Lisa Cahill explains that McCormick was committed to the position that

> there are certain values in the scale which always prevail in conflict cases, so that to choose against one unless it is 'necessary' (in a 'deterministic,' even physical sense) is by definition disproportionate.[165]

An undefended assumption behind this somewhat undeveloped defense seems to be that a moral theory which asserts that a hierarchy exists among the goods agents should pursue, and which does not allow the subordination of any member of an identified set of basic goods to any other member in that hierarchy, is not consequentialist.

The reply to this defense, with its aforementioned assumption, is simple: Why cannot a consequentialist theory identify more than one *maximand* and remain consequentialist? We have seen Neera Kapur explain that some consequentialist theories are "designed to accommodate various things, including friendship, as intrinsic goods."[166] And years ago C.D. Broad noted that a moral theory of this kind may identify several to-be-pursued intrinsic goods.[167] As we shall see when we consider his philosophical anthropology in chapter four, the *ordo bonorum* that McCormick incorporated into his moral theory was understood by him to be ontologically prior to, and independant of, this moral theory. Like the necessity principle and the association of goods, he found the *ordo bonorum* that held sway in his version of proportionalism to be brute fact, something that must be taken into account if one is to arrive at correct assessments of the good and evil promised by one's options. Acknowledgment that there exists a set of basic goods, and that some goods have priority over others, e.g. *life* over *money*, and that some enjoy equality with others, e.g. *life* and *freedom*, and that some are the condition for others, e.g. *life* for *freedom*, does not entail an answer to the question of how one is to judge the moral character of acts that affect instances of these goods. Given this disconnect, one wonders just how McCormick's acknowledgment and acceptance of these prior facts establishes that his moral theory is not consequentialist.

Furthermore, while McCormick may have rjected the subordination of one basic good *simpliciter* to another basic good *simpliciter*, his case analyses show that at times he did advocate the sacrifice of one instance of a basic good for the sake of an instance or instances of another basic good. Cahill herself found McCormick to have maintained that "direct sacrifice of these associated values is justified in certain narrow cases."[168] And when did he call for this sacrificing? When it promised the greatest good among an agent's choices. His position, in Cahill's words, was that

> a nonmoral or premoral good can be directly negated in favor of one which is higher or at least equal. Proportion, not directness of intention, is the key to morally right choice between competing values.[169]

And, in his own words, he explained

> With W.D. Ross we can admit that 'we are faced with great difficulties when we try to commensurate good things of very different types.' Great difficulties? Yes. Insuperable ones? No....What do we do? *Somehow or other*, in fear and trembling, we commensurate. In a sense we *adopt* a hierarchy. We go to war to protect our freedom. That means we are willing to sacrifice life to protect this good....There are human goods that we will die and kill for rather than forfeit—and if that does not involve commensurating, then what is it?[170]

In the end, McCormick's identification of a set of basic and associated goods that are not, in the *ordo essendi*, subordinated one to another, is not enough to save his proportionalism from consequentialism so long as *proportionate reason* remains his criterion for the rightness and wrongness of acts which purposefully sacrifice instances of these goods. Having considered some of the defenses McCormick and Cahill offered against this charge, the most reasonable conclusion is that McCormick's case analyses and his notion of proportionate reason show him to have been a consequentialist, if not a simple utilitarian.

Conclusion

We return now to where we began this chapter, with McCormick's statement of the basic proportionalist position:

> causing certain disvalues in our conduct does not by that very fact make the action morally wrong, as certain traditional formulations supposed. These evils or disvalues are said to be premoral when considered abstractly, that is, in isolation from their morally relevant circumstances. But they are evils....The action in which they occur becomes morally wrong when, all things considered, there is not a proportionate reason in the act justifying the disvalue.[171]

In this chapter we have considered a few elements of McCormick's moral theory: his understanding of *proportionate reason*, the terms and phrases which he at times substituted for it, and his undermining and necessity principles. We have also considered some case analyses where he employed these elements. What the foregoing has shown is that when McCormick claimed that a proportionate reason justifies the purposeful causing of ontic evil, he meant that the promise of a greater good justifies such purposeful harm. But to set this principle as the supreme standard of act assessment, as McCormick did, and to assert that one's primary moral duty is to choose according to it, regardless of what this requires the agent purposefully to do, as McCormick did, is to propose a consequentialist ethical theory. Philip Petit observes that "consequentialists say that the right option in any choice is that which promotes the realization of the relevant valuable properties."[172] Have we not seen McCormick, in so many words, say just that? After one has worked through his somewhat complex assessments of proportion and his somewhat imprecise terminology vis-a-vis *proportionate reason*, it becomes clear that McCormick argued that all choices are to be morally assessed according to the greatest good/ least evil standard typical of consequentialist theories. In the chapters that follow we will see McCormick's basic consequentialist position, outlined above, confirmed again and again in his account of intrinsically evil acts, in his analysis of the distinction between directly and indirectly doing evil, and in his criteria for what is to count as "acting against" a basic human good.

Notes

1 Richard McCormick, "Killing the Patient," in *Considering Veritatis Splendor* John Wilkins (ed.), (Cleveland: The Pilgrimn Press, 1994), 17. Although there were some minor alterations, this is substantially a reprint of an article of the same title in *The Tablet,* (October 30, 1993), 1410-1411.

2 He also claimed that the elements that are to be proportionate to each other are the evil-causing act and the agent's end, but we will see that his other statements and case analyses lead to the conclusion that the to-be-proportioned terms are the good and evil that an act promises, and that, to him, this was equivalent to his notion of act-end proportion.

3 See, for example, Richard McCormick, "Notes on Moral Theology: April-September 1971," *Theological Studies* 33 1 (March 1972),75; "Ambiguity in Moral Choice," in *Doing Evil to Achieve Good* P. Ramsey and R. McCormick (eds.), (Milwaukee: Marquette University Press, 1973.), 41.

4 See, for example, "Ambiguity in Moral Choice," 27-28; "A Commentary on the Commentaries," in *Doing Evil to Achieve Good* P. Ramsey and R. McCormick (eds.), (Milwaukee: Marquette University Press, 1973.), 212, 230, 233-235; "Notes on Moral Theology 1977: The Church in Dispute," *Theological Studies* 39 1 (March 1978), 111.

5 Richard McCormick, *How Brave a New World?* (London: SCM Press, 1981), 428. One may wonder how he would counsel an agent confronted with more than one possible choice in which the good outweighs the evil. While not directly addressing this question, we may infer from what he said in other contexts that he would *require* the doing of that act which promises the greater good in his *ordo bonorum*. More will be said about this below, and in chapter four, when we consider his philosophical/theological anthropology. See also the next footnote.

6 Richard McCormick, "A Commentary on the Commentaries," 263. It may be noted that McCormick's terms here—*lesser, greater*—suggest, although they do not prove, that he was focused exclusively on the alternatives of performing a particular act or not performing that act. This in turn may suggest that he believed that moral decision-making ultimately comes down to a question of whether or not an agent may/should perform a single act, X, in the given circumstances. If this is the case, although it is not certain that it is, it should be noted that McCormick did not explicitly address the issue of how an agent is to narrow her choices in her circumstances to these alternatives, that is, how an agent is to eliminate possibilities W, Y, Z, etc. so that the final decision becomes one of doing or not doing X. Unaware of any principle that he offered to exempt the prior decision to eliminate W, Y, Z, etc., from his criterion for deciding whether or not to do X, and assuming consistency on McCormick's part, we may infer that all possibilities other than X are eliminated through the same greatest good/least evil standard that we shall see determines whether or not X is to be done.

7 Richard McCormick, "Ambiguity in Moral Choice," 27.

8 Ibid., 31.

9 Ibid., 38, 44. McCormick did not explain exactly when, and why, an agent is to seek the greater good instead of the lesser evil (recall from chapter one how these alternatives are not always equivalent, and may indicate different choices in some cases). McCormick's case analyses suggest that when one is confronted with a plurality of options all of which involve some significant evil, one ought to choose the lesser evil, and when one is confronted with a plurality of options all of which represent the fulfillment of a positive duty without involving some significant evil, then one ought to seek and do the greater good. I can say only that McCormick *suggested* this approach because nowhere does he directly address this question, although recall from chapter two that he did claim that "When one is faced with two options both of which involve unavoidable (nonmoral) evil, one ought to choose the lesser evil" ("Notes on Moral Theology 1977: The Church in Dispute," 111). We will also soon see that he claimed that "the rule of Christian reason…is to choose the lesser evil" ("Ambiguity in Moral Choice," 38). This lack of clarity, though, does not effect the case that he was offering a consequentialist ethical theory. The filling of such a lacuna would be necessary were one inquiring

into what precisely he would urge in certain situations. It is not necessary in order to expose the consequentialist principles and analyses he offers.
10 We will see his case analyses dealing with what he considered to be basic human goods, but given his belief in an *ordo bonorum*, he did believe that pursuing a lower good at the expense of a higher one was also disproportionate, i.e. caused greater harm than the alternative of *not* pursuing the lower good at the expense of the higher one. His *ordo bonorum* will be examined in chapter four.
11 Ibid., 45-46.
12 Richard McCormick, "A Commentary on the Commentaries," 201.
13 Ibid. See also his "Ambiguity in Moral Choice," 46: "To see whether an act involving evil is proportionate in the circumstances we must judge whether this choice in the best possible service of all the values the tragic and difficult conflict." Sanford Levy refers to this element in McCormick's theory as "the undermining principle," and we shall do the same; Sanford Levy, "Richard McCormick and Proportionate Reason," *The Journal of Religious Ethics* 13 2 (1985), 259.
14 For an example of McCormick's use of each of these phrases as synonyms of one another, see "A Commentary on the Commentaries," 234. We will return to this point below.
15 Sanford Levy, "Richard McCormick and Proportionate Reason," *The Journal of Religious Ethics* 13 2 (1985), 259.
16 Richard McCormick, "A Commentary on the Commentaries," 228.
17 Ibid. So goes his analysis of the lynch-mob case, as we shall soon see.
18 Ibid., 233.
19 A claim that he believed eliminates his theory from the category of consequentialist ethical theories; we will more fully lay out, and rebut, this claim/defense in chapter 4.
20 Richard McCormick, "A Commentary on the Commentaries," 229-230.
21 Ibid.
22 Richard McCormick, "Notes on Moral Theology 1977: The Church in Dispute," 78, n.9
23 Richard McCormick, "Killing the Patient," 17.
24 McCormick did not deal formally with the issue of how the probability of the greater good or lesser evil being realized is to enter into the assessment. For example, he did not provide us with the wherewithal to deal with the following sort of question: How ought one choose when faced with the alternatives of either purposefully causing disvalue D in order to bring about a proportionate value V when the likelihood of V being realized by doing D is low, or, of not causing D and thereby not having any chance of realizing V while at the same time allowing the disvalue of V's non-realization to obtain? Such would perhaps be the case were one's child ill with a terminal disease that promises to end his life painlessly within several months, and if one were presented with the option of a long and painful procedure (D) which does have a slim chance of curing the child (V) but which would more likely hasten his death. It is perhaps not a weakness of McCormick's theory that it allows for no simple answer to this question. But if some would consider this a fault, one may respond that they may be seeking a degree of certitude and precision that this subject matter does not allow, and that this putative fault is one which has no bearing on our discussion, for McCormick's silence on such an issue may not be taken as any evidence that his theory is non-consequentialist. We will continue to see that what he *did* say clearly places him in the consequentialist camp.
25 We noted in chapter one that our discussion was taking place within the context of normative ethical theories. We also noted that such theories agree that one's duty is to do what is right, and that what separates these theories is their account of what makes a right act right and a wrong act wrong. McCormick, offering a normative ethical theory whose species is in dispute, shared the assumption that one ought to do what is right. In laying out and defending this theory, he stated that "the *rule* of Christian reason...is to choose the lesser evil" (Emphasis mine; "Ambiguity in Moral Choice," 38). Later, he claimed that "When one is faced with two

options both of which involve unavoidable [nonmoral] evil, one *ought* to choose the lesser evil" (Emphasis mine; "Notes on Moral Theology 1977: The Church in Dispute," *Theological Studies* 39 1 [March 1978], 111). Still later, he suggested that "faith and the gospel concretely *demand*" right acts from Christians (Emphasis mine, "Notes on Moral Theology: 1982," *Theological Studies* 44 1 [March 1983], 79). Given the rule of Christian reason previously cited and the criterion of proportionate reason, this demand for morally right acts is a demand/obligation to do those acts which are judged to promise the greater pre-moral good or lesser pre-moral evil.

26 Richard McCormick, "Notes on Moral Theology: April-September 1971," *Theological Studies* 33 1 (March, 1972), 71. We will see in chapter five that McCormick excluded *moral* evil from this claim for a reason entirely consistent with his consequentialism: he believed that *morally* evil acts are inherently disproportionate because there exists no good which is proportionate to moral evil(s). We will also see that McCormick defined some morally evil acts – e.g., *murder*, *theft*, *adultery* – in terms of a disproportion between the nonmoral (ontic) good and nonmoral (ontic) evil promised, making his prohibition on morally evil acts to have been simply a reiteration of his prohibition on acts which promise evil disproportionate to the good sought.

27 Ibid.
28 Ibid., 74.
29 Ibid., 75.
30 A position he would have a difficult time reconciling with his rejection of the position that the death of a person is an *absolute* evil; see Ibid., 71.
31 Albert Outler, "The Beginnings of Personhood: Theological Considerations," *Perkins Journal* 27 (1973).
32 Emphasis mine. Richard McCormick, *How Brave a New World?*, 168.
33 Ibid.
34 Richard McCormick, "Notes on Moral Theology: April-September 1971," 71.
35 In chapter 4 we will see that he did come to grant some moral significance to the distinction between *intentionally doing* an evil and merely *allowing* that same evil. Yet it will be seen that this significance was granted only when, and to the extent that, the distinction was judged to affect the net good and evil an act or omission promises.
36 A prohibition recently formulated as follows: "The deliberate murder of an innocent person is gravely contrary to the dignity of the human being, to the golden rule, and to the holiness of the Creator. The law forbidding it is universally valid: it obliges each and everyone, always and everywhere." *The Catechism of the Catholic Church* (Ligouri, MO: Ligouri Publications, 1994), no.2261. Consider, too, ibid., no.2263: "The legitimate defense of persons and societies is not an exception to the prohibition against the murder of the innocent that constitutes intentional killing."
37 Emphasis mine. Richard McCormick, "Notes on Moral Theology: April - September 1974," *Theological Studies* 36 1 (March 1975), 98. This, too, is a clear example of the act-justifying proportion being between the good and the evil an act promises.
38 Again, more will be said on this in chapter 4.
39 Because the death of the child was caused indirectly and came as unintended effect of the act of saving the mother. A more detailed example of a deontological analysis of this case, an analysis which McCormick explicitly rejected, is found in Germain Grisez' *Abortion: The Myths, the Realities, and the Arguments* (Washington: Corpus Books, 1970), 340.
40 Richard McCormick, "Ambiguity in Moral Choice," 27-28.
41 Later, McCormick incorporated other elements into his analysis of this case. These other elements are what he had in mind when, elsewhere, he appears to have backed off somewhat from the analysis above and wrote that in the abortion dilemma under consideration "the situation is not simply a save-one vs. lose-two dilemma. It is not simply quantitative" ("Notes on Moral Theology 1977: The Church in Dispute," *Theological Studies* 39 1 [March 1978], 111).

He then went on to cite factors that influence the determination of proportion, i.e. the determination of the good and evil connected with the proposed act, in this and similar cases. We will consider some of these factors below, and another will be considered in chapter four. We will see, though, that his consideration of these other elements constitute only a more refined and exhaustive attempt to identify the greater good and/or lesser evil among the alternatives. The basic structure of his moral reasoning that we are noting here will remain unchanged.

42 Recall his words from above as he explained why purposefully *doing* the ontic evil of abortion is licit in those circumstances: "We could *allow* both mother and child (who will perish under any circumstances) to die…" Emphasis mine; see note 41.

43 Richard McCormick, "A Commentary on the Commentaries," 262.

44 Emphasis mine. Richard McCormick, "Notes on Moral Theology: 1976," *Theological Studies* 38 1 (March 1977), 78.

45 Emphasis mine. Richard McCormick, "Ambiguity in Moral Choice," 47.

46 Ibid.

47 Emphasis mine. Richard McCormick, "A Commentary on the Commentaries," 214.

48 As discussed in chapter one, one may agree with a consequentialist that a certain state of affairs is preferable to another state of affairs with respect to the amount or type of ontic evil and good each state contains, and yet disagree that the acts which are required to realize this preferred state of affairs are therefore morally licit.

49 Again, he later indicated some sensitivity to these agent-related considerations but, again, it will be seen that such considerations were incorporated into his assessment of which among an agents options *truly* represents the greater good or lesser evil. The assumption that one ought to *do* that which is judged to be the lesser evil/greater good remained operative. It is this assumption that we are focusing upon here.

50 Richard McCormick, "Notes on Moral Theology 1977: The Church in Dispute," 111.

51 Richard McCormick, "A Commentary on the Commentaries," 212.

52 Richard McCormick, "Notes on Moral Theology 1977: The Church in Dispute," 110.

53 Ibid., 103.

54 Ibid.

55 Richard McCormick, *The Critical Calling: Reflections on Moral Dilemmas since Vatican II* (Washington: Georgetown University Press, 1989), 132.

56 Richard McCormick, "Notes on Moral Theology 1977: The Church in Dispute," 102.

57 Chapter 4 will look closely at this absence of constraint on the purposeful doing of evil.

58 Richard McCormick, *A Commentary on the Commentaries*, 260.

59 Emphasis mine. Richard McCormick, *A Commentary on the Commentaries*, 261. He also referred to this type of relationship as an "essential and necessary causal relationship" (*A Commentary on the Commentaries*, 239).

60 A name given to this element of McCormick's system by Sanford Levy. See Levy's "Richard McCormick and Proportionate Reason," *The Journal of Religious Ethics* 13 2 (1985), 258-278.

61 Emphasis mine. Richard McCormick, "Notes on Moral Theology 1977: The Church in Dispute," 111-112. Elsewhere he said that this case analysis "is made in circumstances where there is an inherent necessity between the means (taking the child's life) and the end (saving the mother where otherwise both mother and child will perish)" ("A Commentary on the Commentaries," 212). Our aim here is not to critique this principle, because whether or not it is plausible is irrelevant to whether or not McCormick's moral theory is consequentialist. We are examining this necessity principle because it is an element in McCormick's moral theory and has a role in our case that this theory is consequentialist. For a critique of the plausibility of this principle, see Levy's "Richard McCormick and Proportionate Reason," *The Journal of Religious Ethics* 13 2 (1985), 258-278.

62 Ibid.

63 Lisa Sowle Cahill, "Teleology, Utilitarianism, and Christian Ethics," *Theological Studies* 42 (1981), 624. His undermining principle and his belief in an association of basic goods are other refinements which Cahill believes keeps McCormick from the utilitarian camp. More will be said on these later.
64 Ibid.
65 We will look closely at his notion of a good being *undermined* in a moment.
66 Richard McCormick, "A Commentary on the Commentaries," 239. Sanford Levy finds McCormick's notion of "necessary" to be vague, the result of various and not easily reconciled phrases that are meant to convey his understanding of necessity ("Richard McCormick and Proportionate Reason," 261).
67 Richard McCormick, "A Commentary on the Commentaries," 262, 263.
68 McCormick treated these as two sides of one criterion ("A Commentary on the Commentaries" 262, 263).
69 Sanford Levy, "Richard McCormick and Proportionate Reason," 268.
70 Richard McCormick, "A Commentary on the Commentaries," 239.
71 Richard McCormick, "Notes on Moral Theology 1977: The Church in Dispute," 111.
72 Emphasis mine. Richard McCormick, "Ambiguity in Moral Choice," 33.
73 Richard McCormick, "Notes on Moral Theology 1977: The Church in Dispute," 113
74 Ibid. The plausibility of this last claim is not the issue here, so we will not linger on it. What is to be noted is how McCormick assessed the ontic evil in the choice to frame given his belief in an association of goods, and how he found this assessment morally decisive.
75 Ibid. One page later he repeated: "...freedom is an associated good which must be asserted and protected if the good of life itself is to survive." See also his "A Commentary on the Commentaries," 229.
76 Paulinus Odozor, *Richard A. McCormick and the Renewal of Moral Theology* (Notre Dame: Notre Dame University Press, 1995), 114-115.
77 Richard McCormick, "Notes on Moral Theology 1977: The Church in Dispute," 113.
78 Richard McCormick, "A Commentary on the Commentaries," 239.
79 Ibid., 260.
80 Ibid.
81 Ibid., 262.
82 Sanford Levy, "Richard McCormick and Proportionate Reason," 262-263.
83 Emphasis mine. Richard McCormick, "Ambiguity in Moral Choice," 33.
84 Ibid.
85 Richard McCormick, "A Commentary on the Commentaries," 250.
86 Ibid.
87 Ibid., 223.
88 A standard perhaps reminiscent of Kant's reasoning to an exceptionless prohibition on lying.
89 Richard McCormick, "Notes on Moral Theology: 1980" *Theological Studies* 42 1 (March 1981), 78.
90 Richard McCormick, *The Critical Calling*, 398.
91 Richard McCormick, "Ambiguity in Moral Choice," 32.
92 Ibid., 28.
93 Richard McCormick, "A Commentary on the Commentaries," 250.
94 Ibid., 263.
95 Although, if it could be established that concepts do suffer harm from some human actions, a moral theory which proposed as the supreme criterion of the rightness and wrongness of human actions the good and evil effect they have on the relevant concepts may yet be consequentialist.
96 Richard McCormick, "A Commentary on the Commentaries," 234.

97 Consider, too, the following passage, offered in a different context, which explicitly equates "disvalue to life" with "ontic evil": "Traditional moral formulations say that indirect killing need not be a violation of right, that it is morally legitimate when proportionately grounded. It can say this, I believe, only after having considered the alternative, scil., what would happen in conflict cases if we did not allow such killing? Because the answer to that alternative possibility is *more disvalue to life itself, more ontic evil*, it was concluded that such killing may be tolerated, and is not therefore a violation of the right of the one indirectly killed" (Emphasis mine; Richard McCormick, "Notes on Moral Theology: April – September 1974," 99).

98 Ibid. It should also be noted that elsewhere he counterposed the paired terms *undermine* and *contradict* with the pair *support* and *maximize* ("Ambiguity in Moral Choice," 10).

99 Emphasis mine. Sanford Levy, "Richard McCormick and Proportionate Reason," 260.

100 Brian Johnstone, "The Meaning of Proportionate Reason in Contemporary Moral Theology," *The Thomist* 49 2 (1985), 247.

101 Richard McCormick, "A Commentary on the Commentaries," 262.

102 Richard McCormick, *How Brave a New World?*, 168. Also, after writing the above he explained that "'human life' refers to individual life from conception..." (ibid.)

103 Sanford Levy, "Richard McCormick and Proportionate Reason," 264.

104 Richard McCormick, "A Commentary on the Commentaries," 260.

105 Ibid., 250.

106 Evidence that he believed abortion to be the taking of a human life can be found in his "Public Policy on Abortion" (*Hospital Progress* 60, 1979) where, after identifying "human life" as a "basic gift and good," he explained that "by 'human life' I mean human life from fertilization or at least from the time at or after which it is settled whether there will be one or two distinct human beings..." (as found in *How Brave a New World?*, 194). Elsewhere, he explained that "'human life' refers to individual life from conception" (*How Brave a New World?*, 168).

107 We will look more closely at this suggestion in a moment.

108 Richard McCormick, "A Commentary on the Commentaries," 239.

109 Ibid., 250.

110 Ibid.

111 As found in, say, John Paul II's *Veritatis Splendor*, no.80.

112 Emphasis mine. Richard McCormick, *The Critical Calling*, 64

113 We will soon see that his qualification "in conflict situations" is misleading given that his theory commits him to a greater good/lesser evil criterion of act assessment in *all* situations of choice.

114 Emphasis mine. Richard McCormick, "A Commentary on the Commentaries," 262. Note too the linking of *undermining* and *disproportionate* with *suffer more*. This linking may be added as evidence in our case that his standard of undermining and serving a value refers to the practical, tangible ontic goods and evils enjoyed or suffered by human beings.

115 He rarely dealt explicitly with the relationship between *rights* and *proportionate reason*. What follows relies upon those few times that he did.

116 "Notes on Moral Theology: April – September 1974," 99.

117 Emphasis mine; Richard McCormick, "A Commentary on the Commentaries," 204.

118 Ibid.

119 Ibid.

120 All of her defenses are against the charge that he is a utilitarian. While we are not making that charge here, her arguments are still relevant enough to merit explicit treatment. Also, our rebuttal of her defense will confirm and add to our case that McCormick is indeed a consequentialist, even if not a utilitarian.

121 Lisa Sowle Cahill, "Teleology, Utilitarianism, and Christian Ethics," 628.

122 Ibid. Elsewhere, in a similar but more general defense of proportionalism that does not focus on McCormick's version of the theory, she refers to this criterion as "a criterion of equal re-

spect for all persons...." ("Contemporary Challenges to Exceptionless Moral Norms," in *Moral Theology Today: Certitudes and Doubts*. St. Louis, Mo.: Pope John Center, 1984: 130).
123 He claimed that all lives are "equally valuable as basic human goods" ("Ambiguity in Moral Choice," 47). Elsewhere, he objected to the omission of life-sustaining treatment on mentally handicapped newborns if this is chosen "simply because the baby is retarded." Such non-treatment, he argued, would be guilty of "fundamentally unequal treatment of equals" ("Saving Defective Infants: Options for Life or Death," *America* 4/23/83: 316).
124 Richard McCormick, "A Commentary on the Commentaries," 247.
125 Ibid., 249.
126 Ibid., 246.
127 Lisa Sowle Cahill, "Teleology, Utilitarianism, and Christian Ethics," 629. See also Cahill's "Contemporary Challenges to Exceptionless Moral Norms," in *Moral Theology Today: Certitudes and Doubts* (St. Louis: Pope John Center, 1984), 131.
128 Richard McCormick, "A Commentary on the Commentaries," 236.
129 Ibid. Here McCormick became somewhat unclear. Referring to McCormick's undermining principle as UP, Sanford Levy writes: "An act-UP principle would say that whether or not an act is permissible depends on whether or not the act itself undermines the kind of value being sought, while a UP-generalization principle would say that it depends on whether or not the universal performance of that kind of act in the situation in question undermines the kind of value being sought. Because McCormick does not explicitly distinguish between act and generalization principles, it is not clear which he accepts" ("Richard McCormick and Proportionate Reason," 264). Yet, whichever McCormick preferred, recall that his assertion that an act which seeks a good actually *undermines* that good means that, overall, the act does not promise lesser evil or greater good than other options vis-a-vis the good being pursued. This being so, whether he ultimately opted for an act-UP or a UP-generalization theory—Levy believes that he preferred the former—his theory will be fundamentally consequentialist, either in an act-utilitarian or a rule utilitarian sense.
130 Richard McCormick, "A Commentary on the Commentaries," 238.
131 J.J.C. Smart and Bernard Williams, *Utilitarianism: For and Against*, 64.
132 Joel Kupperman, *The Foundations of Morality* (London: George Allen & Unwin, 1983) 124.
133 Paul Ramsey, "Incommensurability and Indeterminancy in Moral Choice," in *Doing Evil to Achieve Good: Moral Choice in Conflict Situations* Richard McCormick and Paul Ramsey (eds.), (Chicago: Loyola University Press, 1978) 100; For a confirmation of this principle, by both a utilitarian and a critic of the theory, see J.J.C. Smart and Bernard Williams, *Utilitarianism: For and Against* (Cambridge: Cambridge University Press, 1973) 63, 64, 70, 100, 106.
134 Richard McCormick, "Notes on Moral Theology: April – September 1974," 98.
135 Richard McCormick, "Notes on Moral Theology 1977: The Church in Dispute," 111.
136 Richard McCormick, "Notes on Moral Theology: April – September, 1971," 71. He claims, too, that "value-conflicts are inevitable in human choice" (Ibid.).
137 Richard McCormick, "Notes on Moral Theology: 1980," 78.
138 Louis Janssens, "Ontic Evil and Moral Evil," *Louvain Studies* 4 2 (1972), 134.
139 Peter Knauer, "The Hermeneutic Function of the Principle of Double Effect," *Natural Law Forum* 12 (1967), 145.
140 Richard McCormick, "Notes on Moral Theology: April – September, 1971," 71.
141 Christopher Kaczor, "Double Effect Reasoning From Jean Pierre Gury to Peter Knauer," *Theological Studies* 59 (1998), 303. Kaczor mentioned that he is a former student of McCormick's in personal correspondence between us.
142 Richard McCormick, "The New Medicine and Morality," *Theology Digest* 21, 4 (1973), 316.
143 As opposed to, say, the principle that one ought never purposefully to act against any instance of a basic good. Consider, for example, John Finnis' position that "A basic human good always is a reason for action and always gives a reason *not* to choose to destroy, damage, or im-

pede some instantiation of that good; but since the instantiations of human good at stake in any morally significant choice are not commensurable by *reason* prior to choice, there can never be a sufficient reason not to take that reason-not-to as decisive for choice. Only emotional factors such as desire or aversion could motivate a choice rejecting it" ("Natural Law and Legal Reasoning," in *Natural Law Theory*, Robert George (ed.), [Oxford: Oxford University Press, 1992], 138).

144 Richard McCormick, "A Commentary on the Commentaries," 201.
145 Ibid., 233.
146 Ibid., 201.
147 Ibid., 233.
148 Given that procreation is a good; see Richard McCormick, "A Commentary on the Commentaries," 233.
149 Richard McCormick, "A Commentary on the Commentaries," 233. Elsewhere he wrote: "The incommensurability of goods [procreative, communicative] is reduced by seeing them in interrelationship. And it is this interrelationship that provides the context – a kind of single scale – in which decisions are possible and reasonable…" ("Notes on Moral Theology 1977: The Church in Dispute," 113).
150 Richard McCormick, "A Commentary on the Commentaries," 234.
151 Lisa Sowle Cahill, "Teleology, Utilitarianism, and Christian Ethics," 616.
152 Ibid., 606.
153 Ibid., 619.
154 Ibid. Paulinus Odozor agrees, writing that for McCormick, proportionate reason is "not reducible to a simple utilitarian calculus" (Paulinus Odozor, *Richard A. McCormick and the Renewal of Moral Theology*, 105).
155 Ibid., 627
156 Richard McCormick, *A Commentary on the Commentaries*, 253.
157 Richard McCormick, "Notes on Moral Theology 1977: The Church in Dispute," 110.
158 Bernard Williams, *Utilitarianism: For and Against*, 79.
159 Joel Kupperman, *The Foundations of Morality* (London: George Allen & Unwin, 1983) 70.
160 Neera Badwhar Kapur, "Why It Is Wrong to Be Always Guided by the Best: Consequentialim and Friendship," *Ethics* 101 (April, 1991) 485. Indeed, according to two critics of consequentialism, this type of moral theory "need not be tied to a hedonistic value theory; consequentialism itself perhaps is more plausible than this or that theory of value with which it has been connected" (Germain Grisez and Joseph Boyle, *Life and Death with Liberty and Justice: A Contribution to the Euthanasia Debate* [Notre Dame: University of Notre Dame Press, 1979] 347).
161 Ibid. Kapur's citation is of P. Railton's "Alienation, Consequentialism, and Morality," *Philosophy and Public Affairs* 13 (1984).
162 Sanford Levy, "Richard McCormick and Proportionate Reason," 267.
163 Richard McCormick, *A Commentary on the Commentaries*, 207.
164 Ibid., 228.
165 Lisa Sowle Cahill, "Teleology, Utilitarianism, and Christian Ethics," 619.
166 Neera Badwhar Kapur, "Why It Is Wrong to Be Always Guided by the Best: Consequentialism and Friendship," 485.
167 C.D. Broad *Five Types of Ethical Theory* (New York: The Humanities Press, 1930) 215; see also Ibid., 207.
168 Lisa Sowle Cahill, "Teleology, Utilitarianism, and Christian Ethics," 623.
169 Ibid., 624.
170 Richard McCormick, *A Commentary on the Commentaries*, 227.
171 Richard McCormick, "Killing the Patient," 17; see note 1.
172 Philip Pettit, "Consequentialism and Respect for Persons," *Ethics* 100 (October, 1989), 117

Chapter 4

Purposefully Causing vs. Merely Allowing Ontic Evil

Chapter three went far in making the case that Richard McCormick's proportionalism is a consequentialist moral theory. This chapter will develop the case further. It will be seen that McCormick's consequentialism is apparent not only in his account of the meaning and role of proportionate reason in act assessments, but also in his explanation of when and why there is moral relevance to the distinction between an agent purposefully causing avoidable evil and an agent simply allowing that avoidable evil to occur. Although McCormick's position on this distinction was touched upon in chapter three, it merits a more detailed examination since it adds significantly to the case that his is a consequenialist theory. As we proceed, we will have occasion to consider the philosophical and theological anthropology upon which McCormick rested his proportionalism. Filling-in that as yet unattended area of his moral theory will help fill-out our case that what he proposed is indeed consequentialist.

The Traditional Distinction

In order to more fully develop our argument we will turn to McCormick's rejection of a distinction which often plays an important role in traditional Catholic moral reasoning. Let us begin by noting a point of terminology: Within the Catholic moral tradition, to claim that an agent "directly intended" a particular evil is to claim that this agent purposefully caused the evil, and to claim that an agent "indirectly intended" an avoidable evil is to claim that the agent chose to allow it to occur, although he did not purposefully cause it. The distinction being drawn here is between the choice *to allow* a forseen and avoidable evil to occur (either by not intervening to stop it, or by choosing to perform an act which one believes will cause it as an unintended side-effect) and the choice *purposefully to cause* that same evil as a means to some other end.[1]

The importance of this distinction in traditional Catholic moral reasoning becomes clear when one recalls that the traditional principle of double effect prohibits the intentional (i.e. direct) doing of evil, even as a means to a good end. McCormick provided examples of how this distinction, often referred to as "the traditional distinction," may function as the grounds for deontological prohibitions[2] against certain kinds of choices when he noted that the Catholic moral tradition

> has maintained that if an abortional intervention must be said to be directly intended, it is never permissible. For it involves the direct taking of human life. If, however, the death of the fetus is the forseen but unavoidable byproduct of surgery aimed at removal of a pathological organ (for example, a cancerous uterus), the abortion was said to be only indirectly intended, and justifiable if a truly proportionate reason were present. This same approach was applied in many other areas such as the conduct of warfare, complicity with the evildoing of others, sterilizing interventions, and so on.[3]

The sort of traditional approach that McCormick identified can be found in the *Catechism of the Catholic Church*. There one reads that

> Direct abortion, that is to say, abortion willed either as an end or as a means, is gravely contrary to the moral law.[4]

This distinction between directly and indirectly intended ontic evil, along with an unconditional prohibition on the former and a conditional permitting of the latter, is operative in some other magisterial positions too. Consider:

> whatever its motives and means, direct euthanasia consists in putting an end to the lives of handicapped, sick, or dying persons. It is morally unacceptable. Thus, an act or omission which, of itself or *by intention*, causes death in order to eliminate suffering constitutes a murder....Discontinuing medical procedures that are burdensome, dangerous, extraordinary, or disproportionate to the expected outcome can be legitimate; it is the refusal of 'overzealous' treatment. Here one does not *will to cause* death; one's inability to impede it is merely accepted....The use of painkillers to alleviate the sufferings of the dying, even at the risk of shortening their days, can be morally in conformity with human dignity if death is *not willed* as either an end or a means, but only *forseen and tolerated* as inevitable.[5]

As these examples illustrate, the traditional distinction is understood by some to be morally decisive: the fact that an agent purposefully caused a particular ontic evil (in this case, *death*) makes that choice morally wrong.

McCormick found fault with the understanding of direct and indirect intention reflected in the teachings just cited. He argued that such an understanding

> flies in the face of the meaning of words. For instance, when one administers physical punishment to a refractory child from purely pedagogical motives, should we call the pun-

ishment and pain 'indirect'? Hardly. Rather it has the character of a means, and we speak of an intending will, a direct choice where means are concerned.[6]

McCormick characterized this traditional understanding of direct and indirect intention as "narrow physicalism."[7] He speculated that this physicalism became such an ingrained part of his tradition's moral reasoning simply because so much of the evil caused in the pursuit of good(s) is "genuinely incidental and associated with a permitting will (psychologically)."[8] As a result of the constant conjunction of incidental evil with a permitting (as opposed to an *intending*) will, McCormick believed that "the distinction between direct and indirect came to be identified with proper intentionality."[9] Put simply, McCormick thought that a common fact of human agency, namely, that so much of the evil agents cause is psychologically unintended, gained normative force over time; an *is* became an *ought,* a common characteristic became a necessary one. McCormick rejected this normative turn, asserting that the distinction between directly and indirectly causing evil, in the traditional sense of these terms, is not necessarily morally relevant to act assessments.[10]

Yet despite his rejection of the role played by the direct/indirect distinction in the moral reasoning of his tradition, McCormick seemed unwilling to reject outright the tradition's use of proper intention as a criterion in act assessment. What McCormick took issue with was the inference, implicit in those traditional teachings which rely upon the direct/indirect distinction, that "a disvalue directly caused is one which is therefore directly intended, and therefore part of our purpose or aim."[11] Such a statement suggests that when it came to the assessment of acts, McCormick did maintain some sort of agent-relative requirement of proper intentionality, even in the wake of his rejection of the putative physicalism which his tradition relied upon to specify that intentionality. This suggestion is strengthened when, using the term *integral* and its cognates to refer to morally correct intention, McCormick claimed that

> the moral integrity of one's intentionality cannot be restrictively defined in terms of the psychological indirectness associated with evil-as-an-effect (or aspect) of an indivisible process.[12]

Implicit in this critique of his tradition's criterion for assessing intention (and, in turn, for morally assessing acts) is an acknowledgement of the importance of "the moral integrity of one's intentionality." Such language may suggest to some that McCormick was perhaps preserving his tradition's non-consequentialist, agent-centered criterion of proper intentionality (reflected in the second and third conditions of the principle of double effect). Indeed, Charles Curran notes that "McCormick rightfully insists on a difference between an intending and a permitting will," and believes that this insistence makes it plain that McCormick did not "embrace utilitarianism or...consequentialism."[13] We will soon see, though, that this deontological-sounding demand for proper intentionality is in reality consequentialist, since it reduces to a demand to keep one's purposeful evil-doing proportionate to the good being pursued. In order to more fully appreciate just how this somewhat non-consequentialist sounding requirement of proper intentionality unpacks as a consequentialist notion, let us consider a few more of McCormick's thoughts on the intend/permit distinction.

Recall from chapter three McCormick's non-controversial observation that there are some circumstances in which an agent cannot realize a particular ontic good unless that agent purposefully causes some particular ontic evil. In such cases, the ontic evil would be caused purposefully as a necessary means to a particular end, as in the case of abortion in order to preserve the health of a pregnant woman with a heart condition. In other circumstances, McCormick noted, that same evil may be an unavoidable yet not causally necessary aspect of an act which realizes the same good, as in the death of an unborn child resulting from the health-restoring removal of a pregnant woman's cancerous uterus.[14] In the first case the unborn child is itself the threat to maternal health, and the good that is maternal health cannot be realized except through a termination of the pregnancy. In the second case, it is a cancerous uterus that is threatening maternal health, and the death of the fetus is not chosen a means to maternal health but occurs as an unavoidable side-effect of a hysterectomy.[15] With this distinction in mind, McCormick believed that an agent who purposefully causes ontic evil as a means to some end will have "a different psychological awarenesses" of that evil than an agent who simply allowed that same evil to occur as an unintended side-effect of an act aimed at the same end.[16] This difference in awareness of ontic evil intentionally-caused and ontic evil merely-permitted was what McCormick had in mind when he asserted, seemingly in-step with his tradition, that "there is a real difference between an intending and permitting will."[17] Still, McCormick did not retreat from his rejection of the traditional use of the direct/indirect distinction, arguing that this psychological difference, real as it is, is not sufficient to sustain the position that one may at times permit (as in the hysterectomy case), but never intend (as in the abortion case), ontic evil. He wrote,

> The crucial question is whether (and why) this single form of psychological awareness—that associated with evil as aspect—is normative for a proper human intentionality. The traditional answer has been yes....That is, the evil involved must be unintended *in that one psychological sense*. I believe that there are good reasons to doubt this conclusion...[18]

McCormick's position was that an act which causes evil ought not to be judged morally wrong simply because the agent caused that evil purposefully. His based his argument for this position upon a sense of disapproval that he presumed both evil-intending and evil-permitting agents feel toward the evil they cause. He explained that despite the aforementioned psychological difference between intending and permitting evil, a

> general reluctance that the evil must be brought about (whether 'intended' or 'permitted') is presumably common to both instances.[19]

McCormick characterized this general reluctance as "an attitude of fundamental disapproval"[20] The presence of this attitude in an evil-intending or evil-permitting agent was morally relevant for McCormick in a way that the "psychological awareness" of the agent was not. Indeed, he found this attitude to be "the key element in deciding whether direct (as a means) and indirect intent have *moral* significance as such."[21] And so McCormick replaced the traditional question of whether evil was purposefully caused by an agent with the question of whether the agent *approved* of the evil purposefully caused. Such a move allowed him to argue that,

> in terms of approval and disapproval...permitting and intending as a means can pertain to the same moral category (disapproval) where nonmoral evils are concerned....In this analysis the traditional moral decisiveness of direct (as a means) and indirect intent disappears. If this is correct, we would have to conclude that the mistake of the tradition was to believe that intending as a means necessarily involves approval.[22]

In McCormick's estimation, then, the traditional understanding of the direct/indirect distinction, and the traditional understanding of the role this distinction should play in the moral assessment of acts, misses what is most *morally* significant in acts which cause forseen evil—the agent's attitude toward the evil caused.

This aspect of McCormick's proportionalism is significant because it appears that he was offering a constraint on agents which, although somewhat different and perhaps looser than the traditional prohibition on directly intending evil, nonetheless demanded proper intentionality when purposefully causing evil. In short, he seems to have suggested a prohibition on agents approving the evil that they would purposefully cause as a means to some good(s). If what is suggested is indeed the case, then although McCormick rejected his tradition's deontological prohibition against intentionally causing ontic evil, he offered a somewhat reformulated agent-relative constraint in its place. And as the object of this constraint is the attitude of the agent,[23] and as we have not seen McCormick subordinate this constraint to the demand to maximize good(s) or minimize evil(s), it seems that McCormick may have incorporated a non-consequentialist norm into his moral theory. If this is true, then our argument that he was a consequentialist becomes more difficult to sustain. But, as has been indicated earlier, such is not the case. What will be seen is that McCormick's apparently non-consequentialist requirement of disapproval reduces to his requirement for a proper proportion between the ontic-good and ontic-evil aspects of an act. And, as was seen in chapter three, this requirement for proportion is consequentialist since it in turn reduces to the requirement to maximize ontic good(s)/minimize ontic evil(s).

After rejecting the position that purposefully causing a prohibited evil is always morally wrong due to the agent's intention, and after asserting that an agent's approving or disapproving attitude towards intended evil is more dispositive in the moral assessment of those kinds of choices, McCormick offered this criterion for a proper attitude towards purposefully caused evil:

> integral intentionality traces not to psychological indirectness as such when evil occurs, but *exclusively to the proportionate reason for acting*.[24]

So, like Knauer before him,[25] McCormick appears to have preserved something like the traditional requirement for proper intention in all evil-causing, morally-licit acts. Yet, again like Knauer, he offered the presence of a proportionate reason as the criterion for the proper intention/attitude. So, in the end, what McCormick did was propose a condition of right choice (proper intention, understood as an attitude of disapproval toward all evil caused) that at first glance looks like a deontological constraint on agents but which is, at bottom, simply another way of stating his consequentialist demand that agents are to act in good(s)-maximizing/evil(s)-minimizing ways. Indeed, that such is the case becomes even clearer when one sees that elsewhere McCormick elided the issue of proper attitude altogether and claimed simply that any act in which evil is caused will be justified "if a genuinely proportionate reason (in the sense stated) is present."[26]

The practical import of McCormick's theoretical differences with his tradition on the intend/permit distinction is made plain in his claim that

> killing, for example, is not wrongful simply because it is direct *in the traditional* sense. Concretely, an abortion may be direct and still morally permissible.[27]

And so the permissibility of killing, like all acts of ontic evil-doing, depends "not on the directness or indirectness of intentionality, but on the goodness of the end and the proportion between the means chosen and the end."[28] As for the requirement of proper intentionality (or attitude), we simply cite the following:

> Whether the action so described represents integral intentionality more generally and overall depends on whether it is, or is not, all things considered, the lesser evil in the circumstances.[29]

In sum, then, McCormick rejected the notion that one can judge an act morally wrong simply on the basis of the traditional direct/indirect distinction, that is, he rejected the position that one can say that any act of purposeful killing, for example, is morally wrong *because* in such an act the agent psychologically intended a prohibited evil. McCormick's position was that one may not morally assess an act unless one knows "what is being sought and by what means and in what circumstances."[30] This necessary data reveals

> what other values are at stake, and therefore whether the manner of the pursuit of the good here and now is destructive of it or not. In other words, it reveals whether in the action as a whole the good outweighs the evil, whether there is truly a proportionate reason or not. *And it is the presence or absence of such a reason that determines whether the attitude of the agent is adequate or not, whether he is choosing rightly or wrongly...*[31]

In this way, McCormick offered a greater good/lesser evil standard as the supreme criterion for both act and attitude/intention assessments.

Norms

McCormick's consequentialism becomes even more apparent when one compares his standard of act assessment to that found in John Paul II's *Veritatis Splendor*. There, one finds a restatement of a rather traditional deontological position:

> the natural law expresses the dignity of the human person and lays the foundation for his fundamental rights and duties, it is universal in its precepts and its authority extends to all mankind....The *negative precepts* of the natural law are universally valid. They oblige each and every individual, always and in every circumstance. It is a matter of prohibitions which forbid a given action *semper et pro semper*, without exception, because the choice of this kind of behavior is in no case compatible with the goodness of the will of the acting person, with his vocation to life with God and to communion with his neighbor....there are kinds of behavior which can never, in any situation, be a proper response—a response which is in conformity with the dignity of the person.[32]

Examples of this kind of prohibited behavior are abortion, euthanasia, suicide, indeed "any kind of homocide," slavery, prostitution, physical torture, and mental torture.[33] What is to be noted here is the non-consequentialist reasoning: the universal, exceptionless prohibitions on the behaviors mentioned are neither derived from nor justified by an assessment of their ontic good(s)-producing tendencies. One is not offered an argument which concludes that these acts cannot ever be the option among an agent's possible choices that promises the greatest realization of ontic good or the least amount of ontic evil, and for *that* reason are never licit. Indeed, these acts are prohibited without any mention of the balance of ontic goods and evils they might promise in various circumstances. As John Finnis explains,

> greater and lesser amounts of goodness are not the issue....The moral absolutes call for a refusal to dishonor the basic human good directly at stake in our choice; they call us to leave providence to settle the 'balance' of human goods, a balance which we would merely deceive ourselves if we supposed we could truly see and settle for ourselves.[34]

Finnis goes on to explain that these prohibitions "guide by excluding options," and that

> in adhering to the moral truth articulated by the 'rule,' one honors the value, the person whose good in some fundamental respect one would be choosing to destroy, damage, or impede, by the act which the norm specifies as always to be excluded from deliberation, choice, and action.[35]

In contrast to this reasoning stands McCormick's proportionalism and his call for a reconsideration of any deontological norm that the traditional distinction supported. He explained that one consequence of his proportionate reason-centered rejection of the traditional direct/indirect distinction was that

> those actions considered wrong when involving *direct* intent of the disvalue as a means, and hence giving rise to deontological norms, must be interpreted teleologically.[36]

Now when McCormick called for a teleological reassessment of all acts and norms, he was calling for his standard of proportionate reason to be the final measure of all acts and to supercede the validity of all norms.[37] In his judgment

> a behavioral norm is exceptionless only if it prescribes a value that cannot conflict with other values, or if it does, one that always deserves the preference. *Always deserves the preference* is but a way of saying that (at least in our perspectives) it overrides the other value, is more urgent than the other value, or disallows feature-dependant exceptions. It is a way of saying that choice of the other value would be disproportionate, or, that there is no proportionate reason either thinkable or realistically imaginable for overriding the value. Thus, in summary, proportionte reason is a general term for those characteristics of an action that allow us to conclude that, even though the action involves nonmoral evil, it is morally justifiable when compared to the only alternative (its omission).[38]

As we have seen, McCormick included in the set of acts which "involve" nonmoral evil those acts where the agent purposefully causes the evil. And what is to be noted again is the absence here of the direct/indirect distinction which plays such a crucial role in the act assessments of his tradition. Instead, McCormick invoked his notion of proportionate reason, behind which stood the claim that morally correct choice is a matter of maximizing ontic good(s)/minimizing ontic evil(s).

Consider again, as an example of his moral reasoning, McCormick's argument against bombing civilian populations as a means to shorten a long-lasting, costly war. One popular argument in support of the decision to bomb civilians reasons that such a choice is justified if it saves more lives than it takes. McCormick rejected this moral analysis, claiming that

> even if the good at stake is quantitively proportionate to or greater than the loss, protecting it *in this way* could in the long run undermine this good.[39]

Note again that McCormick's analysis did not invoke a deontological prohibition against purposefully harming innocent people, a prohibition which leads many to conclude that no matter how many lives may be saved by the bombing, such a choice will always be morally wrong. McCormick could not rely upon such a prohibition because his proportionalism would not sustain such an unconditional restriction on choice. His moral theory committed him to acknowledging the possibility, however improbable, that the circumstances surrounding a choice of this kind may be such that the good promised by the bombing would indeed be proportionate to the evil caused, and that therefore the good would not be "undermined" by the proposed bombing; the conclusion, in such circumstances, would be that the choice to bomb is the morally correct one.[40] It is this inability to rule out such choices *a-priori* that left McCormick in a position to say that the norm prohibiting civilian bombing is only "*virtually* exceptionless."[41] He explained that in cases like the one under consideration,

> there are enormous goods at stake, and both our past experience of human failure, inconsistency, and frailty, and our uncertainty with regard to long-term effects lead us to believe that we ought to hold some norms as virtually exceptionless, that this is the conclusion of prudence in the face of dangers too momentous to make risk tolerable.[42]

Taking what appears to be a rule-consequentialist position, McCormick argued that certain norms ought to be followed *because* they are practical, tested guides to good(s)-maximizing/evil(s)-minimizing choices. He found these virtually exceptionless norms to be helpful because they have taken account of "the ordinary circumstances in practical living," thus building confidence that "*ordinarily* a person will achieve the greater good by following the norm, because it incarnates the greater good."[43] Yet it must be remembered that McCormick maintained that these norms are, at best, only *virtually* exceptionless, and that "exception making is traceable to and based on a truly proportionate reason."[44] McCormick asserted that "all concrete rules" are "subsidiary" to the rule that one is to choose that option which promises the lesser evil.[45] It is clear, then, that McCormick offered no restrictions on evil-causing choices that were not subject to the criterion of proportionate reason. This subordination of norms to good(s) maximization/evil(s) minimization confirms that his theory is, at bottom, consequentialist.

Yet despite his rejection of a decisive role for the traditional distinction in act assessments, McCormick did not take the position that direct and indirect intention are "indistinguishable realities and morally irrelevant."[46] While judging the distinction to be somewhat less important than traditionally understood, McCormick nevertheless found it to be

> as *morally* meaningful as the difference between intending (as a means) and permitting can be shown to be.[47]

It will become clear, though, that the only morally relevant difference that McCormick found between permitting evil and intending it as a means was a difference in consequences. He believed that in those cases where intending evil as a means promises different consequences than those promised by merely permitting that same evil, the distinction takes on moral significance. It is for this reason that McCormick was in agreement with at least this practical conclusion of his tradition's moral reasoning: there may be cases where directly intending an evil would be morally unacceptable while merely allowing that same evil would be licit. His reasoning behind this conclusion, however, is altogether consequentialist.

The Moral Relevance of the Traditional Distinction

An important early contribution to the development of proportionalist thought was McCormick's response to an article by another influential member of the movement, Bruno Schuller. In *Direct Killing/Indirect Killing* Schuller argued that the traditional direct/indirect distinction is not relevant to determining whether a choice to cause ontic evil is morally right or wrong.[48] He did, though, find this direct/indirect distinction to be significant in the assessment of *morally* evil acts. He supported an exceptionless prohibition against directly causing or cooperating in the sin, i.e. in the moral evil, of another, believing that

> to affirm evil in this way and to bring it into existence can be nothing else than morally evil....The intrinsic immorality results here simply from the morally evil quality of the intended result of the activity (sin).[49]

Schuller's belief that causing moral evil is always wrong was grounded in his understanding of sin as "an absolute non-value, another's sin no less than one's own. Therefore it must be avoided unconditionally."[50] However, having judged ontic evil to be only a relative disvalue, and referring to it as such, he asserted that

> insofar as it is necessary for the realization of a preferable value, one is allowed to cause a relative disvalue, and at times one *should* cause it.[51]

In brief, Schuller pushed for an exceptionless prohibition on purposefully causing absolute disvalues, and a conditional prohibition on purposefully causing relative disvalues, and he offered the following criterion for determining when an agent may directly cause a relative disvalue (which may be understood as an ontic/physical/non-moral evil):

> ...one may intend a relative disvalue as the consequence of his act, if only it occurs in the service of a proportionately important end.[52]

So, since Schuller held proportionate reason to be the necessary and sufficient condition for the licit, purposeful causing of ontic evil, the question of whether the agent directly or indirectly caused this evil was irrelevant to his moral analyses of the choice in question.

McCormick disagreed with Schuller on this point, arguing that the difference between an agent intending and simply permitting ontic evil can play an important role in determining the moral character of the act in question. He wrote,

> If the distinction between an intending and permitting will is utterly essential and profoundly meaningful where the moral evil (sin) of another is concerned, as Schuller rightly maintains, that can mean but one thing: There is a real difference between an intending and permitting will....Now if there is a real difference between an intending and permitting will, then this difference must show where nonmoral evil is concerned. That in turn means that the human action involving an intending will (of evil) is or at least can be a different human action from that involving a permitting will.[53]

McCormick goes on to explain that an agent's intentional causing of ontic evil (in the psychological sense of *purposefully* causing it) is morally relevant if, and to the degree that, the intending impacts the balance of ontic good(s) and evil(s) promised by the act in question. He claimed that

> where nonmoral evil is concerned, direct voluntariety says but one thing: the evil has a causal relation to the good and is willed as a means. This becomes morally decisive only when the posture of the will affects the determination of what is, all things considered, the lesser or greater evil.[54]

McCormick's complex consequentialism, specifically the complexity of some of his greatest good/least evil assessments, is evident in such reasoning; the moral relevance of an agent's attitude/intentionality toward evildoing is determined by how this attitude affects the balance of ontic good(s) and evil(s). Indeed, in McCormick's estimation, the difference between intending and permitting any particular ontic evil can have enormously different immediate and long-term implications, and therefore generate a quite different calculus of proportion.[55]

It is this last claim which grounded McCormick's observation that

> ...it does not seem to follow that the same proportionate reason which would justify what is indirect (descriptively) would always justify what is direct. In other words, there may be a proportionate reason for doing something in one way which is not proportionate to doing it another way.[56]

This same position was explained somewhat differently when he wrote

> ...since evil-as-means and evil-as-effect are different realities, they may demand different proportionate reasons. What is sufficient for *allowing* an evil may not in all cases be sufficient for *choosing* it as a means.[57]

One may return to the case of purposefully bombing civilian populations in warfare to see concretely what McCormick had in mind when he staked out this position contra Schuller. He wrote:

> Taking innocent human life as a means, for example, to demoralize the enemy, totalizes warfare. The action is radically different in human terms from the incidental death of innocents as one attempts to repel the enemy's war machine, even though the evil effects are numerically the same....Taking innocent human life as a means removes restraints and unleashes destructive powers which both now and in the long run will brutalize sensitivities and take many more lives than we would now save by such action.[58]

Here, McCormick was careful to note that the negative effects of purposefully targeting and killing civilians would in some ways be different than the negative effects of unintentionally killing those same civilians in the bombing of a military target. Although the number of civilians killed in each case would be the same, McCormick argued that the intentional killing would have a damaging effect on agents that the unintentional killing would not. Because this damaging effect would impact the realization of the relevant good(s), the difference between directly and indirectly causing these deaths is, in this case, morally significant. As noted in chapter three, McCormick did not try to make the case that civilian bombing is morally wrong because it violates the rights of the innocent or because it violates some other valid, deontological restriction on agents' choices. Instead, he judged this act to be morally wrong because of the overall negative effects he believed it would have on the relevant good(s), a clearly consequentialist argument.

It should be mentioned again, in fairness to McCormick, that some time after *Ambiguity in Moral Choice* he appears to have deemphasized the role of negative long-term consequences in the moral assessment of acts.[59] Coming closer Schuller's understanding of the moral relevance of the direct/indirect distinction, McCormick wrote:

> I think Schuller is correct in his basic assertion (versus Grisez and Ramsey) that a killing of a human being is not morally wrongful precisely because it is direct....I had attempted [in *Ambiguity*] to show a difference in direct and indirect killing through appeal to deleterious consequences and to assert that these consequences are due precisely to the *directness* of the killing. I then concluded to the practical absoluteness of norms prohibiting direct killing of noncombatants in warfare on the basis of these teleological considerations. I believe this is unsatisfactory.[60]

In this passage McCormick appears to have been ready to disavow the simple consequentialist position he had taken with respect to the moral relevance of the traditional distinction. But, as we shall see, rather than discarding the consequentialism of the earlier position, he simply refined it.

McCormick followed-up his statement of dissatisfaction with his earlier analysis of purposefully (as opposed to incidentally) killing noncombatants with the explanation that the evil of such purposeful killing is

> *disproportionate to the good being sought* because it undermines through the association of basic human goods the very good of life.[61]

Here, one finds McCormick having replaced the long-term effects analysis of just what is wrong with purposefully killing civilians with the now-familiar claim that such purposeful killing "undermines" the good in question (*life*). Yet for McCormick to make this alteration to his analysis is, given his notion of *undermining*, to make a change within consequentialism, but not from consequentialism.[62] As it turns out, his revised position on what is wrong with purposefully killing civilians in order to hasten the end of a war is not at all a fundamental break from his earlier, simpler consequentialist condemnation of this act.[63] As Sanford Levy explains,

> Whatever discounting of consequences and the long run takes place in 'Commentary,' McCormick does not by any stretch of the imagination totally reject them. For the notion of the long run coupled with the notion of undermining is central to the arguments in 'Commentray' that particular acts are wrong.[64]

Indeed, one may well question whether McCormick's ostensive abandonment of his long-term effects analysis in favor of his *undermining* explanation constituted a significant alteration to his moral theory. Even after this theoretical refinement he continued to articulate and to defend the position that a morally wrong act is morally wrong because, with respect to the value being pursued, the act does not yield the greatest good/least evil among the agent's choices. It appears, too, that in *Ambiguity in Moral Choice* McCormick himself predicted both his retention of proportionate reason as the supreme criterion in act assessment and his more nuanced, expanded sense of what must be accounted for when assessing the evil promised by any particular act when he wrote,

> Proportionality is always the criterion where our actions cause damage. Our major problem is to make sure that we do not conceive it narrowly.[65]

Later, in "A Commentary on the Commentaries," he argued

> What is the lesser evil and what is the greater evil is only determinable after the relevance of the permitting and intending will has been established and weighed into the description of the alternatives.[66]

Finally, one may turn to McCormick's post-revision analysis of the civilian bombing case to find confirmation that despite the refinements he made to the "long-term effects" teleology presented in "Ambiguity in Moral Choice," and despite his new sensitivity to the damaging effect that purposefully causing evil may have on agents, his moral theory retained the basic principle that the moral quality of any choice is a function of the ontic good(s) and evil(s) promised by that choice. Recall that in regard to the case of civilian bombing he wrote

> Is anyone willing to assert confidently that there is no connection between Nagasaki-Hiroshima and the senseless slaughters that occurred in South Vietnam? Once the manner of our protection of a basic good reduces or removes by implication the basis for rational limitation of violence (liberty), then irrational (disproportionate) things are going to happen. These irrational things point back to and reveal the disproportion in our original response.[67]

In so taking account of the evil effects on current and future agents brought about by the purposeful killing of civilians, McCormick offered an illustration of his belief that the direct/indirect distinction is, in some cases, morally relevant. He found it morally significant that an agent caused ontic evil intentionally if that purposefulness promised to affect that agent and/or future agents in a manner that would in turn undermine the basic good(s) being pursued.[68] And it is this more nuanced assessment of proportionate reason, rather than a simple body-count, that brought him to say that he could "conceive of no proportionate reason for killing innocent people even during war."[69] In this way, then, despite rejecting the putative physicalism of the traditional distinction between intending and permitting ontic evil, McCormick still found this distinction to be at least somewhat morally relevant at least sometimes, but relevant at times and in a manner that confirms his consequentialism.

McCormick's Philosophical/Theological Anthropology and an Exceptionless Prohibition on Moral Evils

We have seen that McCormick's moral theory does not (and cannot) prohibit *a-priori* the purposeful (direct) causing of any ontic evil. We have also seen that McCormick's explication and defense of his position on the traditional distinction makes apparent the consequentialist nature of his theory. Soon we will see that in spite of this position on causing ontic evil, McCormick did prohibit, without exception, purposefully choosing what he judged to be *morally* evil. Yet we will also see his explication and defense of this exceptionless prohibition confirm our case that his moral theory is consequentialist. But in order to best appreciate just how McCormick's prohibition on moral evil adds to our case that his moral theory is consequentialist, we will consider for a moment his philosophical/theological anthropology. We do this because his anthropology provided him with a value theory to inform his judgments of proportion and was offered as the grounds for his proportionate-reason centered prohibition against purposefully committing moral evil.

It is reasonable to expect that a moral theory which calls for an agent to choose the good(s) maximizing/evil(s) minimizing option open to him would provide this agent with a set of maximands/minimands as well as some way of prioritizing them in cases of conflict. McCormick shared this expectation, noting that in order for an agent to apply his notion of proportionate reason correctly, he must "spell out what evils are greater, what values override others."[70] McCormick looked to his Christian philosophical and theological anthropology, one which views the human person "in terms of the great Christian mysteries: creation—fall—redemption,"[71] to provide the objective set of ordered goods (and the set of evils that these goods imply) that are to inform judgments of proportion.[72] He found that

The Christian story tells us the ultimate meaning of ourselves and the world. In doing so, it tells us the kind of people we ought to be, *the goods we ought to pursue*, the dangers we ought to avoid, the kind of world we ought to seek.[73]

This "outlook on the human"[74] that complements his moral theory was shaped by his religious tradition, a tradition which he explained is

> anchored in faith in the meaning and decisive significance of God's covenant with men, especially as manifested finally in the saving incarnation of Jesus Christ and the revelation of his final coming, his eschatalogical kingdom that is here aborning but will finally only be given.[75]

McCormick suggested how these religious beliefs affected his moral theory when he added that

> faith in these events, love of and loyalty to their central figure yield a decisive way of viewing and intending the world, of interpreting its meaning, of hierarchizing its values, of reacting to its apparent surds and conflicts.[76]

He explained that theology "yields a value judgment and a general policy or attitude. It provides the framework for subsequent moral reasoning."[77] In this way, he continued,

> faith and reason compenetrate to produce a distinct consciousness....[F]aith informs reason. I believe the outcome of such 'informing' is a distinct—though not utterly mysterious—way of viewing the world and ourselves and of hierarchizing values.[78]

Elsewhere, McCormick indicated more explicitly and more precisely just how these religious beliefs were relevant to his moral theory when he asserted that the task for contemporary moral theologians of his tradition, with respect to correctly judging proportion, is to "do all we can to guarantee that our calculus will be truly adequate and fully Christian."[79]

We have seen McCormick argue that one may purposefully cause any type or amount of ontic evil in the pursuit of ontic good(s) so long as the good promised is proportionate to the evil done. For this reason we have said that proportionality is the criterion of right and wrong in McCormick's moral theory. But it should be noted, too, just what McCormick proposed as the criterion of proportionality:

> The criterion of proportionality is that *ordo bonorum* viewed in Christian perspective, for it

is the *ordo bonorum* which is determinative of the good one should attempt to do…[80]

Writing in the first person, McCormick provided an example of how this Christian *ordo bonorum* is to inform judgments of proportion when he assessed the choice to lay down his life for another when it is the only way of saving that other:

> In this instance a good equal to what I sacrifice accrues to another and is the only way of securing that good for him. This is proportionate not because his life is preferable to mine— they are equally valuable as basic human goods—but because in case of conflict, it is a human and Christian good to seek to secure this good for my neighbor even at the cost of my life.[81]

Later he added that

> To deny that such sacrifice could be proportionately grounded would be to deny that self-giving love after the model of Christ is a human good and represents the direction in which we should all be growing.[82]

In McCormick's eyes, then, this case was not simply a matter of one life paid as the price for another; his consequentialist reasoning, set as it is within an "over-all Christian concept of life"[83] is somewhat more complex than that. As he assessed the alternatives he presupposed not only that life itself is a good, but also that the act of giving one's life for another is a good. When the good of self-sacrifice is taken into account, it becomes apparent that the choice to give one's life for another instantiates greater good than the alternative of allowing the other to die and sparing oneself. The reasoning, even with its Christian content, is consequentialist. The alternatives are assessed in terms of the kind and amount of ontic good(s) and evil(s) that are in play, and the balance of ontic good(s) and evil(s) is the supreme criterion for determining the morally correct choice. With this in mind, consider again McCormick's claim that

> Human life, as a basic good and the foundation for the enjoyment of other goods and rights, should be taken only when doing so is the lesser of two evils, all things considered….To qualify as the lesser of two evils there is required, among other things, that there be at stake a human life or its moral equivalent. 'Moral equivalent' refers to a good or value that is, in Christian assessment, comparable to life itself.[84]

Elsewhere he explained that

> The fact that we are pilgrims, that Christ has overcome death and lives, that we will also live with Him, yields a general value judgment on the meaning and value of life as we now live it. It can be formulated as follows: life is a basic good but not an absolute one. It is *basic* because, as the Congregation for the Doctrine of the Faith worded it, it is the 'necessary source and condition of every human activity and of all society.' It is not *absolute* because there are higher goods for which life can be sacrificed (glory of God, salvation of souls, service of others, etc.)....Negatively, we could word this value judgment as follows: death is an evil but not an absolute or unconditional one.[85]

And his expectation was that these faith-based value judgments would function as important principles in moral reasoning:

> What are some of the perspectives and insights that ought to inform our reasoning in the area of biomedicine?....1.*Life as a basic but nor an absolute good*...It is not *absolute* because there are higher goods for which life can be sacrificed (for example, the glory of God, the salvation of souls, or the service of one's brethren).[86]

In the end, then, what differentiates McCormick's proportionalism from other forms of consequentialism is not his notion of what one's basic moral duty is, or his account of the nature of morally wrong choices; these are common to all consequentialist theories and make his proportionalism of-a-kind with them. What distinguishes McCormick's proportionalism from the other members of the consequentialist family is its explicit reliance upon a Christian theological/philosophical anthropology either to provide or to confirm the set of goods that he proposed as the to-be-pursued ends of moral behavior.[87]

Having considered his thoughts on the traditional distinction, and having noted the anthropology which informed his judgments of proportion, we may now turn to McCormick's assertion of an exceptionless prohibition against purposefully choosing *moral* evils, such as adultery and murder.[88] At first glance these prohibitions appear to be consequence-indifferent constraints on agents' choices and, as such, may thus make McCormick's moral theory nonconsequentialist. But as it turns out, McCormick defined these prohibited moral evils in a manner entirely consistent with the consequentialist nature of his moral theory. He wrote,

> when something is described as 'adultery' or 'genocide,' nothing can justify it; for the very terms are morally qualifying terms meaning unjustified killing, intercourse with the wrong person, etc. That is, they are tautological. The question contemporary theologians are facing is rather this: What (in descriptive terms) is to count as murder, adultery, genocide?[89]

McCormick's consequentialism is apparent in his offering of proportionate reason as the standard by which one is to judge whether, say, a particular act of killing was justified or was murder, or whether an instance of engaging in intercourse with someone other than one's spouse constituted an act of adultery. He argued that

> what can justifiably be done at times is not injustice, but killing; not a lie, but a falsehood which in the circumstances is an appropriate use of our expressive powers because it protects the very values veracity is supposed to protect; not an infidelity, but an action which, though it involves nonmoral evil, ought not to be classified as unfaithful.[90]

Here, McCormick was simply recasting in somewhat different language his basic consequentialist position, a position we saw laid out in chapter three: if the ontic good pursued is not proportionate to the ontic evil purposefully caused, then the act is to be judged *morally* evil, *morally* wrong; but if the good pursued is proportionate to the evil purposefully caused, then the ontic evil-doing is justified and the act is not to be judged morally wrong.[91] In Lisa Cahill's words, McCormick was pushing a rather simply formulated proposition: "moral evil consists in choosing a nonmoral evil without sufficient cause."[92] Given this formulation, to prohibit moral evil is to prohibit choosing a nonmoral evil without sufficient cause. And so Cahill adds,

> Thus McCormick would never allow that consequences can justify moral evil; the presence of an overriding reason precludes the existence of moral evil.[93]

As it turns out, then, McCormick's exceptionless prohibition against purposefully choosing moral evil is not an exceptionless, material prohibition against certain specific sorts of behavior, the type of prohibition which characterizes a deontological moral theory. Instead, it is an exceptionless, formal prohibition against purposefully choosing disproportionate acts, i.e. acts which do not promise the greatest ontic good/least ontic evil.

Finally, McCormick confirmed the consequentialist nature of this exceptionless prohibition when, after claiming that such intentional disproportionate evildoing expresses an aversion to God, he argued

> If God is truly the *summum bonum*—source and sum of all good—then sin (*aversio a Deo*, rejection of Him) is the *summum malum*, the very denial of creaturely meaningfulness. Now clearly the *summum bonum* takes precedence over any other human goods, simply because it includes them all, and is greater than all. Therefore, when any action is said to involve a rejection (sin) of the *summum bonum*, it is by definition an action which turns against and rejects the *summum bonum* for something less. One ought never to do that – a matter that is

analytically clear….That means to me that one may never *sin* to bring about some human good or prevent an evil. Or, what is the same, there is never a proportionate reason for sinning or intending another's sin.[94]

Later in this same work he wrote,

> …if sin means free morally bad self-determination, it is difficult to see what nonmoral goods would suffice as commensurate reason,[95]

and this consequentialist explanation simply echoes what he offered a few years earlier:

> there is never any reason for choosing the sin of another in order to realize a 'higher value,' *because there is no higher value*. No good is greater for man than his moral good. Or negatively, sin is an absolute disvalue for man in light of which all other disvalues (e.g., sickness, poverty, death) are relative. *Hence* we may never choose and intend it as we may choose and intend other disvalues.[96]

According to McCormick, then, one may never licitly sin or induce another to sin in order to realize some good *because* there is no good proportionate to that evil. This reasoning is through and through consequentialist and is but another application of his supreme norm *one ought to do that among one's options which promises the greatest good/least evil*. While some might take issue with his theological presuppositions, or his hierarchy of goods, or his judgments of proportion (perhaps arguing that the moral salvation of several people is sufficient to justify purposefully bringing about the moral ruination of one person), we will simply note that such a debate would be carried on among consequentialists, with the disagreement generated not by fundamental differences in concepts of duty or in the nature of morally right and wrong choices, but rather in differing value theories and specific judgments of greatest good/least evil.[97]

Conclusion

In this chapter we have seen McCormick disagree with the moral significance his tradition places on the difference between purposefully causing and merely permitting ontic evil. We have also seen McCormick reject the deontological constraints on agents that this traditional understanding implies. In place of this prohibition against purposefully causing evil, McCormick substituted his own set of conditions governing licit, purposeful evil-causing. We have seen him argue that an agent may intentionally (in the psychological sense) cause ontic evil if: (1) the evil promised is not disproportionate to the good sought and, (2) there is a necessary causal relationship between the evildoing and the good being promoted and, (3) the good pursued is not lower in the hierarchy of goods than the good sacrificed. Yet we have shown that the last two conditions are functions of the first since a violation of (2) unpacks as a violation of (1) given his theory of associated goods, and a violation of (3) also unpacks as a violation of (1) since a lesser good would be preferred to a greater one.[98] In this way, McCormick's critique of his tradition on the moral relevance of the direct/indirect distinction, and the account he offered in its place, depended entirely upon his notion of proportionate reason. But as chapter three has shown, this notion, and the role it plays in determining the moral character of any choice, makes McCormick's proportionalism to be fundamentally consequentialist.

Notes

1. Later, we will see that McCormick used the phrase "psychologically intended" evil to refer to evil "directly intended" in this traditional sense.
2. By 'deontological prohibitions' I mean prohibitions whose force and validity are not based upon, or reducible to, their conduciveness to maximizing ontic goods or minimizing ontic evils.
3. Richard McCormick, *Doing Evil to Achieve Good.* (Chicago: Loyola University Press, 1978), 5. For other examples of this "traditional distinction," see McCormick's "Ambiguity in Moral Choice," ibid., 8.
4. *The Catechism of the Catholic Church* (Ligouri, MO: Ligouri Publications, 1994), no. 2271.
5. Emphasis mine; *Catechism of the Catholic Church,* nos. 2277, 2278, 2279.
6. Richard McCormick, *How Brave a New World* (London: SCM Press, 1991), 420; see also "Ambiguity in Moral Choice," 29-30. This example hardly settles the issue, for one could reasonably argue either (1) that the spanking in this context was not an evil, so it is not an example of doing evil as a means to a good, or (2) that the example indicates that spanking a child is indeed an intentional doing of evil and is, as such, not morally licit.
7. Richard McCormick, "Ambiguity in Moral Choice," 21; see too, Richard McCormick, "Notes on Moral Theology: April-September, 1971," *Theological Studies* 33 (1972), 81.
8. Richard McCormick, "Ambiguity in Moral Choice," 38.
9. Ibid.
10. We will soon see his explanation of when and why this distinction is morally relevant.
11. Richard McCormick, "Notes on Moral Theology: April-September, 1971," *Theological Studies* 33 (1972), 81.
12. Richard McCormick, "Ambiguity in Moral Choice," 40.
13. Charles Curran, *Directions in Fundamental Moral Theology* (Indiana: University of Notre Dame Press, 1985), 187. Christopher Kaczor correctly notes: "From a philosophical perspective, Curran's analysis is confused....[N]o consequentialist would hold that the way in which the end is achieved is not a moral consideration" (*Proportionalism and the Natrural Law Tradition.* [Washington: Catholic University of America Press, 2002] 12, n.9).
14. Ibid., 37.
15. In a moment we will see that McCormick referred to evil purposefully caused, e.g. the abortion in the first case, as "evil as *means.*" Evil unintentionally and unavoidably caused as a side-effect of an act which aims at a good, e.g. the death of the child in the second case, is referred to as "evil as *aspect*" of an act aimed at a good. Alison McIntyre refers to evil caused *instrumentally* and evil caused *incidentally* when dealing with this distinction, language that seems to fit well with how this distinction was understood by McCormick (Alison McIntyre "Doing Away with Double Effect," *Ethics* 111 [January, 2001], 219.
16. Richard McCormick, "Ambiguity in Moral Choice," 37-38.
17. Ibid., 36.
18. Ibid., 38.
19. Ibid., 37.
20. Richard McCormick, "A Commentary on the Commentaries," 264. Here he repeated the claim that "intending as a means and permitting are vehicles of the same mental attitude." See ibid. 256, too, where he wrote that *permitting* an evil and *intending* this evil as a means to some end "may reveal the same basic attitude: 'I would not carry it out if it were possible to achieve the good effect without causing the bad one.'"
21. Ibid., 263. He added that "...the meaning of intending/permitting is found in their relationship to the basic moral attitudes of approval or disapproval" (Ibid.).
22. Ibid., 264. We will note below how McCormick drew from another proportionalist, Bruno Schuller, on this point.

23 I am here treating McCormick's notion of *integral intentionality* as equivalent to his notion of having the proper *attitude of disapproval* toward the evil that one may cause. Nowhere did McCormick explicitly equate the phrase "integral intentionality" with an agent's evil-disapproving attitude, but that these two are equivalent seems clear from his writing. See, for example, "Ambiguity in Moral Choice," p.40, where he wrote "Concretely, it can be argued that where a higher good is at stake and the only means to protect it is to choose to do a nonmoral evil, then the will remains properly disposed to the values constitutive of human good,...that the person's *attitude or intentionality* is good because he is making the best of a destructive and tragic situation." Emphasis mine; see also, "A Commentary on the Commentaries," 261-262.
24 Emphasis mine; Richard McCormick, "Ambiguity in Moral Choice," 40.
25 See chapter two.
26 Richard McCormick, "Ambiguity in Moral Choice," 45.
27 Richard McCormick, "A Commentary on the Commentaries," 263.
28 Ibid., 241.
29 Richard McCormick, "Ambiguity in Moral Choice," 50.
30 Richard McCormick, "Notes on Moral Theology 1977: The Church in Dispute," *Theological Studies* 39 (1978), 115.
31 Ibid.
32 John Paul II, *Veritatis Splendor*, no. 52.
33 Ibid., no.80.
34 John Finnis, *Moral Absolutes: Tradition, Revision, and Truth* (Washington: The Catholic University of America Press, 1991) 12. Finnis is careful to point out that "in this context, 'absolute' is not to be confused with 'absolute' in other contexts, such as the absoluteness of God. The norms in question are not supreme, fundamental, unconditioned; to call them absolute is to say no more than that they are exceptionless" (Ibid., 3).
35 Ibid., 11.
36 Richard McCormick, "A Commentary on the Commentaries," 264.
37 See Richard McCormick, "Ambiguity in Moral Choice," 31-32; "A Commentary on the Commentaries," 264-265.
38 Richard McCormick, "A Commentary on the Commentaries," 232-233.
39 Richard McCormick, "Ambiguity in Moral Choice," 45. In this context, he explicitly cited the case of bombing civilians: "The principle of noncombatant immunity would seem to be an example of this" (Ibid). See also, "A Commentary on the Commentaries," 257.
40 McCormick wrote that one ought to enter every situation with a "strong presumption" that one may not kill, and that one ought to be "budged from this conclusion only by the most extraordinary and tragic circumstances" ("Notes on Moral Theology: April-September, 1971" *Theological Studies* 33 [1972], 85). It seems reasonable to assume that the presumption against civilian bombing was, in his mind, the same sort of conditional presumption.
41 Richard McCormick, "Ambiguity in Moral Choice," 44-45.
42 Ibid., 45.
43 Richard McCormick, "Notes on Moral Theology: April-September, 1971" *Theological Studies* 33 (1972), 77.
44 Richard McCormick, "A Commentary on the Commentaries," 261.
45 Richard McCormick, "Ambiguity in Moral Choice," 39.
46 Ibid., 52, n.51.
47 Richard McCormick, "A Commentary on the Commentaries," 264.
48 Bruno Schuller, "Direct Killing/Indirect Killing," in *Readings in Moral Theology, No.1* C. Curran and R. McCormick (eds.) (New York: Paulist Press, 1979). This article was first published in 1972 in *Theologie und Philosophie* 47 as "Direkte Totung—Indirekte Totung."
49 Bruno Schuller, "Direct Killing/Indirect Killing," in *Readings in Moral Theology, No.1*, 140.

50 Ibid., 141. Schuller did not elaborate on the two categories of values and disvalues he employed—*absolute* values/disvalues and *relative* values/disvalues. He did not, for example, explain whether calling X a relative disvalue means that it is a disvalue in every circumstance but its degree of disvalue varies by circumstance, or that it is only contingently a disvalue and may yet be a value in certain circumstances. He also offered no definition or account of *sin* here, or of how exactly his notion of sin was related to his notion of moral evil. It will be seen, though, that these lacunae are not disruptive to our purposes.

51 Ibid., 143. Here, "to cause" means to cause *directly*, i.e. to cause *purposefully* or *intentionally* in the usual sense of *intentional*. Schuller did not here specify the principles by which one can discern whether one simply *may* or whether one *should* so cause ontic evil in particular circumstances. This, though, is not of great concern to us, since our focus here is McCormick's proportionalism.

52 Ibid., 145. Again, "for the sake of a correspondingly important good," an agent "may intentionally desire and directly cause the non-moral evil" (Ibid., 144).

53 Richard McCormick, "Ambiguity in Moral Choice," 35-36.

54 Ibid., 39.

55 Ibid., 32.

56 Ibid., 31.

57 Ibid., 40.

58 Ibid., 42. This same reasoning is found in his analysis of active and passive euthanasia in "The New Medicine and Morality." There he wrote, "Longwood and Louisell are arguing that direct causing of death involves dangers, especially for the living, not associated with conservative procedures, and that therefore the harm involved in direct termination is disproportionate to the benefit. I believe that they are right and that it is precisely for this reason that we must maintain the moral difference between omission and commission..." "The New Medicine and Morality," *Theology Digest* 21, 4 (1973), 319.

59 This was noted in chapter three.

60 Ibid., 257.

61 Ibid.

62 We have already seen in chapter three that McCormick's *undermining* criterion is consequentialist.

63 There are intimations of the later *undermining* criterion in the earlier work when he claimed that "in the case of indiscriminate warfare, our experience and reflection tell us that all the ends or values will not be best served by such actions" ("Ambiguity in Moral Choice," 44). A natural inference from this argument and analysis is that if our ends or values were "best served" then such actions would be morally licit, even obligatory.

64 Sanford Levy, "Richard McCormick and Proportionate Reason," *Journal of Religious Ethics* 13 (1985), 269.

65 Richard McCormick, "Ambiguity in Moral Choice," 44.

66 Richard McCormick, "A Commentary on the Commentaries," 239-240.

67 Ibid., 238.

68 Such conclusions are "prudential judgments based on both the certainties of history and the uncertainties of the future" (Richard McCormick, "Ambiguity in Moral Choice," 44).

69 Richard McCormick, "Notes on Moral Theology: April-September, 1971" *Theological Studies* 33 (1972), 78.

70 Richard McCormick, "A Commentary on the Commentaries," 232.

71 Richard McCormick "Moral Theology 1940-1989: An Overview," *Theological Studies* 50 (1989), 22.

72 He identified *life, health, mating, raising children, knowledge, friendship, enjoyment of the arts,* and *play* as "the human goods that define our flourishing" ("Theology and Bioethics: Christian Foundations," in *Theology and Bioethics: Exploring the Foundations and Frontiers*. E.E. Shelp [ed.], Dordrect:

D. Reidel Publishing, 1985: 106). For McCormick's explanation/defense of the objectivity of the *ordo bonorum* he employed, see his "Notes on Moral Theology 1977: The Church in Dispute," *Theological Studies* 39 (1978), 92. Also, speaking on behalf of other proportionalists, he wrote: "We understand by 'value' an intrinsic good to man, not something that is good simply because it is evaluated as such by human beings" ("Notes on Moral Theology: 1976," *Theological Studies* 38 [1977], 77). Some examples of values McCormick identified are life, the family, and childbearing ("Notes on Moral Theology 1977: The Church in Dispute," *Theological Studies* 39 [1978], 104).

73 Emphasis mine; Richard McCormick, *Health and Medicine in the Catholic Tradition* (New York: The Crossroad Publishing Co.) 1984, 50.
74 Richard McCormick, *How Brave a New World?* (London: SCM Press Ltd., 1981), 9.
75 Richard McCormick, "The Judeo-Christian Tradition and Bioethical Codes," in *How Brave a New World?* (London: SCM Press Ltd., 1981) 9-10.
76 Ibid., 10.
77 Richard McCormick, *Corrective Vision: Explorations in Moral Theology* (Kansas City: Sheed & Ward, 1994) 147; originally appeared as "Theology and Bioethics," *Hastings Center Report* 19 (1989) 5-10.
78 Ibid., 148.
79 Richard McCormick, "Ambiguity in Moral Choice," 27.
80 Ibid., 47.
81 Ibid.
82 Ibid., 80.
83 Richard McCormick, "Notes on Moral Theology: April-December, 1971," *Theological Studies* 33 (1972), 90.
84 Richard McCormick,"The Abortion Dossier," in *How Brave a New World?* (London: SCM Press Ltd., 1981), 168.
85 Richard McCormick, *Corrective Vision: Explorations in Moral Theology*, 146.
86 Richard McCormick, *Health and Medicine in the Catholic Tradition* (New York: The Crossroad Publishing Co., 1984) 51. Contrast this allowance for the licit *sacrificing* of life with the following: "…the dignity of human persons is protected by moral absolutes. Among those absolutes, we believe, is one which forbids choices to destroy human lives. Killing people is not a permissible means to promote other goods or prevent other evils." John Finnis, Joseph Boyle, Germain Grisez, "A Sounder Theory of Morality," in *Readings in Moral Theology No.11: The Historical Development of Moral Theology in the United States* Richard McCormick and Charles Curran (eds.) (New York: Paulist Press, 1999) 217.
87 For example, he wrote that "faith that God loves each individual and calls each to salvation deepens our insight into the worth of the individual" (Richard McCormick, "Notes on Moral Theology1977: The Church in Dispute," *Theological Studies* 39 [1978], 77). Such is an example of a value being grounded and ratified in revelation. Relevant here, too, is the following statement: "I believe and do not apologize for the fact that our emotions and religious commitments do function in our value judgments in a way that is sometimes beyond reduction to reasoning processes or analytic arguments" (Richard McCormick, "A Commentary on the Commentaries," 250).
88 Examples of *moral* evil provided by McCormick are: adultery, genocide, murder, lying, infidelity, theft; Richard McCormick, "Notes on Moral Theology1977: The Church in Dispute," *Theological Studies* 39 [1978], 93; *How Brave a New World?*, 417.
89 Richard McCormick, "Notes on Moral Theology1977: The Church in Dispute," *Theological Studies* 39 [1978], 93.
90 Richard McCormick, "A Commentary on the Commentaries," 222.
91 One may recall McCormick's summation and endorsement of Peter Knauer's position on what constitutes *moral* [as opposed to *ontic*] evil: "…a lie consists in telling what is false *without*

commensurate reason and therefore directly or formally causes the error of another. Theft is the taking of the property of another *without commensurate reason*. Mutilation is surgery *without commensurate reason*. Murder is killing *without commensurate reason*. Contraception is intervention into the fertility of the conjugal act *without commensurate reason*." (emphasis mine; Richard McCormick, *How Brave a New World?*, 417)

92 Lisa Sowle Cahill, "Teleology, Utilitarianism, and Christian Ethics," *Theological Studies* 42 (1981), 614.
93 Ibid.
94 Ibid., 222-223.
95 Ibid., 258.
96 Emphasis mine; Richard McCormick, "Notes on Moral Theology: April-December, 1971," *Theological Studies* 33 (1972), 72.
97 One such potential area of disagreement is McCormick's necessity principle. He relied explicitly upon his Christianity to elucidate and validate this principle, a notion which played a crucial role in his argument that bombing noncombatants is disproportionate: "There is no *necessary connection* between our doing harm to noncombatants (e.g. killing innocent civilians to stop that nation) and that nation's ceasing unjust aggression. To say that there is would be to insult the humanity of the aggressor by denying his liberty; for unjust aggressors are free to cease unjust aggression. Christ did not invent that idea, of course, but by his graceful redemption he powerfully restated it to a world that too often came to terms with its inhumanities as 'necessary,' 'culturally imposed,' etc. And by denying the agressors freedom, we deny our own by implication, thus removing the conditions for any rationality in war. That is why, I believe, the Christian judges attacks upon noncombatants as disproportionate" (Richard McCormick , "Notes on Moral Theology1977: The Church in Dispute," *Theological Studies* 39 [1978], 115). His claim that "it is the Christian's faith that another's ceasing from his wrongdoing is *never* dependent on my doing nonmoral evil" (Ibid., 114) does not separate his moral theory *in principle* from other consequentialist ethical theories. Instead, this claim is simply one of the philosophical/theological anthropological beliefs which McCormick's consequentialist ethic presupposed.
98 Consider his explanation of licit, intentional killing: "Obviously, life itself or a value quite as urgent (adoption of a hierarchy) must be at stake. Killing for lesser reason is unnecessary and disproportionate" (Richard McCormick, "A Commentary on the Commentaries," 262).

Chapter 5

Acting Against Basic Goods and Intrinsically Wrong Acts

In the last chapter we considered McCormick's norm prohibiting the choice of moral evil and saw how it is entirely consistent with his consequentialism. In this final chapter we will consider McCormick's norm prohibiting "acting against" a basic good, as well as his account of intrinsically wrong acts. These two elements of his thought deserve our attention because, like other aspects of his thought that we have already considered, they may appear to some to be non-consequentialist elements within his moral theory, a theory that we have argued is consequentialist. This apparent problem will soon disappear, though, because a close examination of these two elements will show them to be reducible to the greatest good/least evil standard of proportionate reason that is at the heart of his account of morally wrong acts.

Acting Against a Basic Good

Keeping in mind the set of basic human goods identified in his philosophical and theological anthropology, consider McCormick's claim that

> all would grant that repudiation or rejection of a basic human good like procreation is morally wrongful.[1]

Elsewhere, he asserted that "an action, like killing, is morally wrongful when it must be said to turn against a basic good."[2] These statements suggest that McCormick accepted the formal norm that *one ought not turn against, repudiate, or reject any basic human good.* That he accepted such a norm, and that he considered it to be exceptionless, is apparent in his assertion that "...we must never choose against a basic good."[3] To act in this prohibited way towards any basic human good is to commit a morally wrong act.

Because McCormick did not explicitly subordinate this somewhat vaguely stated norm to the duty to maximize ontic good(s)/minimize ontic evil(s), this aspect of his moral theory may, on first read, seem non-consequentialist. Were one to consider only the just-cited basic goods-protecting prohibition, one might reasonably conclude that McCormick was offering restrictions on agents that are neither conditioned upon, nor justified by, the amount and type of ontic good(s) and evil(s) they promise. In reality, though, this norm prohibiting repudiating, rejecting, or turning against a basic good in one's choices is consequentialist. This becomes clear when it is understood that, for McCormick, to turn against, repudiate, or reject a basic human good is to act in a manner that does not promise to maximize the net realization of, or minimize the net damage to, that good. Given this criterion for determining what counts as the prohibited behavior, the norm turns out to be a rather natural elaboration on McCormick's fundamental, consequentialist principle that ontic good is to be maximized/ontic evil minimized.

McCormick's position on acting against basic goods may be better understood if compared to the position of some of his contemporaries. Russell Shaw and Germain Grisez, the latter singled out by McCormick as one moralist with whom he disagreed in this matter,[4] go right to the heart of the dispute by asking a rather simple question:

> Is any action whatsoever allowable, at least in certain circumstances? Or are there actions which it is never morally right to perform?[5]

Relying upon the traditional understanding of the direct/indirect distinction, one which we have seen equates *directly intending X* with *purposefully doing X*, Grisez and Shaw assert "unequivocally" that there are actions which are never morally right to perform.[6] They explain that their position "may be put quite simply: it is never right to act directly against one of the fundamental human goods,"[7] and they make clear what they mean by the phrase *acting against* when they stipulate that

> to act directly against one of the fundamental goods is to violate an actual or possible aspect of the personhood of a real person or persons: to violate 'life,' for example, means violating somebody's life.[8]

John Finnis agrees:

> One of morality's principles...excludes acting against a basic reason by choosing to destroy or damage any basic human good in any of its instantiations in any human person....These instantiations of human good constitute *reasons against* any option which

includes choosing (intending) to destroy or damage any of them.⁹

The position shared by Grisez, Shaw, and Finnis is clear: to act against even a single instance of a basic human good is to act against this good, and one may never purposefully do that. It is important to notice, too, that the validity of this prohibition is not conditioned upon its conduciveness to the maximum realization of the ontic goods at play or the maximum diminishment of the relevant ontic evils. This position is perhaps just what Philip Pettit has in mind when he notes that deontologists reject the consequentialist belief that "the right option in any choice is that which promotes the realization of the relevant valuable properties," and argue instead that

> in some cases at least, the right option is that which honors a relevant value by exemplifying respect for it *in this particular instance, whether or not honoring the value in this way promotes its realization overall.*[10]

Indeed, Boyle, Grisez, and Finnis maintain that

> if an action's description, however limited, makes plain that such an action involves a choice to destroy, damage, or impede *some instance* of a basic human good, the wrongness of any action which meets the description is settled. Additional factors may affect the degree of wrongness, but further description of the act cannot reverse its basic moral quality.[11]

Here again their criterion for what is to count as the prohibited *acting against* a basic good is clearly indicated—to act purposefully against a single instance of a particular good, e.g. purposefully to take one person's life, counts as acting against that good (*life*), and such choices are morally excluded.

McCormick fundamentally disagreed with this criterion. He rejected the position that "one must be said to turn against (or set oneself against) a basic good when one directly intends a nonmoral evil in the traditional sense."[12] Believing that "what is to count as 'turning against a basic good' is, of course, the crucial moral question in some concrete and controversial discussions,"[13] he argued, contra Grisez *et al.*, that to destroy or harm an instance or instances of any basic good is not necessarily to act against that good in the prohibited, moral sense of the phrase. Perhaps unsurprisingly, McCormick explained that

> it is the presence or absence of a proportionate reason which determines whether my action—be it direct or indirect psychologically or causally—involves me in turning against a basic good in a way which is morally reprehensible.[14]

And it is just this proportionate reason standard which lead him to maintain that "suppressing a value, or preferring one to another in one's choice cannot simply be identified with turning against a basic good."[15] His position on this issue was clearly stated and repeated often, as when he argued that when one purposefully acts against an instance or instances of a basic good, it is the presence or absence of a proportionate reason which

> determines whether the attitude of the agent is adequate or not, whether he is choosing rightly or wrongly, whether he remains open to the basic goods or closes one of them off in pursuit of another, whether or not one chooses against a basic good...[16]

For McCormick, then, one who makes a choice purposefully to destroy or damage an instance of a basic good does not violate the norm that one ought not act against or "spurn"[17] this good so long as the choice in question promises a good proportionate to the evil purposefully caused. By making the presence or absence of a proportionate reason the element which alone determines whether a purposeful harming of an instance of a basic good constitutes an instance of the prohibited acting against that basic good, McCormick subordinated the norm prohibiting acting against basic goods to his greatest ontic-good/least ontic-evil standard. This subordination confirms what has been pointed out in previous chapters, namely, that in McCormick's moral theory, there is no constraint on the principle that the morally correct and obligatory choice among an agent's options is that option which promises the maximization of ontic good(s) or the minimization of ontic evil(s).

McCormick's analysis of one particular act of purposeful killing provides a concrete example of how proportionate reason stood in his mind as the criterion for what counted as *acting against* a basic good. Recall the abortion case in which the choice is between allowing both the mother and child to die or aborting the child in order to save the mother. Recall, too, that in defending the choice to abort, McCormick wrote:

> What is the justification—or proportionate reason?...Is it not because, all things considered, abortion is the lesser evil in this tragic instance? Is it not precisely for this reason, then, that abortion in this instance is proportionate?...And is it not for this reason that abortion in these circumstances does not involve one in turning against a basic good?[18]

Here, we see the ostensive fact that abortion is the lesser ontic evil among the agent's alternatives both justifying that choice and preventing it from being a legitimate instance of turning against the basic good *life*. Several years later

McCormick repeated this analysis, asking

> [H]ow does one establish that those who choose to end the life of an unborn baby by abortion always 'set themselves against life'? If abortion is the only life-saving, life-serving option available (as in the classical case: allow both to die vs. save the one [mother] that can be saved), one would think that the intervention is just the opposite of 'setting oneself against' life.[19]

Convinced that a proportionate reason is both necessary and sufficient to justify purposefully causing the evil of death, and convinced that there exists in this case a proportionate reason purposefully to abort (namely, the good of saving the mother's life), McCormick wondered, "How does one possibly establish the conclusion that one 'sets oneself against life'" by choosing to abort here?[20] He judged abortion to be the morally correct choice in these circumstances (and not an instance of turning against the basic good *life*) because he believed abortion to be that act among the agent's choices which would yield the best results (or, as he phrased it, "the lesser evil").[21] Such reasoning makes clear that in McCormick's version of proportionalism the norm prohibiting an agent from acting against a basic good is, effectively, nothing else than a reformulation of the norm not to choose to cause an amount or type of ontic evil that is disproportionate to the good being pursued.

McCormick also employed this *act against* terminology in his justification of one particular choice which promised to cause a tremendous amount of unintended (in the psychological sense) evil, but this justification also indicates that he found proportionate reason, and not the agent's intention, to be morally decisive. Looking back at World War II, he defended the position that

> the entry of the United States into the war against the Axis aggressor was a morally right decision, even though this was accompanied with the foreknowledge that thousands of American troops would perish in the effort.[22]

He explained that in such a decision

> somehow or other, in fear and trembling, we commensurate. In a sense we adopt a hierarchy. We go to war to protect our freedom. That means we are willing to sacrifice life to protect this good.[23]

It is significant that McCormick here did not state simply that one may *risk* death if the reason is proportionate. Instead, he wrote that life may be *sacrificed* if the good for which it is sacrificed is proportionate. This term, *sacrifice*, used as it is in this passage, brings with it connotations of purposeful killing which we may presume were not lost on McCormick. Consistent with this suggestion that a proportionate reason makes licit the purposeful taking of life is McCormick's assertion that "...if the cost is proportionate one does not turn against human life in exacting it..."[24] The reasoning here, just like the reasoning in the abortion case considered earlier, demonstrates that McCormick believed that the fact that a particular act involved an agent in psychologically intending damage to a concrete instance or instances of a human good was insufficient to make this act an instance of the prohibited *turning against* that good. These case analyses add flesh to McCormick's earlier claim that it is the presence or absence of a proportionate reason which alone determines whether a particular choice is guilty of the prohibited *turning against* a basic human good; and, it should be noted, this position is itself entirely consistent with his earlier claim that "...we may directly will and directly cause a nonmoral evil if there is a proportionate reason for doing so"[25]

It seems, then, that when considering whether McCormick's proportionalism is consequentialist in nature, one must be careful not to be misled by some possibly confusing terminolgy. When one considers his prohibition on acting against, undermining, etc. basic goods, and when one considers his claim that any act that violates this norm is morally wrong, one must keep in mind what we have demonstrated, namely, that his claim that a particular act attacks, undermines, acts against, etc. a basic good is simply a claim that this act is disproportionate, which itself means that the act is not that one among the agent's choices which promises the greatest realization of ontic good(s) or the greatest diminution of ontic evil(s). The norm in question, therefore, is far from being a consequence-indifferent constraint on certain types of behavior. Instead, it is simply another expression of McCormick's consequentialist understanding and use of proportionate reason.

Intrinsically Evil Acts

Like his norm prohibiting acting against any basic human good, McCormick's position on intrinsically evil acts may on first glance appear to be a non-consequentialist element within his moral theory. Lisa Cahill believes McCormick tried to separate himself from consequentialism by taking the very non-consequentialist sounding position that there are certain acts that are wrong absolutely, even though these acts can be specified only if some accompanying circumstances are known.[26]

Indeed, it is just this element in McCormick's moral theory that Baruch Brody cites when he writes,

> It is clear that McCormick is not a consequentialist. He believes that certain types of actions are intrinsically right or wrong and that we can know this without having to consider their consequences.[27]

However, McCormick's account of what it means to call a category of acts *intrinsically evil* (or, as he prefers, *intrinsically wrong*[28]), as well as his critique and rejection of the position that certain acts are "intrinsically (always, whatever the circumstances) morally evil,"[29] will in the end support our case that his moral theory is consequentialist.

The understanding of intrinsically evil acts that McCormick rejected allows one to identify certain physical behaviors that one ought never purposefully engage in; these are physical behaviors which are never morally right to choose. The principles which support such a position are rather broadly laid out in Pope John Paul II's *Veritatis Splendor*. Although Michael Quirk is correct in his observation that this encyclical "is not primarily a technical treatise on normative ethical and moral epistemological topics,"[30] it nevertheless gives us a good sense of the type of act assessments McCormick rejected. The encyclical explains that

> The morality of the human act depends primarily and fundamentally on the 'object' rationally chosen by the deliberate will....The object of the act of willing is in fact a freely chosen kind of behavior....that object is the proximate end of a deliberate decision.[31]

Having thus stipulated the meaning of *object* in this context, the encyclical continues:

> Reason attests that there are objects of the human act which are by their nature 'incapable of being ordered' to God, because they radically contradict the good of the person made in his image. These are acts which, in the Church's moral tradition, have been termed 'intrinsically evil' (*intrinsece malum*).[32]

Once one inserts the aforementioned definition of *object*, the position here is clear: there are certain types of physical behaviors which one should never choose to do because such behaviors, by their very nature, "radically contradict" the good of the person who is the image of God.[33] Listed among these behaviors are "any kind of homicide" and, more specifically, abortion.[34] The prohibition on the choice of these behaviors is grounded in a judgment that each behavior possesses, in Jean Porter's words, an "intrinsic inconsistency with the good of the human person."[35] Furthermore, these prohibitions are not subordinated to a demand to maximize ontic good(s) or to minimize ontic evil(s), a fact which allows one to judge *a-priori* that any choice to kill, for example, is morally wrong regardless of the amount or type of ontic good(s) that such a choice may promise.[36] *Veritatis Splendor* identifies and flatly rejects the proposition that one may purposefully choose intrinsically evil behaviors so long as these behaviors are employed as well-intentioned means to a sufficiently good end:

> human activity cannot be judged as morally good merely because it is a means for attaining one or another of its goals, or simply because the subject's intention is good.[37]

So while acknowledging the possibility that some well-intentioned agents may at times choose intrinsically evil behaviors, and while allowing that such behaviors may indeed be efficacious in achieving these well-intentioned agents' ends, it is maintained that, nevertheless, these contingent facts do not alter the intrinsic moral defect in the choice to engage in such behaviors. Such choices will be morally wrong

> *always and per se*, in other words, on account of their very object, and quite apart from the ulterior intentions of the one acting and the circumstances.[38]

It is just this understanding of intrinsically evil acts that McCormick opposed. Twenty years prior to *Veritatis Splendor* he had taken a position from which he did not budge:

> a means can be judged to be evil *only if it is caused without commensurate reason*. One cannot, in other words, isolate certain physical evils and say of them that they are, in all circumstances, moral evils.[39]

By establishing proportionate reason as the sole determinant of the moral quality of acts, McCormick committed himself to the position that act assessments must compare all promised ontic evil(s) to the ontic good(s) being pursued.[40] Given this requirement, no instance of purposefully choosing ontic evil(s) can be morally assessed *a-priori* because that *a-priori* assessment would ignore that which determines the moral quality of these choices, namely, the amount and/or type of ontic good(s) for the sake of which the evil was chosen.[41] And so McCormick's rejection of the idea that the choice of some behaviors can be morally ruled out *a-priori* was grounded in his belief that the moral assessment of any concrete choice is the assessment of the amount and/or type of ontic good(s) and evil(s) at play in that choice. This rejection of the very possibility of *a-priori* moral assessments of particular behaviors and of the subsequent identification of some choices as *intrinsically* wrong further supports the case that McCormick's proportionalism is a consequentialist theory since it highlights once again the consequentialist nature of McCormick's account of what it is that determines the moral quality of an agent's choices: proportionate reason.

Yet despite his dissatisfaction with the understanding of intrinsically evil acts reflected in *Veritatis Splendor*, McCormick did not entirely abandon the idea that some acts may be, in a real sense, always morally wrong, that is, *intrinsically* wrong.[42] Recall from chapter three his analysis of the choice to sacrifice an innocent man in the lynch-mob case. Believing that the choice to kill in this situation would be act of extortion, he wrote

> ...what appears to be a lifesaving action by the judge is really at odds with the very value of life — is disproportionate. I have suggested above why I believe that is the case, namely, extortion by definition accepts the necessity of doing nonmoral evil to get others to cease their wrongdoing. The acceptance of such a necessity is an implied denial of human freedom. But since human freedom is a basic value associated with other basic values (in this case, life), undermining it also thereby undermines life.[43]

McCormick also described this act of extortion as "wrong in itself," but it is important to note again that it was not the *purposeful* aspect of the killing that lead to this description.[44] Indeed, we have already seen him reject the proposition that "directly intended killing is evil in se"[45] and argue instead that

> some killings are justified. That is, we know that there is a proportionate reason for taking human life at times.[46]

Instead of focusing upon the intention of the agent when judging the moral quality of this act, McCormick focused upon the act's effectiveness at maximizing the relevant ontic good(s). In addition to claiming that extortion contains an implied denial of human freedom, a denial which is itself an ontic evil, he also claimed that the basic human goods *freedom* and *life* are so related that any act which undermines *freedom* will also undermine *life*, thereby adding to the ontic evil promised by this choice. The upshot of McCormick's analysis of this act of extortion, then, is that the association of goods ensures that the ontic good of making an evildoer cease their evildoing will not be proportionate to the ontic evil promised by the act's denial of human freedom.[47] So, given his belief that acts of extortion, by their very nature, yield disproportionate evil, and given his belief that the presence or absence of a proportionate reason determines an act's moral quality, it is not unreasonable for McCormick to have concluded that acts of extortion are *by their very nature* morally wrong. But what must be kept in mind is that this conclusion means simply that any act of extortion, i.e. any act which "accepts the necessity of doing nonmoral evil to get others to cease their wrongdoing," promises to cause a type or amount of ontic evil that is disproportionate to any ontic good that the act might realize.

The consequentialist character of this account of intrinsically wrong acts is most apparent in McCormick's assertion that "when an action is always morally wrong," it is so "because when *taken as a whole*, the nonmoral evil outweighs the nonmoral good, and therefore the action is disproportionate."[48] Keeping in mind this explanation of disproportion, consider his claim, offered a few years later, that

> if an action in all thinkable situations is disproportionate, I would think one could say of it that it is 'immoral in principle.'[49]

In this same vein he maintained that

> there are many acts that could be called 'intrinsically evil' if their circumstances are exhaustively included in the description of the action.[50]

Such passages make clear that McCormick's account of intrinsically evil acts was both grounded in and consistent with his prior convictions about proportionate reason and the nature of morally wrong acts, convictions which we have shown to be consequentialist.

Turning again to the issue of abortion will allow us to emphasize this point. Immediately after classifying abortion as a "killing act," McCormick offered the following caveat: "by saying that abortion is a 'killing act' I do not mean to imply that it cannot be justified at times."[51] We have already considered one of the cases where McCormick judged this killing act to be justified, namely, when purposefully killing an unborn child promises to save the mother's life and is the only alternative to allowing both mother and child to die. McCormick believed that abortion in these circumstances promises the lesser evil among the alternatives and is therefore justified. Elsewhere, McCormick claimed that an abortion is not justified if chosen as a means to avoid the considerable medical bills promised by carrying a pregnancy to term. He believed that choosing to kill for that reason is "always wrong—and, if one wishes, intrinsically wrong."[52] His claim seems to have been that any act of the form *K for the sake of M*, where *K* is killing and *M* is money, will be disproportionately evil given the fact that *K* is a basic good while *M* is merely an instrumental good.[53] This interpretation is supported by his assertion that when instrumental and basic goods conflict, "one sacrifices the instrumental for the basic, because instrumental goods are lesser in the order of goods."[54] Further support for this interpretation is found in his claim that "*lesser* goods such as convenience, avoidance of shame, and health are not to be preferred to life."[55] Recall, too, his claim that any act of rejecting God for some other good

> is by definition an action which turns against and rejects the *summum bonum* for something less. One ought never to do that—a matter that is analytically clear.[56]

So, given the *ordo bonorum* he endorsed, it is not unreasonable for McCormick to have concluded that certain acts, like those that may be characterized as *K for the sake of M*, will always cause disproportionate evil. In this way, then, these kinds of acts will be unavoidably disproportionate, that is, unavoidably morally wrong in that consequentialist sense.[57]

Here seems to be the best place to consider another of McCormick's defenses against the charge that his proportionalism is consequentialist in nature. McCormick believed that consequentialist theories were committed to the principle that all acts are neutral in themselves and derive their meaning—good or evil—from their consequences Using a promise as an example, he claimed that a "straightforward consequentialism" would maintain that

> a promise gets its meaning from consequences, that it is to be kept or not depending on whether keeping it would produce better net results than not keeping it.[58]

In contrast to this, he believed that "a promise has an inherent meaning and binding force; breaking a promise is always a disvalue."[59] Perhaps conflating the notions *intrinsically right/wrong* and *intrinsically good/evil*, McCormick thought that since his version of proportionalism holds that some acts have an inherent meaning, it is not a form of consequentialism.

When considering this defense one should note that McCormick made two claims here; one has to do with the inherent value of a promise, the other with what determines whether a particular promise binds. McCormick's first claim, or perhaps *suggestion*, is that a consequentialist cannot with consistency maintain that certain acts have inherent value. To this one may well reply, Why not? What defining, necessary consequentialist principle does such a value judgment contradict? McCormick did not answer these questions. We have seen that the defining mark of a consequentialist ethical theory is not that it cannot consider an act to be inherently valuable, but that it understands choices to be morally right or wrong according to their effect on the realization of values. And we have shown that McCormick's proportionalism bears this mark. Consider, for example, the consequentialist who identifies *truth* as an inherently good *maximand*. Such a position invites the judgment that any act of truth-telling is inherently valuable in the sense that by definition it yields the *maximand*. But this value judgment about acts of truth-telling is not incompatible with the belief that in certain circumstances a lie, rather than truth-telling, will *maximize* the production of *truth*, i.e. will yield more truth in those circumstances than an act of truth-telling. The consequentialist would judge that in those circumstances one's duty is to lie. This judgment of duty, though, does not entail the proposition that truth-telling in the aforementioned situation is *not* inherently valuable in the sense specified above. The judgment of duty is simply the judgment that in the circumstances *more* good will be realized by lying than by truth-telling. The act of truth-telling *simpliciter* may still be judged inherently valuable because all such acts, by definition, yield the intrinsic good *truth*. As C.D. Broad wrote,

> Teleological theories hold that the rightness or wrongness of an action is always determined by its tendency to produce certain consequences which are *intrinsically* good or bad.[60]

So if an act by its very nature produces consequences which are intrinsically good, that type of act should be judged intrinsically good in the sense specified above. How is this incompatible with consequentialism? Returning to the example of promising, Sanford Levy points out that

> ...[N]othing in a maximizing reading forces us to say that promises do not have 'inherent meaning.' All it says is that this inherent meaning can be overridden to maximize the kind of value that is being sought, and McCormick himself says that the inherent meaning of promises can be overridden.[61]

Furthermore, McCormick's defense here appears to conflict with a position he took elsewhere, namely, that sexual intercourse "has a sense and meaning prior to the individual purposes of those who engage in it," and that this act ought to be restricted to marriage.[62] In defending the restriction of this act to marriage, he wrote

> How was this judgment derived? It seems that it is the conclusion of long experience and reflection, especially about consequences. In other words, the experience of centuries has led us to conclude that unless this type of intimacy is restricted to the marriage relationship, the integrity of sexual language will be seriously threatened. Such a judgment is clearly a form of consequentialism. 'What would happen if...?' It is precisely here that a consequentialist methodology appears to me absolutely correct.[63]

And so McCormick brought together, without apparent contradiction or inconsistency, a judgment that a certain act has inherent value, and a consequentialist norm governing behavior vis-à-vis that value. He found no problem with such juxtaposition, and rightly so.

The second of the two claims in McCormick's defense here is that a consequentialist ethical theory must hold that the question of whether a promise is to be kept depends upon "whether keeping it would produce better net results than not keeping it."[64] This is true, but it is also a position that McCormick himself embraced:

> There are times, however, when it is reasonable and right to visit the disvalue of a broken promise on the promisee, times when he would be unreasonable to expect and insist on the keeping of the promise. Those are times when some urgent value overrides the covenant established in a promise....By saying some values take precedence over others they are saying nothing more or less than one who says lesser evil or proportionate reason.[65]

And he went on to maintain that to require that all promises be kept would be counterproductive with respect to certain goods:

> If all promises had to be kept, no matter what, then people would not make promises and that means *undermining the good of promise keeping by removing from our midst the goods we secure through covenants* among one another. In other words, in the example above, breaking the promise, while involving nonmoral evil, is not disproportionate.[66]

If one recalls that he explained *proportionate reason* to mean greater good (or lesser evil), then one can better see that his position was that one may purposefully cause the ontic evil of promise-breaking in order to realize a greater good (or in order to avoid the realization of a greater evil). His claim, then, that a promise has an inherent value cannot keep him from being placed among the ranks of the consequentialists, and his position on purposefully causing the ontic evil of breaking a promise is fundamentally indistinguishable from the position that whether or not a promise is to be kept depends on whether or not keeping it would produce better results than not keeping it.

What hopefully has become clear from the foregoing is that McCormick's account of acts that are *always* morally wrong is a reasonable and rather unsurprising corollary to his account of the nature of morally wrong acts, an account that we have shown to be consequentialist. Earlier in this study it was pointed out that McCormick found the moral defect of morally wrong acts to be that these acts promise an amount or type of ontic evil that is disproportionate to the ontic good they promise. It has just now been shown that McCormick found *intrinsically* wrong acts to be those which, by their very nature, will unavoidably bring about an amount or type of ontic evil that is disproportionate to the ontic good they promise. It seems, then, quite reasonable to consider McCormick's account of intrinsically wrong acts to be no more than an acknowledgment and elaboration on his belief that, in the words of Michael Quirk,

> it is entirely possible that no goods one could cite on behalf of an action would outweigh its associated bads: such an action would indeed be *malum in se*.[67]

Now since McCormick rested these theoretical refinements upon his own set of debatable prior convictions (his anthropology and its *ordo bonorum*, his necessity and undermining principles, and the association of basic goods) it bears mentioning that the issue at hand is not whether these prior convictions are plausible. What we have been focused upon is the structure of McCormick's moral reasoning and his account of what makes intrinsically wrong acts be intrinsically wrong. In short, what we have seen is that for McCormick to have identified an act as intrinsically wrong was for him to make a consequrntialist assessment, or perhaps a consequentialist prophecy, and claim that due to the nature of these acts they cannot ever yield an amount or type of ontic good that would justify the ontic evil they entail.

We saw in earlier chapters that McCormick offered and applied the consequentialist belief that the specifying defect of a morally wrong act is that the evil it promises is greater than the amount or type of good it would realize. It was then argued that McCormick's prohibitions on intending ontic evil (in the moral sense of *intend*) and on engaging in moral evil are, despite initial appearances, entirely consistent with this foundational belief. In this chapter, we have seen this pattern continue. McCormick's norm prohibiting acting against any basic good may on first-read appear to function deontologically and enjoy a validity which is not derived from his consequentialist greater good/lesser evil standard. Yet once the criterion for what constitutes this prohibited behavior is identified, it becomes clear that the norm is reducible to the fundamental position that purposeful evildoing is justified by a proportionate good. In similar fashion, McCormick's claim that certain acts may indeed be intrinsically wrong is to be understood simply as the claim that certain kinds of choices will always be disproportionately evil due to the nature of the act and to some inescapable realities of the world in which agents find themselves, including the *ordo bonorum*. Here once again, one sees the primacy of proportionate reason, i.e. of the greatest good/least evil standard, not abandoned but affirmed once the meaning behind the norm or notion is understood.

Conclusion

We began this study by considering two fundamentally different types of normative ethical theories: consequentialist and deontological. We saw that one of the two defining marks of consequentialist theories is their assertion that every agent's primary moral obligation is to act in ways that either maximize the realization of a particular good or set of goods, or minimize the realization of correlative evil(s). The other defining mark of consequentialist theories has to do with act assessments and the nature of morally right/wrong acts. Each of these theories maintains that acts are morally specified, and assessable, according to their productivity of the to-be-pursued good(s) or the to-be-avoided evil(s) identified by that particular theory. Our aim in identifying these defining marks of consequentialist ethical theories was to make plain that Richard McCormick's brand of proportionalism bears each of them. I believe that has now been accomplished. What we have seen is that in McCormick's theory, proportionate reason reigns supreme in all act assessments. There are a number of elements within his theory that may, on first look, obscure its fundamentally consequentialist character, elements like his necessity principle, his assertion of an association of goods, his somewhat vague prohibitions on "undermining a good" and "denying a value," his notion of intrinsically wrong acts, his norm forbidding without exception the choice of moral evil, and his argument for the moral relevance of the distinction between an agent merely allowing a particular ontic evil and that agent purposefully causing that evil. As we moved through these and other elements of his theory, though, we again and again saw them either subordinated or reduced to proportionate reason, the eponym that we have seen McCormick himself repeatedly equate with *the greater good* and/or *the lesser evil.* In the end, then, all of the theoretical complexities and refinements of McCormick's moral theory, along with his theological and philosophical anthropology, serve one purpose: to identify correctly in an often complicated world which among an agent's choices promises the greatest good or the least evil, with the assumption being that there lies the morally right and obligatory act. This is why McCormick's proportionalism is to be considered a consequentialist ethical theory.

Notes

1 Richard McCormick "Notes on Moral Theology 1977: The Church in Dispute," *Theological Studies* 39 1, 95.
2 Richard McCormick, "A Commentary on the Commentaries," 261.
3 Richard McCormick, *How Brave a New World?* (London: SCM Press, 1981) 6.
4 Ibid., 6.
5 Germain Grisez, Russell Shaw, *Beyond the New Morality* (Notre Dame: University of Notre Dame Press, 1974) 129.
6 Ibid.
7 Ibid. The basic goods that they identify are *life, play, aesthetic experience, speculative knowledge, integrity, authenticity, friendship,* and *religion* (ibid., 72-73). Whether and how this set of goods overlaps with McCormick's is not important here, what is important is the shared belief that there are some fundamental human goods, necessary for human fulfillment, that agents can, in some sense, act against.
8 Ibid., 130
9 John Finnis, "Natural Law and Legal Reasoning," in *Natural Law Theory: Contemporary Essays*, Robert George (ed.) (Oxford: Clarendon Press, 1992) 147.
10 Emphasis mine; Philip Pettit "Consequentialism and Respect for Persons," *Ethics* 100 (October, 1989), 117.
11 Emphasis mine; John Finnis, Joseph Boyle, Germain Grisez, "A Sounder Theory of Morality," in *Readings in Moral Theology No.11: The Historical Development of Moral Theology in the United States* Richard McCormick and Charles Curran (eds.) (New York: Paulist Press, 1999) 216.
12 Richard McCormick, "A Commentary on the Commentaries," 263; see also "Ambiguity in Moral Choice," 27 where he rejected the notion that when it comes to doing evil purposefully, "an intending will necessarily involves one in turning against a basic good." In this context, too, he wondered "why one must be said to turn against a basic good when the evil occurs as a means, and is the object of an intending will." Elsewhere he expressed somewhat more concretely this same thought: "Why, it has been asked, does every concrete choice to speak a falsehood or take a life necessarily involve one in directly rejecting the basic good of truth itself or the good of life?" ("Some Early Reactions to *Veritatis Splendor*," *Theological Studies* 55 [1994], 503).
13 Richard McCormick, *How Brave a New World?* (London: SCM Press, 1981) 6.
14 Richard McCormick, "Ambiguity in Moral Choice," in *Doing Evil to Achieve Good*, Richard McCormick and Paul Ramsey (eds.) (Chicago: Loyola University Press, 1973) 28-29.
15 From his article in *Personal Values and Public Policy*, John Haughey (ed.), reprinted in *Introduction to Christian Ethics* Ronald Hamel and Kenneth Himes (eds.) (New York: Paulist Press, 1989) 142.
16 Emphasis mine; Richard McCormick "Notes on Moral Theology 1977: The Church in Dispute," *Theological Studies* 39 1, 115; see also ibid., 95.
17 From his article in *Personal Values and Public Policy* John Haughey (ed.), reprinted in *Introduction to Christian Ethics*, 142.
18 Richard McCormick, "Ambiguity in Moral Choice," 27-28.
19 Richard McCormick, *The Critical Calling: Reflections on Moral Dilemmas Since Vatican II* , (Washington: Georgetown University Press, 1989) 229.
20 Ibid., 230.
21 Recall that he considered "the rule of Christian reason" to be "to choose the lesser evil" ("Ambiguity in Moral Choice," 38).
22 Richard McCormick, "A Commentary on the Commentaries," 226,
23 Ibid., 227.
24 Ibid., 226. He later repeated this point when he added, "when the proportion is there, there is no turning against the good of life" (Ibid.).

25 Richard McCormick, "Notes on Moral Theology: April – September, 1971," 71.
26 Lisa Sowle Cahill, "Teleology, Utilitarianism, and Christian Ethics," *Theological Studies* 42 (1981), 618. Cahill's claim that McCormick's position on intrinsically evil acts was his attempt to separate his proportionalism from consequentialism is interesting in that I am unaware of any place where McCormick featured this part of his theory in a defense against the charge that it is consequentialist.
27 Baruch Brody, "The Problem of Exceptions in Medical Ethics," in *Doing Evil to Achieve Good*, 55. In this vein James Walter writes, "…one reason why proportionalists are not consequentialists is because they maintain that actions which realize or cause premoral values/disvalues are not entirely neutral" ("The Foundation and Formulation of Norms." *Moral Theology: Challenges for the Future.* Charles E. Curran [ed.] [New York: Paulist, 1990], 129).
28 We note here that in this discussion, *intrinsically evil* and *intrinsically wrong* were used interchangeably.
29 Richard McCormick, *Health and Medicine in the Catholic Tradition* (New York: The Crossroad Publishing Co., 1984) 97. Elsewhere he made reference to acts which are "always wrong regardless of circumstances or consequences" ("Notes on Moral Theology 1977: The Church in Dispute," 103), and acts which are "…always morally wrong with no exceptions" ("Birth Regulation, *Veritatis Splendor,* and Other Ways of Viewing Things," *Eglise et Theologie* 26 [1995], 32).
30 Michael J. Quirk, "Why the Debate on Proportionalism is Misconceived," *Modern Theology* 13 4, 504.
31 Pope John Paul II, *Veritatis Splendor*, 98-99. Elsewhere, the notion of *freely choosing* a certain behavior is expressed as a *deliberate consent* to that behavior, and a *deliberate choice* of that behavior (See ibid., 96, 97).
32 Ibid., 101.
33 What precisely is meant by an act *contradicting* the good of the person as the image of God is not explained. However, what seems clear from a reading of the encyclical is that this notion of an act *contradicting* the good of the person is not equivalent to McCormick's notion of an act *undermining* a particular good. We have seen that McCormick's notion of an act undermining the good(s) it seeks centered around the act's effects vis-à-vis the realization of the relevant good(s). *Veritatis Splendor*'s notion of an act contradicting the good of the person focuses upon the consistency or "fit" between the act and the ontological status of the agent as an image of God.
34 Ibid., 101.
35 Jean Porter, "The Moral Act in *Veritatis Splendor* and Aquinas's *Summa Theologiae*: A Comparative Analysis," in *Readings in Moral Theology No.11: The Historical Development of Moral Theology in the United States*, 225.
36 It is for this reason that those who would defend such a moral theory demand at the same time a sensitivity to the traditional distinction between *intending* and *allowing* evil in one's choices. Such sensitivity is necessary because, as Finnis, Boyle, and Grisez point out, "one cannot act at all without accepting some bad side effects. In any choice, one at least devotes part of one's limited time and other resources to the pursuit of a particular good, and leaves unserved other goods for which one might have acted. So there could not be a general moral principle entirely excluding the willing of every negative impact on a basic human good. One sometimes can accept bad side effects as inevitable concomitants of a fully reasonable response to the intelligible requirements of goods. Thus, the principle that evil may not be done that good may come of it applies only to the *choice* of a means to an ulterior end, not to the acceptance of side effects." Emphasis mine; John Finnis, Joseph M. Boyle, Jr., Germain Grisez "A Sounder Theory of Morality," in *Readings in Moral Theology No.11: The Historical Development of Moral Theology in the United States*, Richard McCormick and Charles Curran (eds.) (New York: Paulist Press, 1999) 215.

37 Pope John Paul II, *Veritatis Splendor*, (Boston: Pauline Books & Media, 1993) 92.
38 Ibid., 101. Perhaps seeking to emphasize the point by repeating it, soon after one again reads: "...the Church teaches that 'there exist acts which per se and in themselves, independently of circumstances, are always seriously wrong by reason of their object" (Ibid).
39 Emphasis mine; Richard McCormick, "Ambiguity in Moral Choice," in *Doing Evil to Achieve Good*, (Chicago: Loyola University Press) 1973, 10. This quote was McCormick's summation of one part of Peter Knauer's moral theory, a summation that McCormick embraced. Here it may be interesting to note these words of Pope John Paul II: "...the opinion must be rejected as erroneous which maintains that it is impossible to qualify as morally evil according to its species the deliberate choice of certain kinds of behavior or specific acts, without taking into account the intention for which the choice was made or the forseeable consequences of the act for all persons concerned" (Pope John Paul II, *Veritatis Splendor*, 103).
40 Recall that McCormick's anthropology did enable him to identify *a-priori* certain choices as choices of ontic evil. For example, any choice to kill a human being is the choice of an ontic evil because human life is an ontic good..
41 And we have seen that a logical conclusion of this position is that no material norms are exceptionless, but only *virtually* exceptionless; see ch.4, sec. *ii* above. See also "Notes on Moral Theology: April – September 1974," *Theological Studies* 36 1, 88; "Notes on Moral Theology 1977: The Church in Dispute," *Theological Studies* 39 1, 93; "A Commentary on the Commentaries," in *Doing Evil to Achieve Good*, (Chicago: Loyola University Press, 1973), 232,261,264; *The Critical Calling: Reflections on Moral Dilemmas Since Vatican II*, (Washington: Georgetown University Press, 1989) 132-134.
42 He referred to these acts in different ways at different times, sometimes calling them *intrinsically evil*, other times *intrinsically wrong*, and other times *evil in principle* or *evil in se*. We will see an example of each in what follows.
43 Richard McCormick, "A Commentary on the Commentaries," 260. Recall from chapter three that McCormick's notion of *undermining a good* referred to substantive harm to concrete instances of this good. Recall, too, his claims that "one who unjustifiably takes human life also undermines other human goods, and these human goods, once weakened or undermined, will affect the very good of life itself" (Richard McCormick "Notes on Moral Theology 1977: The Church in Dispute," 112), and that "I would argue that because of the association of basic goods, an assault on one (liberty) will bring harm to another (life) and that therefore judicial murder is in itself a disproportionate means" ("A Commentary on the Commentaries," 250).
44 Ibid., 260, 261.
45 Richard McCormick, "Ambiguity in Moral Choice," 27.
46 Richard McCormick "Notes on Moral Theology 1977: The Church in Dispute," 93. Elsewhere he explained that "the presumption against taking human life is the principle (or substance) of Catholic teaching in this matter. The rule, on the other hand, ('no direct taking of innocent human life'), is a kind of formulation-application of this substance....Such concrete rules...will not always share the same force or universality as the substance" ("Pluralism Within the Church," in *Catholic Perspectives on Medical Morals*. E. Pellegrino, J. Langan, J Harvey [eds.], Netherlands: Kluwer Academic Publishers, 1989: 157).
47 As noted when we were considering McCormick's notion of an association of basic good and his undermining principle, our concern here is the nature of McCormick's moral reasoning, not the plausibility of the principles he employed.
48 Richard McCormick, "Notes on Moral Theology 1977: The Church in Dispute," 103.
49 Richard McCormick, "Notes on Moral Theology: 1981," 80.
50 Richard McCormick, "Notes on Moral Theology: 1982," 77, n.22. To appreciate the consequentialist character of this claim, one should recall from chapter three that McCormick understood an act's morally relevant circumstances to be those factors which affect in any way the amount/proportion between the ontic good(s) and evil(s) promised in that act. See his

"Notes on Moral Theology: 1981," p.86, where he listed "side effects, possible consequences, intentions, etc." as included in the notion of "morally relevant circumstances."
51 Richard McCormick, *Corrective Vision: Explorations in Moral Theology* (Kansas City: Sheed & Ward, 1994) 191.
52 Richard McCormick "Notes on Moral Theology 1977: The Church in Dispute," *Theological Studies* 39 1, 103.
53 I say that his claim *seems* to have been this because despite his allowance that one may consider this act to be *intrinsically* wrong, he did not elaborate on what precisely was wrong with it. I am simply applying his proportionate reason standard and the rather commonplace value judgments that life is a fundamental good while money is an instrumental good. Supporting my speculation that the problem here lies in the sacrificing of a greater good for a lesser one is his claim that "if there is a truly proportionate reason for acting, *the agent remains properly open and disposed toward the ordo bonorum* whether the evil occurs as an indivisible effect or as a means within the action." Emphasis mine; Richard McCormick "Ambiguity in Moral Choice," 40.
54 Richard McCormick, "Notes on Moral Theology 1977: The Church in Dispute," 112.
55 Emphasis mine. Richard McCormick, "Ambiguity in Moral Choice," 26-27.
56 Richard McCormick, "A Commentary on the Commentaries," 222-223.
57 One may argue against others that a sufficient quantity of a lower-ranked good in the *ordo bonorum* would justify the sacrificing of a higher-ranked good, but this debate would be among consequentialists and would be about what precisely is meant by the notions *greater evil, lesser evil, greater good,* and *lesser good.*
58 Richard McCormick, "A Commentary on the Commentaries," 235.
59 Ibid., 235. See also, "Bioethics and Method: Where Do We Start?," *Theology Digest* 29, 4 (1981): 315. Elsewhere he offered this same sort of defense and based it upon his claim that there is an inherent value in keeping secrets and an inherent disvalue in breaking them ("Notes on Moral Theology: April – September 1974," 97).
60 C.D. Broad, *Five Types of Ethical Theory*, 206.
61 Sanford Levy, "Richard McCormick and Proportionate Reason," 271.
62 Richard McCormick, "Notes on Moral Theology: April – September 1971," 82. See also his article "Human Significance and Christian Significance," in *Norm and Context in Christian Ethics*, Paul Ramsey and Gene Outka (eds.) (New York: Scribners, 1968) 619.
63 Ibid., 83.
64 Richard McCormick, "A Commentary on the Commentaries," 235.
65 Ibid.
66 Emphasis mine; Ibid.
67 Michael Quirk, "Why the Debate on Proportionalism is Misconceived," *Modern Theology* 13 4, 506.

Bibliography

Adams, Robert Merrihew. "Motive Utilitarianism," *The Journal of Philosophy* 73 (1976): 467-481.

Allsopp, Michael. "Deontic and Epistemic Authority in Roman Catholic Ethics: The Case of Richard McCormick," *Christian Bioethics* 2, 1 (1996): 97-113.

Aquinas, Thomas. *Summa theologiae* translated by the Fathers of the English Dominican Province (1947), Hypertext Version Copyright 1995, 1996 New Advent Inc.; <*http://www.newadvent.org*>

Ashley, Benedict, O'Rourke, Kevin. *Ethics of Health Care*. Washington, D.C.: Georgetown University Press, 1994.

Bentham, Jeremy. *An Introduction to the Principles of Morals and Legislation*, in *The Utilitarians*. New York: Doubleday & Company, Inc., 1961.

Bourke, Vernon. "Is Thomas Aquinas a Natural Law Ethicist?" *Monist* 58 (1974): 52-66.

Boyle, Joseph, Germain Grisez and John Finnis. "A Sounder Theory of Morality," in *Readings in Moral Theology No.11: The Historical Development of Fundamental Moral Theology in the United States* New York: Paulist Press, 1999: 200-218.

———. "Intentions, Christian Morality, and Bioethics: Puzzles of Double Effect," *Christian Bioethics* vol.3, no.2 (1997): 87-88.

———. "Who Is Entitled to Double Effect?" *The Journal of Medicine and Philosophy* 16 (1991): 475-494.

———, Germain Grisez and John Finnis. "Incoherence and Consequentialism (or Proportionalism)—a Rejoinder," *American Catholic Philosophical Quarterly* 64 (1990): 271-77.

———. Germain Grisez and John Finnis. "Practical Principles, Moral Truth, and Ultimate Ends," *The American Journal of Jurisprudence* 32 (1987): 99-151.

———. "Toward Understanding the Principle of Double Effect," *Ethics* 90 (1980): 527-538.

———, and G. Grisez. *Life and Death With Liberty and Justice: A Contribution to the Euthanasia Debate*. Notre Dame: University of Notre Dame Press, 1979.

Broad, C.D. *Five Types of Ethical Theory*. New York: The Humanities Press, 1930.

Brody, Baruch. "The Problem of Exceptions in Medical Ethics," *Doing Evil to Achieve Good: Moral Choice in Conflict Situations*. McCormick and Ramsey (eds.), Chicago: Loyola University Press, 1978: 193-267.

Brown, N. "Teleology or Deontology?" *Irish Theological Quarterly* 53 (1987): 36-51.

Cahill, Lisa Sowle. "On Richard McCormick: Reason and Faith in Post-Vatican II Catholic Ethics," in *Theological Voices in Medical Ethics*. A. Verhey and S. Lammers (eds.) Grand Rapids, MI: Eeerdmans Publishing Co., 1993, 78-105.

———. "Contemporary Challenges to Exceptionless Moral Norms," in *Moral Theology Today: Certitudes and Doubts*. St. Louis, Mo.: Pope John Center, 1984: 121-135.

———. "Teleology, Utilitarianism, and Christian Ethics," *Theological Studies* 42 (1981): 601-29.

Carney, Frederick. "On McCormick and Teleological Morality," *Journal of Religious Ethics* 6 (1978): 81-107.

Clark, Peter A. *To Treat or Not to Treat: The Ethical Methodology of Richard A. McCormick, as Applied to Treatment Decisions for Handicapped Newborns*. Omaha: Creighton University Press, 2003.

Connery, John R. "Catholic Ethics: Has the Norm for Rule-Making Changed?" *Theological Studies* 42 (1981): 232-50.

———. "Morality of Consequences: A Critical Appraisal," *Readings in Moral Theology No. 1: Moral Norms and Catholic Tradition*. Charles E. Curran and Richard A. McCormick (eds.) New York: Paulist Press, 1979, 244-66.

———. "The Teleology of Proportionate Reason," *Theological Studies* 44 (1983): 489-96.

Curran, Charles. *The Living Tradition of Catholic Moral Theology*. Indiana: University of Notre Dame Press, 1992.

———. "Notes on Richard A. McCormick," *Theological Studies* 61 (2000).

———. (ed.) *Moral Theology: Challenges for the Future: Essays in Honor of Richard A. McCormick*. Mahwah, N.J.: Paulist Press, 1990.

———. *Directions in Fundamental Moral Theology*. Indiana: University of Notre Dame Press, 1985.

———. "Utilitarianism and Contemporary Moral Theology: Situating the Debates," *Readings in Moral Theology No. 1: Moral Norms and Catholic Tradition*. Charles E. Curran and Richard A. McCormick (eds.) New York: Paulist Press, 1979, 294-340.

Di Ianni, Albert M. "The Direct/Indirect Distinction in Morals," *The Thomist* 41 (1977).

Ellis, Brian. "Retrospective and Prospective Utilitarianism," *Nous* 15 (1981): 325-339.

Filteau, Jerry. "Theologians Discuss Criteria for Voters When Candidates Back Abortion," *CNS*, 9/29/04, <http://www.catholicnews.com>.

Finnis, John M., and Germain Grisez and Joseph Boyle. "A Sounder Theory of Morality," in *Readings in Moral Theology No.11: The Historical Development of Fundamental Moral Theology in the United States*. New York: Paulist Press, 1999: 200-218.

———. "Beyond the Encyclical," in *Considering Veritatis Splendor*. John Wilkins (ed.) Cleveland: The Pilgrim Press, 1994: 69-76.

———. "Object and Intention in Moral Judgments According to Aquinas," *The Thomist* 55 (1991): 1-27.

———. *Moral Absolutes: Tradition, Revision, and Truth.* Washington, D.C.: The Catholic University of America Press, 1991.

———, G. Grisez and J. Boyle. "Incoherence and Consequentialism (or Proportionalism)—a Rejoinder," *American Catholic Philosophical Quarterly* 64 (1990): 271-77.

———, G. Grisez and J. Finnis. "Practical Principles, Moral Truth, and Ultimate Ends," *The American Journal of Jurisprudence* 32 (1987): 99-151.

———. *Fundamentals of Ethics.* Washington, D.C.: Georgetown University Press, 1983.

Frankena, William K. "McCormick and the Traditional Distinction," in *Doing Evil to Achieve Good.* Richard A. McCormick and Paul Ramsey (eds.) Chicago: Loyola University Press, 1978, 145-64.

Grisez, Germain, J. Finnis and J. Boyle. "A Sounder Theory of Morality," in *Readings in Moral Theology No.11: The Historical Development of Fundamental Moral Theology in the United States* New York: Paulist Press, 1999: 200-218.

———. "Are There Exceptionless Moral Norms?" in *The Twenty-Fifth Anniversary of Vatican II: A Look Back and a Look Ahead.* Braintree, Mass.: The Pope John Center, 1990, 117-35.

———, J. Finnis and J. Boyle. "Incoherence and Consequentialism (or Proportionalism)—a Rejoinder," *American Catholic Philosophical Quarterly* 64 (1990): 271-77.

———. "A Contemporary Natural-Law Ethics," in *Moral Philosophy: Historical and Contemporary Essays.* William C. Starr and Richard C. Taylor (eds.) Milwaukee: Marquette University Press, 1989, 125-43.

———, J. Boyle, and J. Finnis. "Practical Principles, Moral Truth, and Ultimate Ends," *The American Journal of Jurisprudence* 32 (1987): 99-151.

———. "Infallibility and Specific Moral Norms: A Review Discussion" *The Thomist* 49 (1985): 248-87.

——— and J. Boyle. *Life and Death With Liberty and Justice: A Contribution to the Euthanasia Debate* Notre Dame: University of Notre Dame Press, 1979.

———. "Against Consequentialism," *The American Journal of Jurisprudence* 23 (1978): 21-72.

———. "Choice and Consequentialism," *Proceedings of the American Catholic Philosophical Association* 51 (1977): 144-52.

——— and Russell Shaw. *Beyond the New Morality.* Notre Dame and London: University of Notre Dame Press, 1974.

———. *Abortion: The Myths, the Realities, and the Arguments.* Washington: Corpus Books, 1970.

Hallett, Garth L. *Greater Good: The Case for Proportionalism.* Washington: Georgetown University Press, 1995.

———. "The Place of Moral Values in Christian Moral Reasoning," *Heythrop Journal* 30 (1989): 129-49.

———. *Christian Moral Reasoning: An Analytic Guide*. Notre Dame: University of Notre Dame Press, 1983.

Hill, J. "The Debate Between McCormick and Frankena," *Irish Theological Quarterly* 49 (1982): 121-133.

Hoose, Bernard. "Proportionalists, Deontologists, and the Human Good," *Heythrop Journal* 33 (1992): 175-191.

———. *Proportionalism: The American Debate and Its European Roots*. Washington: Georgetown University Press, 1987.

Hurley, Paul. "Agent-Centered Restrictions: Clearing the Air of Paradox," *Ethics* 108 (October, 1997), 120-146.

Irving, Dianne. "Comments: 'Catholic' Bioethicist Thomas Shannon's 'Implications of the Papal Allocution on Feeding Tubes'" <http://www.lifeissues.net/writers/irvi/irvi_63thomasshannon.html>.

Jackson, Frank. "Decision-theoretic Consequentialism and the Nearest and Dearest Objection," *Ethics* 101 (April, 1991): 461-482.

Janssens, Louis. "Ontic Good and Evil—Premoral Values and Disvalues," *Louvain Studies* 12 (1987): 62-82.

———. "St. Thomas and the Question of Proportionality," *Louvain Studies* 9 (1982): 26-46.

———. "Ontic Evil and Moral Evil," *Louvain Studies* 4 (1972): 115-156.

John Paul II. *Veritatis Splendor*. Vatican trans. Boston: Pauline Books and Media, 1993.

Johnson, Mark.. "Proportionalism and a Text of the Young Aquinas: Quodlibetem IX, Q.7, A.2," *Theological Studies* (53): 683-699.

Johnstone, Brian V. "The Meaning of Proportionate Reason in Contemporary Moral Theology," *The Thomist* 49 (1985): 223-47.

Kaczor, C. *Proportionalism and the Natrural Law Tradition*. Washington: Catholic University of America Press, 2002.

———. *Proportionalism: For and Against*. Milwaukee: Marquette University Press, 2000.

———. "Proportionalism and the Pill: How Developments in Theory Lead to Contradictions in Practice," *The Thomist* 63 (1999), 269-281.

———. "Double-Effect Reasoning from Jean Pierre Gury to Peter Knauer," *Theological Studies* 59 (1998): 297-316.

Kalbian, Aline. "Where Have All the Proportionalists Gone?" *Journal of Religious Ethics* 30, 1 (2002): 3-22.

Kapur, Neera B. "Why It Is Wrong to Be Always Guided by the Best: Consequentialism and Friendship," *Ethics* 101 (April, 1991): 483-504.

Keane, Philip. "The Objective Moral Order: Reflections on Recent Research" *Theological Studies* 43 (1982): 260-278.

Kiely, Bartholomew M. "The Impracticality of Proportionalism," *Gregorianum* 66 (1985): 655-86.

Knauer, Peter. "The Hermeneutic Function of the Principle of Double Effect," *Natural Law Forum* 12 (1967): 132-161.
Kramer, Matthew. "How Not to Oppugn Consequentialism," *The Philosophical Quarterly* 46 (1996): 213-220.
Kupperman, Joel. *The Foundations of Morality*. London: Allen & Unwin, 1983.
———. "A Case for Consequentialism," *American Philosophical Quarterly* (1981): 305-313.
———. "Vulgar Consequentialism," *Mind* (1980): 321-337.
Langan, John. "Catholic Moral Rationalism and the Philosophical Bases of Moral Theology," *Theological Studies* 50 (1989): 25-43.
Levy, Sanford S. "Richard McCormick and Proportionate Reason," *Journal of Religious Ethics* 13 (1985): 258-78.
Mangan, Joseph. "An Historical Analysis of the Principle of Double Effect," *Theological Studies* 10 (1949): 41-61.
Marquis, Donald. "Four Versions of Double Effect," *The Journal of Medicine and Philosophy* 16 (1991): 515-544.
Marshner, William. "Aquinas on the Evaluations of Human Actions," *The Thomist* 59 (1995): 347-370.
May, William E. *Moral Absolutes: Catholic Tradition, Current Trends, and the Truth*. Milwaukee: Marquette Univ. Press, 1989.
McBrien, Richard. "Is Cardinal Ratzinger a Proportionalist?" *The Tidings*, 10/8/04, <http://www.the-tidings.com/2004/1008/essays.htm>
McCormick, Richard. "Birth Regulation, *Veritatis Splendor*, and Other Ways of Viewing Things," *Eglise et Theologie* 26 (1995): 31-42.
———. *Corrective Vision: Explorations in Moral Theology*. Kansas City: Sheed and Ward, 1994.
———. "Some Early Reactions to *Veritatis Splendor*," *Theological Studies* 55 (1994): 481-506.
———. "Killing the Patient," *The Tablet* (10/30/93): 1410-1411.
———. "Pluralism Within the Church," in *Catholic Perspectives on Medical Morals*. E. Pelligrino, J. Langan, J Harvey (eds.), Netherlands: Kluwer Academic Publishers, 1989: 147-167.
———. "Moral Theology 1940-1989: An Overview," *Theological Studies* 50 (1989): 3-24.
———. *The Critical Calling: Reflections on Moral Dilemmas since Vatican II*. Washington: Georgetown University Press, 1989.
———. "Self Assessment and Self Indictment" *Religious Studies Review* 13 (1987): 37-39.
———. "Theology and Bioethics: Christian Foundations," in *Theology and Bioethics: Exploring the Foundations and Frontiers*. E.E. Shelp (ed.), Dordrect: D. Reidel Publishing, 1985: 95-113.
———. *Notes on Moral Theology 1981 through 1984*. Lanham, MD: University Press of America, 1984.

———. *Health and Medicine in the Catholic Tradition* New York: The Crossroad Publishing Co., 1984.

———. "Notes on Moral Theology: 1982," *Theological Studies* 44 (1983): 71-122.

———, and John Paris. "Saving Defective Infants: Options for Life or Death," *America* 4/23/83: 313-317.

———. *How Brave a New World?* London: SCM Press, 1981.

———. *Notes on Moral Theology 1965 through 1980.* Lanham, Md: University Press of America, 1981.

———. "Notes on Moral Theology: 1981," *Theological Studies* 43 (1983).

———. "Notes on Moral Theology: 1980," *Theological Studies* 42 (1981).

———. "Bioethics and Method: Where Do We Start?," *Theology Digest* 29, 4 (1981), 303-318.

———. "Reflections on the Literature," *Readings in Moral Theology, No. : Moral Norms and Catholic Tradition* McCormick and Curran (eds.) New York:Paulist Press, 1979. 294-340.

———. "Moral Theology Since Vatican II: Clarity of Chaos" *Cross Currents* 29 (1979) 15-27.

———. "Notes on Moral Theology 1977: The Church in Dispute," *Theological Studies* 39 (1978), 76-138.

———. "A Commentary on the Commentaries," in *Doing Evil to Achieve Good: Moral Choice in Conflict Situations.* McCormick and Ramsey (eds.) Chicago: Loyola University Press, 1978: 193-267.

———. "Ambiguity in Moral Choice," in *Doing Evil to Achieve Good: Moral Choice in Conflict Situations.* McCormick and Ramsey (eds.), Chicago: Loyola University Press, 1978: 7-53.

———. "Notes on Moral Theology: 1976," *Theological Studies* 38 (1977): 57-114.

———. "Notes on Moral Theology: April-September 1974," *Theological Studies* 36 (1975), 77-129.

———. "The New Medicine and Morality," *Theology Digest* 21, 4 (1973), 308-321.

———. "Notes on Moral Theology: April-September, 1971," *Theological Studies* 33 (1972), 68-119.

McDonnell, Kevin. "The Consequentialist Controversy" *The Modern Schoolman* 61 (1979): 201-215.

McIntyre, Alison. "Doing Away With Double Effect," *Ethics* 111 (January, 2001): 219-255.

McKeever, Paul E. "Proportionalism as a Methodology in Catholic Moral Theology," *Human Sexuality and Personhood.* St. Louis: Pope John Center, 1981: 211-222.

McKim, Robert and Peter Simpson. "On the Alleged Incoherence of Consequentialism," *New Scholasticism* 62 (1988): 349-52.

McKinney, Ronald H. "The Quest for an Adequate Proportionalist Theory of Value," *The Thomist* 53 (1989): 56-73.

Melchin, Kenneth R. "Revisionists, Deontologists, and the Structure of Moral Understanding," *Theological Studies* 51 (1990): 389-416.
Mill, John Stuart. *Utilitarianism*, in *The Utilitarians*. New York: Doubleday & Company, Inc., 1961.
Moore, George Edward. *Principia Ethica*. Cambridge: Cambridge University Press, 1980.
Odozor, Paulinus. "Proportionalists and the Principle of Double Effect: A Review Discussion," *Christian Bioethics* 3 (1997): 115-130.
Pettit, Philip. "Consequentialism and Respect for Persons," *Ethics* 100 (October, 1989): 116-126.
Porter, Jean. "The Moral Act in *Veritatis Splendor* and Aquinas's *Summa Theologiae*: A Comparative Analysis," in *Readings in Moral Theology No.11: The Historical Development of Fundamental Moral Theology in the United States* New York: Paulist Press, 1999: 219-241.
———. "Moral Rules and Moral Actions: A Comparison of Aquinas and Modern Moral Theology," *The Journal of Religious Ethics* 17 (1989): 123-150.
Portmore, Douglas W. "Position-Relative Consequentialism, Agent-Centered Options, and Supererogation," *Ethics* 113 (January, 2003): 303-332.
———. "Can an Act-Consequentialist Theory Be Agent Relative?" *American Philosophical Quarterly* 38 (October, 2001): 363-377.
Quay, Paul M. "Morality by Calculation of Values" *Readings in Moral Theology No.1: Moral Norms and Catholic Tradition* McCormick and Curran (eds.), New York: Paulist Press (1979): 267-93.
Quirk, Michael J. "Why the Debate on Proportionalism is Misconceived," *Modern Theology* 13 4 (1997): 501-515.
Ramsey, Paul. "Incommensurability and Indeterminancy in Moral Choice," in *Doing Evil to Achieve Good: Moral Choice in Conflict Situations*. McCormick and Ramsey (eds.), Chicago: Loyola University Press, 1978: 69-144.
Ratzinger, Joseph. "Worthiness to Receive Holy Communion – General Principles," *L'espresso*, June, 2004. <http://www.catholicculture.org/docs>
———, et al. *Catechism of the Catholic Church* trans. by United States Catholic Conference, Missouri: Ligouri Publications, 1994.
Rawls, John. *A Theory of Justice*. Cambridge: Harvard University Press, 1971.
Rhonheimer, Martin. "Intentional Actions and the Meaning of Object: A Reply to Richard McCormick," *The Thomist* 59 (1995): 279-311.
———. "'Intrinsically Evil Acts' and the Moral Viewpoint: Clarifying a Central Teaching of *Veritatis Splendor*," *The Thomist* 58 (1994): 1-39.
Ross, W.David. *Foundations of Ethics*. Oxford: The Clarendon Press, 1963.
Salzman, Todd. "The Basic Goods Theory and Revisionism: A Methodological Comparison on the Use of Reason and Experience as Sources of Moral Knowledge," *The Heythrop Journal* 42, 4 (2001): 423-450.
———. *Deontology and Teleology: An Investigation of the Normative Debate in Roman Catholic Moral Theology*. Leuven: Leuven University Press, 1995.

Scheffler, Samuel. *The Rejection of Consequentialism: A Philosophical Investigation of the Considerations Underlying Rival Moral Conceptions.* Oxford: Clarendon, 1982.

———, ed. *Consequentialism and Its Critics.* Oxford: Oxford University Press, 1988.

Schuller, Bruno. "Direct Killing/Indirect Killing" in *Readings in Moral Theology No. 1: Moral Norms and Catholic Tradition.* Charles E. Curran and Richard A. McCormick (eds.), New York: Paulist Press, 1979: 139-157.

———. "The Double Effect in Catholic Thought" in *Doing Evil to Achieve Good.* Richard A. McCormick and Paul Ramsey (eds.) Chicago: Loyola University Press, 1978: 165-91.

Sen, Amartya. "Informational Analysis of Moral Principles," *Rational Action.* New York: Cambridge University Press, 1979.

Sidgwick, Henry. *The Methods of Ethics,* 7th ed. Chicago: The University of Chicago Press, 1962.

Smart, J.J.C. and Williams, Bernard. *Utilitarianism: For and Against.* Cambridge: Cambridge University Press, 1973.

———. "Extreme and Restricted Utilitarianism," *Theories of Ethics.* Philippa Foot (ed.) Oxford: Oxford University Press, 1967: 171-183.

Sparks, R.C. "The Storm Over Proportionalism: Choosing the Lesser of Two Evils," *Church* 5 (1989): 9-14.

Tubbs, James B. "Moral Epistemology in Richard McCormick's Ethics," *Christian Bioethics* 2 (1996): 114-126.

Ugorji, Lucius. *The Principle of Double Effect. A Critical Appraisal of its Traditional Understanding and Its Modern Interpretation.* Frankfurt and New York: P. Lang, 1985.

Vacek, Edward. review of "Proportionalism: For and Against," *Theological Studies* 63 (2002), 651.

———. "Proportionalism: One View of the Dabate," *Theological Studies* 46 (1985): 287-314.

Walter, James. "The Foundation and Formulation of Norms ,"*Moral Theology: Challenges for the Future.* Charles Curran (ed.) New York: Paulist, 1990: 125-54.

———. "Response to John C. Finnis: A Theological Critique," *Consistent Ethic of Life.* Thomas G. Fuechtmann.(ed.) Kansas City, Mo.: Sheed and Ward, 1988: 182-95.

———. "Proportionate Reason and its Three Levels of Inquiry: Structuring the Ongoing Debate," *Louvain Studies* 10 (1984), 30-40.